"Gordley provides scholars, students, and also those concerned with Christian worship today, with a richly informed, balanced, and stimulating study of earliest Christian hymnic praise. He shows how, whether or not given New Testament texts were actual hymns, they incorporate and reflect hymnic expressions and features, and so at least give us indirect evidence of earliest Christian worship. His additional emphasis on these texts as expressive of a 'spirituality of resistance' (to Roman imperial claims) is a fresh contribution. This is now the go-to book on the texts often cited as New Testament hymns."

L. W. Hurtado, emeritus professor of New Testament Language, Literature, and Theology at the University of Edinburgh

"Scholars have identified several New Testament passages (e.g., Phil 2:6-11; Col 1:15-20; John 1:1-18) as Christological hymns or hymn-like compositions that very likely originated in the setting of early Christian worship. These are some of the most theologically dense Christological passages in Scripture. Matthew Gordley, an expert on the subject (he has published two important and well-received monographs on ancient didactic hymnody), has now crowned his previous work on the subject with an indispensable and up-to-date discussion of a dozen of the most important of these hymnic texts, providing a carefully nuanced and judicious reading of these hymnic passages in the context of their overlapping Jewish, Greco-Roman, and early Christian settings."

David E. Aune, Walter Professor of New Testament and Christian Origins, emeritus, University of Notre Dame

"Although the question of whether or not certain passages in the New Testament give us access to actual hymns used in the early church's worship remains hotly contested, I find it to be of great value to give careful attention to those places where we hear the authors of the New Testament 'sing,' even if the words are of their own composition. When it comes to the study of worship, ancient or modern, the hymn deserves as close a study as the sermon or the creed, and it is most often the *hymn* that survives the longest in the worshiper's consciousness and exercises the greatest impact upon his or her formation. Here is a thoroughly researched study of the hymnic passages in the New Testament that can teach us about this important dimension of early Christian religious experience—an important commentary on those passages of Scripture. I believe it is also an important window into Christian worship in its most formative generations. Every chapter is relevant to the church's ongoing quest to find authentic expressions of worship in the twenty-first century, forcing us to ask whether our own hymnody or praise song repertoire reflects the broad Scriptural understanding of the significance of the Son's incarnation, death, resurrection, and ascension that is necessary to guide our own lives as disciples redeemed from the powers of this age to serve a very different kingdom."

David A. deSilva, Trustees' Distinguished Professor of New Testament and Greek, Ashland Theological Seminary

"Drawing on an impressive breadth of scholarship, Gordley offers a mature and careful study of an important field of research, with implications for early Christology, liturgy, and much more besides. He is to be congratulated for producing such a useful, learned, and constructive work that also makes important and pointed criticisms of recent scholarship. Gordley has written a book that will need to be consulted by all engaged in these and related debates."

Chris Tilling, graduate tutor and senior lecturer in New Testament studies at St. Mellitus College

"In this volume, Gordley opens up the rich world of ancient hymnody. After taking the reader on a learned and fascinating tour of early Jewish and Greco-Roman hymns, Gordley turns to the New Testament. His investigation goes well beyond formal analysis to a deep appreciation of the purpose and effect of the earliest Christian hymns. I was particularly drawn in by Gordley's analysis of how the hymns' artistry shaped worshipers' imaginations, often by functioning as resistance literature that countered imperial ideology and other competing worldviews. Combining rigorous, wide-ranging scholarship with insightful conclusions about contemporary practice, this book is invaluable both for readers who care about ancient worship and for anyone thinking about Christian worship today."

Kindalee De Long, professor of religion at Pepperdine University, author of *Surprised by God: Praise Responses in the Narrative of Luke-Acts*

"According to Matthew Gordley, the devotional practices of the first Christians centered on God's salvific work in Christ while simultaneously extending, engaging in, and resisting the cultural contexts of the day. His comprehensive study of the New Testament christological hymns should be carefully studied by biblical scholars and leaders of corporate worship who desire liturgical and theological guidance from the first followers of Jesus."

Jeremy Perigo, director of music and worship programs and lecturer in theology, music, and worship at the London School of Theology

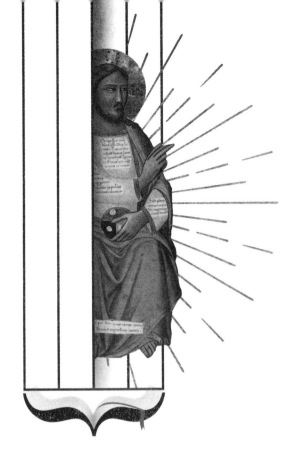

𝔑ew 𝔗estament

CHRISTOLOGICAL HYMNS

Exploring Texts, Contexts, and Significance

MATTHEW E. GORDLEY

IVP Academic

An imprint of InterVarsity Press
Downers Grove, Illinois

InterVarsity Press
P.O. Box 1400, Downers Grove, IL 60515-1426
ivpress.com
email@ivpress.com

*InterVarsity Press® is the book-publishing division of InterVarsity Christian Fellowship/USA®, a
movement of students and faculty active on campus at hundreds of universities, colleges, and schools
of nursing in the United States of America, and a member movement of the International Fellowship
of Evangelical Students. For information about local and regional activities, visit intervarsity.org.*

All Scripture quotations, unless otherwise indicated, are the author's translation.

Cover design: David Fassett
Interior design: Jeanna Wiggins
Images: gold surface: © FrankvandenBergh / E+ / Getty Images
      yellowed paper background: © ke77kz / iStock / Getty Images Plus
      *Christ in heaven: Illustration of Christ in Heaven in "Address in verse to Robert of Anjou" / British Library,
      London, UK / © British Library Board. All Rights Reserved / Bridgeman Images*

ISBN 978-0-8308-5209-3 (print)
ISBN 978-0-8308-8002-7 (digital)

Printed in the United States of America ∞

*InterVarsity Press is committed to ecological stewardship and to the conservation of natural resources
in all our operations. This book was printed using sustainably sourced paper.*

Library of Congress Cataloging-in-Publication Data
A catalog record for this book is available from the Library of Congress.

P   25   24   23   22   21   20   19   18   17   16   15   14   13   12   11   10   9   8   7   6   5   4   3   2   1
Y   37   36   35   34   33   32   31   30   29   28   27   26   25   24   23   22   21   20   19   18

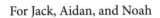

For Jack, Aidan, and Noah

CONTENTS

ACKNOWLEDGMENTS

𝔐 y fascination with understanding early Christian praise of Jesus in light of its broader cultural context began in Ross Wagner's 2001 doctoral seminar, Earliest Christianity in Its Greco-Roman Setting, at Princeton Theological Seminary. It was in this class that I first read ancient hymns written in honor of the Egyptian goddess Isis and was struck by the surprising familiarity of the language. Though there was no borrowing of specific phrases or exact expressions, the Isis aretalogies showed a way of praising a divine savior that seemed to breathe a similar air to the praise passages in the New Testament oriented around Jesus as Savior. What was the nature of the relationship between these very different kinds of texts from antiquity? I explored these ideas further in my doctoral studies at the University of Notre Dame and, under the guidance of David Aune, wrote my dissertation on Colossians 1:15-20 in its Jewish and Greco-Roman hymnic and epistolary contexts. That volume was subsequently published in 2007 as *The Colossian Hymn in Context: An Exegesis in Light of Ancient Jewish and Greco-Roman Hymnic and Epistolary Conventions.* From there it was a natural step to expand my explorations of the use and functions of hymnody in antiquity, the results of which are reflected in my 2011 *Teaching Through Song in Antiquity: Didactic Hymnody Among Greeks, Romans, Jews, and Christians.*

Though it had been in my mind for some time to produce a survey of the New Testament christological hymns that would bring to bear the findings of other studies to discuss the significance of the phenomenon of New Testament hymns more adequately, I owe the creation of the present book to Larry Hurtado and Dan Reid. It was Dan Reid, a student of Ralph Martin and well acquainted with his work on the Philippian hymn, who saw the need for a contemporary study of this kind. Larry suggested my name to Dan as someone who might be willing to write such a book. Since the publication of a book provides an opportunity to publicly recognize the individuals who have shaped it, I must certainly start then by acknowledging Larry Hurtado, Dan Reid, and the staff of IVP Academic who have brought this book to completion. Dan's editorial work from the start and his suggestions in the shaping of the final version of this book improved it immensely from what I had envisioned originally. The same can be said of the anonymous reviewers who offered many excellent suggestions for strengthening this book.

There are many individuals who have shaped my development as a biblical scholar, and to be able to name some of these individuals here is a small indication of my gratitude for their impact on my life. Among these are my outstanding professors from college, seminary, and graduate school including David Aune, Gregory Sterling, Jim VanderKam, Jerry Neyrey, Hindy Najman, Hugh Page, Gary Anderson, Mary Rose D'Angelo, Robin Darling Young, Rabbi Michael Signer, Don Juel, Ross Wagner, James Charlesworth, William Crockett, David Denyer, Bryan Widbin, Gerald Hawthorne, and Gary Burge. I cannot imagine a finer list of teachers. No less important have been my classmates at Notre Dame who have remained a vital part of my intellectual community across many miles: Jack Conroy, Kindy De Long, Dan Machiela, Brian Han Gregg, Ardea Caviggiola Russo, Steve Schweizer, Brant Pitre, Alison Schofield, Jonathan Lawrence, and Todd Hanneken. My fine colleagues during my years at Regent University School of Divinity have likewise influenced this work, especially Archie Wright, Brad Embry, Kevin Spawn, Graham Twelftree, Bill Lyons, Peter Gräbe, and Michael Palmer. I must express my thanks to graduate students who had a role in various stages of this project including Lance Hand and Sean Ireland. At Carlow University, where the entirety of the book was written, this project was made possible through the excellent work of librarians Emily Szitsas and Andrea Leyko. I wish also to express sincere thanks to my executive assistant, Ada Lovo-Martinez, for outstanding administrative support of this project and of all my efforts since my arrival at Carlow. Without her skillful support this project would not have been possible.

Finally, I would like to express my gratitude to my wife, Janine, for all the many ways in which she inspires me, encourages me, and keeps me dreaming big. Understanding the importance of this research to me, she has helped me to persevere and overcome the inevitable obstacles that arose in the process of writing and completing this book. For that and for so much else, I am grateful every day. And I wish to dedicate this book to the three amazing young men who make every day of my life so rewarding and who make each day an adventure just by being who they are: to my sons, Jack, Aidan, and Noah.

ABBREVIATIONS

JOURNALS AND SERIES

A(Y)B	Anchor (Yale) Bible
ABRL	Anchor Bible Reference Library
AJEC	Ancient Judaism and Early Christianity
AnBib	Analecta Biblica
ANTC	Abingdon New Testament Commentaries
ATDA	Das Alte Testament deutsch Apokryphen
AUSS	*Andrews University Seminary Studies*
BBR	*Bulletin of Biblical Research*
BGBE	Beiträge zur Geschichte der biblischen Exegese
Bib	*Biblica*
BiBInt	*Biblical Interpretation*
BibSac	*Bibliotheca Sacra*
BibSem	Biblical Seminar
BNTC	Black's New Testament Commentaries
BR	*Biblical Research*
BZNW	Beihefte zur Zeitschrift für die neutestamentliche Wissenschaft
CBQ	*Catholic Biblical Quarterly*
CBQMS	Catholic Biblical Quarterly Monograph Series
CRINT	Compendia Rerum Iudaicarum ad Novum Testamentum
CSHJ	Chicago Studies in the History of Judaism
CTR	*Criswell Theological Review*
CurBR	*Currents in Biblical Research*
CurTM	*Currents in Theology and Mission*
DCLS	Deuterocanonical and Cognate Literature Studies
ECC	Eerdmans Critical Commentary
ECL	Early Christianity and Its Literature
EJL	Early Judaism and Its Literature
FN	*Filologia Neotestamentaria*
FRLANT	Forschungen zur Religion und Literatur des Alten und Neuen Testaments
GRBS	*Greek, Roman, and Byzantine Studies*
HNT	Handbuch zum Neuen Testament
IBC	Interpretation: A Bible Commentary for Teaching and Preaching

ICC	International Critical Commentary
JAJ	*Journal of Ancient Judaism*
JBL	*Journal of Biblical Literature*
JCTCRS	Jewish and Christian Texts in Contexts and Related Studies
JRS	*Journal of Roman Studies*
JSJSup	Supplements to Journal for the Study of Judaism
JSTNSup	Journal for the Study of the New Testament Supplement Series
JSOTSup	Journal for the Study of the Old Testament Supplement Series
JSP	*Journal for the Study of the Pseudepigrapha*
JTC	*Journal for Theology and the Church*
JTS	*Journal of Theological Studies*
KEK	Kritisch-exegetischer Kommentar über das Neue Testament
LJPSTT	Literature of the Jewish People in the Period of the Second Temple and the Talmud
NICNT	New International Commentary on the New Testament
NIGTC	New International Greek Testament Commentary
NovTSup	Supplements to Novum Testament
NTAbh	Neutestamentliche Abhandlungen
NTL	New Testament Library
NTOA	Novum testamentum et orbis antiquus
NTS	*New Testament Studies*
OCM	Oxford Classical Monographs
PRSt	*Perspectives in Religious Studies*
SC	Sources chrétiennes
SNT	Studien zum Neuen Testament
SNTSMS	Society for New Testament Studies Monograph Series
SP	Sacra Pagina
SPhiloA	Studia Philonica Annual
STAC	Studien und Texte zu Antike und Christentum
STDJ	Studies on the Texts of the Desert of Judah
StPatr	*Studia Patristica*
SUNT	Studien zur Umwelt des Neuen Testaments
TSAJ	Texts and Studies in Ancient Judaism
VC	*Vigiliae Christianae*
VTSup	Supplements to Vetus Testamentum
WBC	Word Biblical Commentary
WMANT	Wissenschaftliche Monographien zum Alten und Neuen Testament
WUNT	Wissenschaftliche Untersuchungen zum Neuen Testament

ANCIENT WORKS

1 En.	*1 Enoch*
Clem.	Seneca, *De clementia*
Conf.	Philo, *De confusione linguarum*
Contempl.	Philo, *Vita contemplativa*
Det.	Philo, *Quod deterius potiori insidari soleat*
Did.	Didache
Ecl.	Calpurnius Siculus, *Eclogues*
Ep.	*Epistulae*
Fort. Rom.	Plutarch, *De fortuna Romanorum*
Fug.	Philo, *De fuga et inventione*
Hist. eccl.	*Eusebius of Caesarea, Historia ecclesiastica*
IEph	*Inscriptions from Ephesus*
Ign. *Eph.*	Ignatius, *To the Ephesians*
Ign. *Phld.*	Ignatius, *To the Philadelphians*
Ign. *Rom.*	Ignatius, *To the Romans*
Ign. *Trall.*	Ignatius, *To the Trallians*
IPergamon	*Inscriptions from Pergamon*
Inst.	Quintilian, *Institutio oratoria*
Legat.	Philo, *Legatio ad Gaium*
LXX	Septuagint
OGIS	*Orientis Graeci Inscriptiones Selectae.* Edited by Wilhelm Dittenberger. 2 vols. Leipzig: Hirzel, 1903–1905
Or.	Aristides, *Orationes*
Paed.	Clement of Alexandria, *Paedagogus*
P.Oxy.	*Papyrus Oxyrhynchus*
Princ. iner.	*Plutarch, Ad principem ineruditum*
Rep.	*Plato, Republic*

– One –

THE PLACE OF HYMNS IN THE NEW TESTAMENT AND IN SCHOLARSHIP

*T*he Christian church began with song."[1] So claimed Ralph Martin, and from the witness of the New Testament, we may readily agree. The songs sung by Mary, Zechariah, Simeon, and the angelic host in Luke's Gospel and the hymns recited before the throne in Revelation mark the advent of Christ and the exaltation of Christ, respectively, as events that were generative of hymnic praise. The importance of the Psalms of the Jewish Scriptures to the early Christians is also widely known, and their significance to the writers of the New Testament can readily be seen from the frequency with which they are quoted. The practice of the singing of psalms, hymns, and spiritual songs is likewise clear to any reader of the New Testament (see Col 3:16). But the idea that some of the newly composed hymns of the early Christians may be preserved in whole or in part in certain New Testament passages is a relatively recent one that has only become widely discussed in the last one hundred years.[2] This book is a study of those New Testament passages that have

---

[1] Ralph P. Martin, *Worship in the Early Church* (Grand Rapids: Eerdmans, 1974), 39.

[2] For a summary of the history of early scholarship, see Reinhard Deichgräber, *Gotteshymnus und Christushymnus in der frühen Christenheit*, SUNT 5 (Göttingen: Vandenhoeck & Ruprecht, 1967), 11-21; Jack T. Sanders, *The New Testament Christological Hymns: Their Historical Religious Background*, SNTSMS 15 (Cambridge: Cambridge University Press, 1971), 1-5. Deichgräber pointed to the pioneering work of Eduard Norden in the first decade of the twentieth century, which was broadened and furthered by the 1920/1921 publication of Josef Kroll, *Die*

captured the attention of biblical scholars and that have been identified as christological hymns—hymns in praise of Christ.[3]

Before diving into the necessary preliminary matters in this introductory chapter, it is important to outline several features of these texts that make the study of them so imperative. First, based on their contents alone these are some of the richest and deepest passages in the New Testament. Even a casual reading of these passages puts the reader in touch with some of the earliest and most profound strands of reflection on the person and work of Christ. A closer reading of these passages with attention to their hymnic features as well as their cultural, literary, and theological contexts can yield penetrating insights into the ways in which the earliest Christians understood Jesus and his significance for themselves and for humanity as a whole.

Second, these hymnic passages are among the most debated passages in the New Testament in terms of their background, origin, meaning, and significance. Scholarly consideration of these passages continues to bring new perspectives to bear that help illumine their meaning and that also challenge earlier views. As we will see below, the very idea that some or all of these passages reflect early Christian hymnody, while still accepted by many, is an idea that has been subjected to significant and increasing criticism within the last decade. Sustained engagement with these critiques is now needed in order to be able to speak in a meaningful way about the existence of early Christian hymns in the New Testament.

Third, given that the practice of hymn writing and hymn singing has continued to be a feature of Christian worship throughout the centuries, the worship practices of the earliest Christians continue to be of pressing interest for Christians today. Deep study of these passages can reveal insights into the nature of early Christian worship and its relationship to early Jewish and Greco-Roman practices. These insights have the potential to lend texture and meaning to the worship practices of contemporary worshipers as they engage with modern cultures that are quite different from the cultural milieu of the first century. While the modern world will not be the focus of the chapters that follow, my concluding chapter will allow room for imagining how these findings may be of use to contemporary worshipers.

---

christliche Hymnodik bis zu Klemens von Alexandria (Darmstadt: Wissenschaftliche Buchgesellschaft, 1968).

[3]As I explain below, we will look specifically at Phil 2:5-11; Col 1:15-20; Jn 1:1-18; Eph 2:14-16; 1 Tim 3:16; Heb 1:1-4; and 1 Pet 3:18-22. We will also examine Lk 1:46-55; 1:68-79; 2:14; 2:29-32 as well as the hymns in Rev 4–5.

Fourth, scholarly studies of these hymns, extensive as they are, have tended to focus on individual passages to the neglect of the larger phenomenon of early Christian hymnody. This is not a bad thing in itself and is a natural product of the rich contents of each individual passage. Each hymn requires careful and detailed study in its own right. However, as a result of this dynamic very little work has been done in terms of putting the pieces together in a meaningful way. Some studies of larger scope have been written, but many of these, valuable as they are, are significantly dated, particularly given the amount that has been written on New Testament hymns in recent years, not to mention the methodological and other advances in the field of biblical studies.[4] As a result, one is hard-pressed to find a current monograph that both attends to the current state of the discussion of individual hymns while at the same time providing an overall synthesis that attempts to makes sense of the phenomenon of early Christian hymns as a whole. This book fills that gap, providing both detailed analysis of New Testament hymnic passages in light of current research and a larger perspective on the significance of these passages and their presence in the New Testament.

Recognizing the richness and complexity of these passages, the scholarly debates they have engendered, and their potential to shed light on some of the worship practices of the earliest Christians, I begin this chapter with a brief overview of the texts under consideration and my aims in studying them. I will then step back to consider the larger context of early Christian worship and the place of hymns within that milieu. I then turn to address some methodological concerns and respond to important criticisms that have been brought forward against the idea that there are early Christian hymns embedded within the New Testament. At the end of the chapter I will summarize my own position and approach to the passages under discussion in the remainder of the volume.

CHRISTOLOGICAL HYMNS IN THE NEW TESTAMENT: OVERVIEW

That there are psalms and hymns in the New Testament has long been recognized. Depending on which scholar you consult, some of the earliest hymnic compositions of the first Christians may actually be quoted and preserved in

---

[4]The important works noted above by Deichgräber and Sanders were written half a century ago. More than two decades have passed since the insightful but more devotionally oriented volume by Robert J. Karris, *A Symphony of New Testament Hymns* (Collegeville, MN: Liturgical Press, 1996).

whole or in part in the New Testament. By hymns I refer to short compositions that have their focus on praise of the divine in second- or third-person address and that describe the actions and attributes of the one being praised in an elevated prose or poetic style. Although they share some common features, hymns may be distinguished from other similar kinds of passages such as prayers, blessings, doxologies, confessions, and acclamations.[5] The New Testament hymns naturally have their focus on the praise of God and the praise of Jesus. Because I am exploring christological hymns, I will focus specifically on those passages that offer praise of Christ in hymnic style.[6] The earliest examples are passages preserved in the letters of Paul, both in genuine Pauline letters and in letters for which Pauline authorship is disputed. Later examples of christological hymns are to be found in Hebrews, the Gospels of Luke and of John, and in Revelation. In this volume I explore hymnic passages from each of these New Testament writings. Three of these passages are both influential and somewhat lengthy: the Philippian hymn (Phil 2:5-11), the Colossian hymn (Col 1:15-20), and the Johannine prologue (Jn 1:1-18). Because of the complexity and significance of each of these passages, I devote a chapter to each one. I will also examine other instances of New Testament christological hymns or hymn fragments that are shorter in length or appear to be partial in nature. These passages include Ephesians 2:14-16; 1 Timothy 3:16; Hebrews 1:1-4; and 1 Peter 3:18-22. I will also include some New Testament hymns that are found in a context with other hymnic passages and that are not as explicitly christological or are focused on Christ to a lesser extent. In this vein I will consider the psalms and hymns of the Lukan infancy narrative: the Magnificat (Lk 1:46-55), the Benedictus (Lk 1:68-79), the Gloria in excelsis (Lk 2:14), and the Nunc Dimittis (Lk 2:29-32). I will also take note of some of the instances of hymnic praise in Revelation, especially the hymns around the throne in

---

[5]For discussion of these various genres see Richard N. Longenecker, *New Wine into Fresh Wineskins: Contextualizing the Early Christian Confessions* (Peabody, MA: Hendrickson, 1999), 7-23. In spite of their differing lengths and stylistic features he proposes to "give priority to content and classify all these materials under the generic rubric 'early Christian confessions'—that is, to speak of them as formulaic statements that express the essential convictions of the earliest believers in Jesus" (24). While that is appropriate for Longenecker's purpose, for the purposes of this volume more specificity is necessary.

[6]A study of hymns in praise of God would be another task altogether. Among the hymns to God in the New Testament, see Rom 11:33-36, as well as possible hymn fragments in 2 Cor 1:3-4; Eph 1:3-14; Col 1:12-14; 1 Pet 1:3-5; and Acts 26:18. These and others are explored at length in Deichgräber, *Gotteshymnus und Christushymnus*, 60-105. Longenecker adds Rev 15:3-4 in this category (*New Wine*, 10-11).

Revelation 4–5. I will examine these shorter passages and the associated psalms from Luke and Revelation in a chapter that takes a wider look at the phenomenon of hymnic passages in the New Testament.

As I look at these passages, my aim is to provide a comprehensive, comparative, and exegetically informed analysis of New Testament christological hymns in light of their cultural, literary, and theological contexts. I will endeavor to situate them within the cultural matrices of Greco-Roman praise and also of early Jewish worship, and argue that understanding those broader contexts allows for a richer understanding of how these passages functioned within their epistolary contexts and also within the early Christian communities. In this way I will show the value and benefit of reading these passages as hymns, while at the same time considering the limitations of a hymnic designation. Reading them with an awareness of what hymnody was and how it functioned in the ancient world will ultimately lead us to a greater appreciation of their significance "then and there," and potentially "here and now." We will also see that the meaning conveyed in these passages comes not just through their words and concepts but also through their authors' use of hymnic forms, which tap into common cultural norms regarding the expression of praise of the divine.

LOCATING NEW TESTAMENT HYMNS WITHIN EARLY CHRISTIAN WORSHIP

To begin, I will set the stage by talking briefly about the larger context of early Christian worship. After providing a definition of worship that accounts for the plurality of worship practices as well as the worldview assumptions that lie behind acts of worship, I move on to describe what we know about hymn singing and hymn composition within the early Christian communities.

Worship: basic understandings. In this volume I understand worship as a practice of affirming, proclaiming, and confessing an allegiance to God that, among other things, enables worshipers to see themselves as part of a reality that is larger than the visible reality on offer within the world in which the worshipers live. Worship, in this sense, may include words, actions, and rituals, together with an overall pattern of values that constitute the orientation of one's life.[7] Each of these dimensions or aspects of worship were part of the

---

[7]On the many complexities of defining the concept of worship, both in ancient and modern contexts, see Andrew B. McGowan, *Ancient Christian Worship: Early Church Practices in Social,*

experience of individuals in the earliest Christian communities.[8] Depending on the cultural and social world in which worshipers find themselves, not only may worship facilitate the broadening of one's view of reality to include invisible, spiritual realities, but it may also take on the role of countering other claims that are on offer within the worshiper's world. This is particularly the case when what is affirmed, proclaimed, and confessed about God in worship runs counter to affirmations, proclamations, and confessions that are accepted, or vying for acceptance, within society as a whole. As we will see, early Christian worship thus had very tangible and visible manifestations in words, actions, and rituals that made sense in the first century CE. It also offered a revolutionary worldview and countercultural perspective to those who participated in it.

Studies of the contours of early Christian worship include a broad spectrum of practices that were a part of worship in the first century, including baptism, meals, the Eucharist, footwashing, anointing with oil, reading of biblical texts, preaching, prayer, and singing.[9] Many studies of these activities appropriately seek to position early Christian practices within the larger context of Greco-Roman culture as well as Jewish tradition. Such an approach is vital for a nuanced understanding of early Christian worship since, regardless of their devotion to Jesus, Christians of all backgrounds were already deeply immersed in larger cultural and social contexts.

Historical, and Theological Perspective (Grand Rapids: Baker Academic, 2014), 2-8. While McGowan ends up focusing his study on worship on the "practices that constitute Christian communal and ritual life" irrespective of what the New Testament connotes as worship (7), he acknowledges that within the ancient world and within the New Testament, the terms that we translate as "worship" have a broader scope: "not a specific realm of activity like 'liturgy' but the orientation of all forms of human activity, including the liturgical or ritual, toward a particular allegiance" (4). As we will see, that broader notion of orientation is an important concept for interpreting the New Testament hymns. On the New Testament concept of worship, see James D. G. Dunn, *Did the First Christians Worship Jesus? The New Testament Evidence* (Louisville, KY: Westminster John Knox, 2010), 7-28.

[8]Seminal studies of worship in the New Testament by Gerhard Delling, *Worship in the New Testament* (London: Darton, Longman & Todd, 1962); Martin, *Worship in the Early Church*. More recently, see Paul F. Bradshaw, *Reconstructing Early Christian Worship* (London: SPCK, 2009); Larry W. Hurtado, *Lord Jesus Christ: Devotion to Jesus in Earliest Christianity* (Grand Rapids: Eerdmans, 2003); McGowan, *Ancient Christian Worship*.

[9]See, for example, David E. Aune, "Worship, Early Christian," in *Anchor Bible Dictionary*, ed. David Noel Freedman (New York: Doubleday, 1992), 6:973-89; Larry W. Hurtado, *At the Origins of Christian Worship: The Context and Character of Earliest Christian Devotion* (Grand Rapids: Eerdmans, 2000); Paul F. Bradshaw, *The Search for the Origins of Christian Worship: Sources and Methods for the Study of Early Liturgy* (New York: Oxford University Press, 2002); McGowan, *Ancient Christian Worship*.

In the first-century-CE Greco-Roman world, worship of gods and deified rulers played a pivotal role in the daily life of the individual within his or her household, in the functioning of the polis, and in the ordering and maintenance of empires.[10] As N. T. Wright explains, for Greeks and Romans, worship "would have been a feature of everyday life, bringing the gods, both local and national and increasingly . . . transnational, into touch with all other elements of life, business, marriage, home and hearth, death and birth, travel and festival."[11] In addition to the worship practices and the beliefs that support those practices at all levels of society, comprehensive studies of ancient worship have also considered the spaces allotted for worship, the people and positions assigned to individuals in regulating and leading worship activities, and the specific words associated with worship. By "words" I include both how the ancients described their worship practices and also the words they used: the prayers, hymns, and other compositions that were included within the realm of worship of the divine.

If it is true for the Greeks and Romans that worship included words, actions, and rituals that affected all of life, it is similarly true for ancient Jews. The Jewish concept of worship of God likewise involved rituals, actions, and practices affecting all levels of society. Likewise, worship practices took place in key places (home, synagogue, temple), involved key personnel, and involved words of various kinds: prayers, psalms, and sacred texts of many genres.

These widespread and varied practices that constitute ancient worship and concern many aspects of human existence do not stand on their own. Beliefs and assumptions—some more explicit, some more implicit—about the nature of the gods, about humanity, and about the interrelationships of the human and divine spheres stand alongside the specific worship practices of cultures and peoples. Rituals and actions of worship are often undergirded by a particular set of worldview assumptions.[12] At the same time, the practices of worship themselves serve to reinforce those worldviews. Therefore one way that ancient worship can be approached fruitfully is by considering both the

---

[10]On religion and the household, see John P. Bodel and Saul M. Olyan, *Household and Family Religion in Antiquity*, Ancient World—Comparative Histories (Malden, MA: Blackwell, 2008). On the place of the emperor in Roman worship, in particular, see Ittai Gradel, *Emperor Worship and Roman Religion*, OCM (Oxford: Clarendon, 2002).

[11]N. T. Wright, *Paul and the Faithfulness of God* (Minneapolis: Fortress, 2013), 36.

[12]On worldview issues in approaching the world of the early Christians, see ibid., 24-36. See also the useful analysis of Wright's approach to worldview issues in Samuel V. Adams, *The Reality of God and Historical Method: Apocalyptic Theology in Conversation with N. T. Wright*, New Explorations in Theology (Downers Grove, IL: IVP Academic, 2015), 44-64.

concrete actions of worship and the abstract worldview frameworks that support those actions.

For purposes of this volume, my focus is primarily on the verbal aspect of early Christian worship. More specifically, I am examining the words that survive in the hymnic compositions within the New Testament. Even so, it is vital that the words of worship (i.e., the words used in prayers, psalms, hymns) be understood within the larger conceptual framework of ancient religious worship, which, as we have just seen, involved people, places, practices, and worldviews. Thus I begin with some discussion about the place of hymns within early Christian worship.

Hymn singing and hymn composition in early Christian worship. With this broader understanding in place, what part did the composition and singing of hymns play within this context? Hermut Löhr recommends that we make a distinction between hymnody (the practice of singing hymns) and hymnography (the practice of composing hymns).[13] These are rightly understood as two distinct though interrelated practices. With this caution in mind we can see that if there are hymns embedded in the New Testament, then the New Testament gives us more evidence and material for consideration of hymnography (composition) rather than hymnody (singing or practice). We have the written evidence that certain individuals crafted hymnic passages (whatever we wish to call them), which spoke of Christ using elevated language and expressions. We have much less direct evidence about the actual practice of singing hymns.

Nevertheless, though the evidence for the singing of hymns in the early church is limited, there is indication enough to suggest the importance of hymnody.[14] The bulk of this evidence is found within the New Testament itself, as multiple writers refer to the singing of hymns. Within the Pauline tradition, for example, the exhortation to sing "psalms, hymns, and spiritual songs" (Eph 5:19; Col 3:16) is well-known.[15] Paul himself references his own singing

---

[13]Hermut Löhr, "What Can We Know About the Beginnings of Christian Hymnody?," in *Literature or Liturgy? Early Christian Hymns and Prayers in Their Literary and Liturgical Context in Antiquity*, ed. Clemens Leonhard and Hermut Löhr, WUNT 2/363 (Tübingen: Mohr Siebeck, 2014), 157-74.

[14]See the overviews in Hurtado, *At the Origins*, 86-92, and Richard Bauckham, "The Worship of Jesus in Early Christianity," in *Jesus and the God of Israel: God Crucified and Other Studies on the New Testament's Christology of Divine Identity* (Grand Rapids: Eerdmans, 2009), 127-51.

[15]On the background and later Christian developments relating to these terms, see Antoon A. R. Bastiaensen, "*Psalmi, Hymni* and *Cantica* in Early Jewish-Christian Tradition," *StPatr* 21 (1989): 15-26.

(1 Cor 14:15) and mentions a psalm as one item that believers could contribute for the good of all (1 Cor 14:26). The epistle of James advocates that the cheerful ought to sing songs of praise (Jas 5:13). Jesus and the disciples are remembered singing a hymn in Mark 14:26.

Other early Christian writings from the first few centuries CE attest to the widespread practice of hymn singing. Musical imagery is prominent in the letters of Ignatius, as is the inclusion of hymnic passages similar to the christological hymns of the New Testament.[16] In Acts of John 94–96 Jesus sings a hymn to the Father holding hands with the disciples and with their responding "amen." In Acts of Paul 9 we read of a communal meal to the accompaniment of psalms and songs. Likewise references to singing are found in the Odes of Solomon (7.22-23; 16.1-3; 41.1-2, 16).[17] Outside of the early Christian literature, scholars frequently point to Pliny's famous statement about the singing of a hymn to Christ as evidence for the widespread nature of Christian hymn singing.[18] Taken together, this evidence from the first two centuries suggests the vitality of hymn singing as part of the early Christian experience of communal worship.[19]

Beyond this evidence from early Christianity, the practices of Jews and Gentiles in their own worship settings should also be considered as evidence. In fact, music and song appears to have been an important part of Greco-Roman worship, one that Gentile followers of Jesus would have been very comfortable bringing into their new associations with other followers.[20] By contrast, there is very little evidence to suggest the presence of hymn singing within early Jewish synagogues.

J. A. Smith has explored this issue particularly with regard to the question of the extent to which early Christian singing was similar to or reflected

---

[16]Musical imagery suggestive of Christian worship settings can be found in Ign. *Eph.* 4.1-2, Ign. *Phld.* 1.2, and Ign. *Rom.* 2.2. For analysis of hymnic passages in the letters of Ignatius, see Matthew E. Gordley, *Teaching Through Song in Antiquity: Didactic Hymnody Among Greeks, Romans, Jews and Christians*, WUNT 2/331 (Tübingen: Mohr Siebeck, 2011), 351-58.

[17]Stephen G. Wilson, "Music in the Early Church," in *Common Life in the Early Church: Essays Honoring Graydon F. Snyder*, ed. Julian V. Hills and Richard B. Gardner (Harrisburg, PA: Trinity Press International, 1998), 390-401, here 394.

[18]Pliny, *Ep.* 10.96.7. Cf. Ralph P. Martin, *A Hymn of Christ: Philippians 2:5-11 in Recent Interpretation and in the Setting of Early Christian Worship* (Downers Grove, IL: InterVarsity Press, 1997), 1-9; Martin Hengel, "The Song About Christ in Earliest Worship," in *Studies in Early Christology* (Edinburgh: T&T Clark, 1995), 227-91, esp. 262-64.

[19]For more on the development of hymnody in the second and third centuries, see chap. 7.

[20]Wilson, "Music in the Early Church," 398-400.

characteristics of contemporary Jewish singing.[21] On the basis of a comparison of New Testament and early Jewish vocabulary with reference to the practice of singing, he concludes, surprisingly, that a connection cannot be claimed. He writes, "Neither the use of common Greek terms to designate religious singings, nor the presence of Jewish-Christian hymnic passages in the New Testament, is sufficient to prove that first-century Christian singing had elements in common with contemporary Jewish religious song."[22] This finding seems counterintuitive considering the otherwise close connections between early Judaism and early Christian belief and practice. It is worth exploring further to ensure we understand what the evidence will allow.

The problem Smith identifies is that the terms used for singing "elude clear individual definition in both ancient Jewish and early Christian literature" and so there is no basis for comparing different types of singing or song that may be implied.[23] Further, he finds that the Jewish-Christian hymns embedded in the New Testament "either lack demonstrable association with singing, or else defy attempts to connect their singing with the material world."[24] Odes of Solomon provides later instances, but due to its date these passages are not direct evidence of what was occurring in the first century. Smith thus concludes, "Given that Christianity originated within Judaism it seems a reasonable assumption that the singing of the earliest church originated in—indeed to a large extent probably was—Jewish singing. But this is an assumption precisely because there is insufficient evidence available from the first century to confirm it as fact."[25] Even so, the assumption seems a safe starting point provided that we recognize the limitations of the evidence.

Although it is likely that Jewish practices provide much helpful context for early Christian worship, we can also consider concrete evidence from later centuries of Christian practice. As with the preceding kinds of considerations, this data is suggestive of earlier Christian practices, but not definitive. For example, early Christian collections of biblical odes, including both Old

---

[21]J. A. Smith, "First-Century Christian Singing and Its Relationship to Contemporary Jewish Religious Song," *Music and Letters* 75 (1994): 1-15; Smith, "The Ancient Synagogue, the Early Church, and Singing," *Music and Letters* 65 (1984): 1-16.

[22]Smith, "First-Century Christian Singing," 14.

[23]Ibid.

[24]Ibid.

[25]Ibid.

Testament and New Testament texts, offer tantalizing hints about Christian worship in the early centuries.[26] One of the earliest surviving Christian hymns that includes musical notation is also instructive. P.Oxy. 1786 is a late third-century hymn of Egyptian provenance and written in Greek poetic meter. The hymn contains musical notation but no instructions about the occasion of the hymn.[27] Charles Cosgrove notes that since its "text seems suitable for a variety of settings, it is impossible to know whether the hymn was intended for a particular liturgical event and, if so, which event."[28] The hymn includes mention of themes and practices of early Christian worship such as hymning the Trinity, using doxologies, and keeping silence. However, as Cosgrove points out, these are projected onto an imaginal world in which these things are occurring in the cosmic realm. Thus it is difficult to read back from the hymn into actual liturgical practice. However, Cosgrove rightly notes that the events described in the imaginal heavenly realm of the hymn "have *associations* with actual liturgical practice."[29] This conclusion, while intriguing, does not allow for a mirror reading in which the hymn enables us to see an exact reflection of worship in the activities of the congregation.

However, it is significant to note a salient issue that P.Oxy. 1786 raises. Cosgrove notes an important distinction between what is fictional and what is imaginal. Thus, "For ancient singers/hearers, picturing the imaginal world of P.Oxy. 1786 would have meant conceiving *themselves* as part of a cosmic liturgy involving nature and angelic beings."[30] Further, Cosgrove explains,

> Those who used the hymn of P.Oxy. 1786 may have differed in how literally they interpreted its language, but common tenets of Christian faith in the third and fourth centuries provided reasons for them to believe that what the hymn describes of a reverent natural world and worshiping angels who join the church in a unified liturgy was in some way a true description of the real and the actual in their own worship.[31]

---

[26]Jennifer Knust and Tommy Wasserman, "The Biblical Odes and the Text of the Christian Bible: A Reconsideration of the Impact of Liturgical Singing on the Transmission of the Gospel of Luke," *JBL* 133 (2014): 341-65. See the variety of early Christian worship practices analyzed recently by McGowan, *Ancient Christian Worship*.

[27]Charles H. Cosgrove, *An Ancient Christian Hymn with Musical Notation: Papyrus Oxyrhynchus 1786: Text and Commentary*, STAC (Tübingen: Mohr Siebeck, 2011).

[28]Ibid., 147.

[29]Ibid., 149 (emphasis added).

[30]Ibid., 80.

[31]Ibid., 81.

It is interesting to note a parallel here with the earlier phenomenon of the Qumran community members' experience of worshiping alongside a heavenly chorus of angelic worshipers. As we will see, there are hints in the christological hymns of the New Testament that the earliest Christians saw their earthly worship as somehow mirroring unseen heavenly realities.

In attempting to position P.Oxy. 1786 in historical context, Cosgrove provides a helpful review of other examples of early Christian hymn singing and pays special attention to Clement of Alexandria's "Hymn to Christ the Savior" at the end of the *Paedagogus* (*Paed.* 3.12.101).[32] Clement's is the earliest complete christological hymn composed in Greek meter and replete with Greek literary allusions. Cosgrove concludes, "From the second through the fifth centuries, Christians with a Hellenistic education and a poetic bent composed hymns and other spiritual works in Greek meter. Some of the shorter and more accessible hymns of this sort were undoubtedly sung in devotional settings of various kinds, including worship."[33] However, Cosgrove also notes that by the fourth century, in contrast to the popularity of singing of biblical psalms, the composing and singing of original hymns "fell into disfavor due to concerns that non-biblical hymns were seductive vehicles for heresy."[34] This third- and fourth-century evidence is interesting in its own right, but only indirectly sheds light on the first-century Christian practices hinted at in the New Testament.

At the very least, in light of the evidence from within the New Testament, and the Jewish and later Christian information from outside the New Testament, we can be quite certain that the singing of hymns, that is, hymnody, was an important feature of early Christian worship.[35] With Löhr's distinction between hymnody and hymnography in mind, however, we must note that there is some debate as to whether the New Testament actually provides any evidence of hymnography—that is, hymn writing. Ralph Brucker, for example, argues that the passages of praise found in the New Testament are not liturgical

---

[32]See my discussion of the importance of this hymn in Gordley, *Teaching Through Song in Antiquity*, 371-81.

[33]Cosgrove, *Ancient Christian Hymn*, 156.

[34]Ibid. Indeed, teachers like Marcion, Valentinus, and Bardesanes made significant use of hymns and original psalms. See John Anthony McGuckin, *The Path of Christianity: The First Thousand Years* (Downers Grove, IL: IVP Academic, 2017), 824-27; Gordley, *Teaching Through Song in Antiquity*, 358-63.

[35]On this point, see the survey of the material to support this conclusion in Bauckham, "Worship of Jesus," 135-39.

at all, but rather literary.[36] Using the concept of epideictic rhetoric, Brucker argues that the closest analogues to the so-called New Testament hymns are not hymns and psalms at all but rather short rhetorical units of praise (Greek: *epainos*) found in many literary compositions. While Brucker's drawing attention to the concept and practice of epideictic rhetoric to shed light on these passages is useful, his reasons for dismissing the hymnic dimension of these passages are not compelling. Though I will address these issues more fully below, it is sufficient to note here that he relies on the strictest possible definition of a hymn, insisting that a hymn must be poetic, which in turn is signaled by adherence to meter. He also argues that a hymn must have a standard tripartite structure. By these criteria the passages commonly identified as hymns in the New Testament do not stand the test and thus there is no hymnography in the New Testament. However, Brucker does not take into account as fully as is warranted that these passages do evidence other features common to ancient hymns, especially features common to early Jewish psalmody. These features will be explored more fully in chapter two, but for now it is important to recognize the extent to which Greek rhetoric and Jewish psalmody are often considered worlds apart, as Brucker suggests. And yet, it seems that the early Christians somehow married the two. An a priori decision to make a sharp distinction is a decision as to what the outcome of any analysis of these passages will be.

To what extent do the passages under consideration here reflect the practices and features of early Christian worship? With the christological hymns of the New Testament, it is simply not possible to know with certainty if they represent word-for-word transcriptions of the actual prayers and songs of the early Christians. Some of them may indeed, but the evidence just does not allow for a strong conclusion in that direction. However, we are surely on much more solid ground to make a claim in the other direction. It is more certain that the worship practices of the early Christians (the complex of ways in which they affirmed, proclaimed, and confessed allegiance to God)

---

[36]See the full-length study in Ralph Brucker, *"Christushymnen" oder "epideiktische Passagen"? Studien zum Stilwechsel im Neuen Testament und seiner Umwelt*, FRLANT 176 (Göttingen: Vandenhoeck & Ruprecht, 1997). This is now summarized and updated in Ralph Brucker, "'Songs,' 'Hymns,' and 'Encomia' in the New Testament?," in Leonhard and Löhr, *Literature or Liturgy*, 1-14. He concludes, "Solemn passages praising Christ or God in the New Testament writings are not quotations of 'songs' or 'hymns' (and hence traces of early Christian liturgy), but rather examples of a literary phenomenon that has numerous analogies in other ancient texts" (10).

influenced their epistolary compositions. Thus, we may consider that these hymnic passages, even if not proved to be actual songs of praise, most certainly *do* reflect aspects of the worship practices of the early Christians. In addition, they point to an awareness of a larger spiritual reality—an imaginal world—in which Christian devotion to Jesus made sense. Viewed in this way the New Testament christological hymns can illumine our understanding of what early Christian worship was about. Taking this approach, in this study I will point to a number of conclusions about early Christian worship, its features, its emphases, and its focus. Next, however, I turn to address in more detail some important criticisms that have been raised with regard to the attempt to discover christological hymns in the New Testament. As we look at these criticisms we will see that, while they bring to light important limitations to studying these texts as hymnic, they do not undermine the enterprise as a whole. In fact, the critical comments of a number of scholars actually help to sharpen the focus of the present study as they point out some of the errors that we will be seeking to avoid.

A CRITICAL APPROACH TO THE STUDY OF NEW TESTAMENT HYMNS

At the turn of the century it was safe to say that a majority of scholars accepted the view that in passages such as Philippians 2:6-11, Colossians 1:15-20, and others, the authors of the epistles were drawing on preexisting material of some kind.[37] These preexisting materials were often identified as early Christian hymns or even pre-Christian hymns adapted by early followers of Jesus. The case was made by appealing to a number of features of the texts under consideration. These features have been spelled out by a number of scholars over the years and have been summarized by David Aune. Citing the approach of Ethelbert Stauffer, who listed criteria for identifying hymns or, more broadly, creedal material, the following can be said about these creedal materials or hymns:

  1. They are often inserted and introduced by such words as "deliver," "believe," or "confess" (see Rom 10:9).

---

[37]Stephen Fowl, though critical of the enterprise, wrote in 2005, "Indeed, the majority of modern scholars believe that Phil 2:6-11 represents preexisting material that Paul is quoting and/or redacting." Stephen E. Fowl, *Philippians*, Two Horizons New Testament Commentary (Grand Rapids: Eerdmans 2005), 110.

2. They are often marked by contextual dislocations (e.g., 1 Tim 3:16).

3. They often do not fit into the context syntactically (e.g., Rev 1:4).

4. They often exhibit a different linguistic usage, terminology, or style from their contexts (e.g., 1 Cor 16:22).

5. They sometimes repeat the same formula in very similar form (e.g., 2 Cor 5:21).

6. They often exhibit simple syntax, avoiding particles, conjunctions, complicated constructions, preferring parataxis to hypotaxis, and the thought proceeds by thesis rather than argument (e.g., Acts 4:10).

7. They often stand out because of stylistic construction; that is, they favor antithetic or anaphoral style (e.g., 1 Tim 3:16).

8. They are often rhythmical in form, by the number of stresses or even words (e.g., 1 Cor 15:3).

9. They are often arranged in lines and strophes (e.g., Col 1:15-20).

10. They are often marked by their preference for appositions and noun predicates (e.g., Ign. *Eph.* 7.2).

11. They frequently favor participles and relative clauses (e.g., Rom 1:3).

12. They refer to the elementary truth and events of salvation history as norms (e.g., Ign. *Trall.* 9.1-2).[38]

For many scholars, a preponderance of the features noted above was sufficient to justify a claim that a particular passage was an early Christian hymn or psalm of some kind. For passages such as Philippians 2, Colossians 1, and John 1, use of these criteria led a majority of scholars to recognize them as being reflective of early Christian hymns. Analyses of these passages include more or less extensive discussions about the nature of the text. Often, a sketch of the main hymnic features has been considered sufficient to explain why the passage was viewed in this way.

However, there has also long been a minority of scholars who raised critical questions about this approach, its underlying assumptions, and its results in terms of understanding and evaluating certain New Testament passages.[39]

---

[38] Adapted from David E. Aune, "Hymn," in *The Westminster Dictionary of New Testament and Early Christian Literature and Rhetoric* (Louisville, KY: Westminster John Knox, 2003), 222-24. See a slightly different list in Longenecker, *New Wine*, 10-11.

[39] See, for example, Gordon D. Fee, "Philippians 2:5-11: Hymn or Exalted Pauline Prose," *BBR* 2 (1992): 29-46; N. T. Wright, "Poetry and Theology in Colossians 1:15-20," *NTS* 36 (1990): 444-68. For a particularly sharp critique of "hymn-hunting" in 1 Peter, see C. J. A. Lash, "Fashionable

Within the last decade a handful of articles have been published that have given voice to serious problems with the whole business of finding hymns in the New Testament.[40] Yet in spite of these criticisms, many scholars continue to find it useful to refer to passages like Colossians 1:15-20 or Philippians 2:6-11 as hymns.[41]

In this section I will review and respond to some of the criticisms that have been raised. My response will show that not all of these criticisms hold equal weight, and some are misguided. Some of the criticisms, however, are well-grounded and require a critical response. In addition, I will point forward beyond "hymn hunting" to the real exegetical and interpretive value of using hymn language with regard to some of these texts. In particular the language and form of many of these hymnic passages can be understood within the framework of Jewish resistance poetry—a tradition that has deep roots within the biblical tradition and within early Judaism in particular. Rather than a form-critical approach that seeks to reconstruct a lost original version by identifying and removing redactional material, the identification of passages with features of hymns and psalms as we envision it invites reflection on how this material functioned for the author of the epistle or narrative in which it is included. Whether preexisting or composed for the occasion, the features of these passages provide clues toward their functions within their larger literary contexts.

In short, I will argue for a broad understanding of the concept of *hymn* based on the breadth of application of the term in antiquity.[42] The result of such

---

Sports: Hymn-Hunting in 1 Peter," in *Studia Evangelica*, vol. 7, *Papers Presented to the Fifth International Congress on Biblical Studies*, ed. E. A. Livingstone, TUGAL 126 (Berlin: Akademie-Verlag, 1982), 293-97.

[40]See, for example, Michael Peppard, "'Poetry,' 'Hymns' and 'Traditional Material' in New Testament Epistles or How to Do Things with Indentations," *JSNT* 30 (2008): 319-42; Benjamin Edsall and Jennifer R. Strawbridge, "The Songs We Used to Sing? Hymn 'Traditions' and Reception in Pauline Letters," *JSNT* 37 (2015): 290-311; Brucker, "'Songs,' 'Hymns,' and 'Encomia.'"

[41]Michael Wade Martin and Bryan A. Nash, "Philippians 2:6-11 as Subversive *Hymnos*: A Study in the Light of Ancient Rhetorical Theory," *JTS* 66 (2015): 90-138. As an example of scholars still apparently happy to call Col 1:15-20 a hymn see Michael F. Bird, *Colossians and Philemon*, New Covenant Commentary (Havertown, UK: Lutterworth, 2011), 47; Ulrich Huttner, *Early Christianity in the Lycus Valley*, trans. David Green, AJEC 85 (Leiden: Brill, 2013), 119.

[42]In this we are not far from the pioneering work of Josef Kroll, who noted in *Die christliche Hymnodik* both the song aspect of hymnody ("A hymn is first and foremost praise, a praise song of God" [10]) as well as the tradition of prose hymnody: "A hymn is therefore a praise of God in elevated—metrical or stylistic prose—diction" (11). This broad understanding is reflected in my own definition of didactic hymnody in Gordley, *Teaching Through Song in Antiquity*, 4-9.

a broad understanding is, for my purposes, that if a passage contains many of the features associated with hymns, then it can be considered a hymn or at least hymnic in nature. Such a conclusion about any one passage is not significant in and of itself. More significant questions also need to be asked such as: If this passage is hymnic in nature, what kind of hymn is it? What kind of ancient hymn does it most resemble? What specific features does it utilize to tap into the discourse of hymns in the ancient world? And finally, how does the inclusion of a passage with these hymnic features contribute to an author's larger composition? Taking this measured approach and asking these questions, we will see that many of the criticisms that have been raised against the prospect of identifying hymns in the New Testament lose their force.

The case against New Testament hymns. I begin by pointing out a fundamental flaw in some of the approaches to New Testament christological hymns taken in the past: they have often manifested a concern to identify preexisting material. Such an approach has been joined together with the recognition that there are passages that have a significant accumulation of poetic features that reflect the features of ancient psalms and hymns. The result has been to identify these passages as preexisting hymns. This flawed approach to studying these passages is what has called forth the most serious criticisms since it has led to a number of serious interpretative and methodological problems, which will be outlined below. My contention is that the conflation of these two issues—the identification of preexisting material and the recognition of hymnic passages—is at the root of the critiques offered by scholars like Stephen Fowl and Michael Peppard. Once the two issues are separated, it can be seen that the majority of critiques apply to the identification of preexisting materials and not to the identification of hymnic features in New Testament passages.

As a representative of scholars critical of the preexisting hymn approach, Stephen Fowl has voiced these concerns coherently and concisely, claiming that identifying preexisting material in the New Testament is impossible, pure conjecture, and of no value.[43] His points may be summarized briefly: (1) there is no convincing argument that a passage is drawn from a piece of preexisting material; (2) even if it were, the attempt to reconstruct an original and discuss its setting in earliest Christianity is purely speculative; (3) the results of such

---

[43]Fowl, *Philippians*, 108-13.

a process are without value since the function of the passage must be understood and evaluated in its current context, not in a hypothetical other setting.
In the context of his discussion in his Philippians commentary these critical
concerns relate primarily to Philippians 2:6-11. However, the same arguments
must be addressed in the study of any New Testament passage that scholars
claim is a citation of a preexisting text.

The following section is an argument in favor of continuing with the study
of New Testament hymns, but in a nuanced way that acknowledges the limitations of what may be claimed based on the nature of the evidence available. I
respond here most directly to Fowl's criticism and then interact with variations of these concerns raised by other scholars. As noted above, scholars who
identify hymns in the New Testament and engage in this kind of analysis point
to a number of criteria as indicative of hymnic material. Fowl disputes the two
criteria that he suggests scholars most often attend to for making their claims:
uniqueness of vocabulary and evidence of redactional activity based on stylistic abnormalities.[44] Here Fowl is already off track since he ignores several
other major indicators that, taken together, actually do make a stronger case
than Fowl allows for. Nevertheless, here I will address the two criteria that
Fowl challenges directly.

Uniqueness of vocabulary is an observable factor in many so-called
hymnic passages. As such it is to some degree an objective criterion in that
scholars can at least agree when unique vocabulary is being utilized. In the
christological hymns of the New Testament, there is no question that rare
vocabulary is present in high doses.[45] Fowl's point, which is apt, is that the
appearance of unusual vocabulary can be explained plausibly in several ways.
The presence of unusual vocabulary in the Philippian hymn, for example,
does not necessarily point to the conclusion that someone other than Paul
must have written it. Paul himself could have written the passage using unusual vocabulary. While this is an excellent point, Fowl does not go far
enough and he mistakes the value of this observation for the task at hand.
The uniqueness of the vocabulary simply points to the fact that the passage
under consideration is distinctive in some way. Thus this is not really a point

---

[44]Ibid., 111.
[45]However, note the criticism of Lash, who suggests that the sample size for comparison for some
New Testament authors, particularly in 1 Peter, is just too small to make a persuasive argument
about unusual vocabulary. See Lash, "Fashionable Sports," 295.

about authorship. Paul could have utilized unique vocabulary himself for emphasis; or someone else could have. This is in no way a decisive point. It is simply an objective observation about the nature of the passage. Its significance must then be assessed.

Fowl also criticizes the claims that stylistic abnormalities in the passages point to redaction on the part of Paul in citing the earlier text. I agree with Fowl that this is problematic in that it presupposes a standard of what is stylistically conventional.[46] He points out that in terms of both Jewish and Greco-Roman stylistic conventions, purported redactional activity based on the violation of stylistic standards is off the mark.[47] Again, I must agree on this point. The identification of supposed redactional activity can in no way be used as a criterion for deciding whether a passage is a preexisting hymn of some kind. Identification of redactional insertions could potentially be considered as a later step after one has found convincing reasons for determining that a passage consisted of preexisting material. But to reverse the process is methodologically unsound.

Fowl has raised two important points that are valid as far as they go. If these were the only criteria for recognizing New Testament hymns, the game would be over. However, uniqueness of vocabulary is but one indicator of the elevated style of the passage; evidence of redactional activity is not a criterion at all, but a result of a later step in the analysis. So in terms of identifying hymns in the New Testament Fowl's criticisms fall short. He focuses solely on identifying preexisting material, and there are many other criteria besides the ones he criticizes.

At this point we can return to the list of criteria I mentioned at the beginning of this section.[48] A problem with these lists, and this would be a further objection some might raise, is that while they point to observable features in each text, how one interprets the presence of these features is what is at stake. Unique vocabulary, elevated style, hymnic form, and christological content do not in and of themselves justify the conclusion that a passage is preexisting material.

---

[46]Fowl, *Philippians*, 111.

[47]Ibid., 112.

[48]W. Hulitt Gloer, "Homologies and Hymns in the New Testament: Form, Content and Criteria for Identification," *PRSt* 11 (1984): 115-32; Ethelbert Stauffer, *New Testament Theology*, trans. John Marsh (London: SCM, 1955), 338-39; Longenecker, *New Wine*, 10-11, 15-16. Aune cites these as well, but with recognition of the challenges they present; Aune, "Hymn."

Another major critic, Ralph Brucker, claims that the following criteria are problematic when used to identify traditional material: exuberant style, rhythm, parallelism, relative clauses, and the use of participles.[49] As he explains, "They prove themselves to be rather weak and eventually based on mere feeling, since all of them are to be found in prose as well."[50] This is an excellent point in and of itself, but not as much of a concern if one is prepared, as I am, to recognize the importance of prose hymnody in the ancient world and for the early Christians.

Brucker goes on to suggest that the use of rhetorical categories does not help the case for identifying these passages as hymns. If encomium is invoked, for example, Brucker argues that it is a category of prose, not poetry. And for Brucker, poetry must be composed with regular meter; parallelism (a common feature of Jewish psalmody) is not enough to consider a passage as poetry.[51] Accordingly, these passages may be praise, in Brucker's view, but they cannot be hymns. Brucker is emphatic here: "Solemn passages praising Christ or God in the New Testament writings are not quotations of 'songs' or 'hymns' (and hence traces of early Christian liturgy), but rather examples of a literary phenomenon that has numerous analogies in other ancient texts."[52] In his view, they are best identified as epideictic passages using the label *epainos* (praise) rather than *encomium* since in rhetorical theory and practice the latter term is used for longer and more elaborate praise of individuals rather than the shorter kinds of passages found in the New Testament. This works out in practice in his analysis of Philippians 2:6-11. As his critique above suggests, he prefers to call this passage a "praise of Christ." Interestingly, Brucker does acknowledge a "hymnic style" in the passage but claims that it is not poetic and not a hymn.[53]

Brucker's analysis is valuable as he explicitly brings into the discussion other ancient examples and discussions of praise from the realm of rhetoric.[54]

---

[49]Brucker, "'Songs,' 'Hymns,' and 'Encomia,'" 3.

[50]Ibid.

[51]Ibid., 4.

[52]Ibid., 10.

[53]Ibid., 7.

[54]Brucker is not the only one to bring these rhetorical perspectives into the discussion. See my own analysis of these materials in Matthew E. Gordley, *The Colossian Hymn in Context: An Exegesis in Light of Jewish and Greco-Roman Hymnic and Epistolary Conventions*, WUNT 2/228 (Tübingen: Mohr Siebeck, 2007), 111-24. More recently, see the same material discussed in Martin and Nash, "Subversive *Hymnos*," esp. 93-109.

I will return to these in greater detail in chapter two. However, what is important to note here is that Brucker, like Fowl, also conflates the two issues. He argues plausibly that it is problematic to use any list of criteria to identify preexisting material; but he also uses that point to draw the faulty conclusion that the New Testament passages in "hymnic style" (his term) cannot justifiably be called hymns. I suggest that the two issues—preexisting materials and hymns—need to be considered separately. Brucker also unnecessarily restricts the application of the category of hymn to poetic texts, essentially ignoring the tradition of prose hymnody in antiquity.

The critique offered by Peppard is similar, in part because he draws on the earlier work of Brucker and cites his approach with approval. At the heart of his critique is the claim of circularity along with a lack of awareness by scholars of faulty assumptions they are making when claiming that these passages are hymns. Using the influential work of Ralph Martin on the Philippian hymn as an example, he asks: "Which seems to come first: a critical method to distinguish poetry from prose, a hymn from an epistle, or rather Martin's convictions about what a hymn should look like?"[55] He also laments that there is not a scientific (i.e., repeatable) method for distinguishing New Testament hymns. Like Fowl and Brucker he identifies a number of problems with the usual criteria that are invoked. Some, he notes, are "vague and applicable to too many kinds of texts," adding that these "should be discounted immediately."[56] In this camp he includes parallelism (which he dismisses with a footnote), a series of threes, unusual vocabulary, figurative language, theological or christological concepts, and careful construction. Why vagueness and applicability to other kinds of texts is a problem is not stated. Without any argument, Peppard asks readers to discount six features, most of which are common to each New Testament hymnic passage. And yet, surely the presence of these common features is noteworthy and ought to be considered in interpreting these texts.

Peppard devotes more attention to a second list of problematic criteria, some of which are on Brucker's list as well. These are use of rhythmical style, presence of an introductory formula, setting in a cultic milieu, and beginning with a relative pronoun.[57] Unlike the preceding list of criteria, which Peppard

---

[55]Peppard, "Poetry," 323.
[56]Ibid., 324.
[57]Ibid., 324-25.

dismissed without argument, here he argues against each in turn. For example, he points out that rhythm is a quality of well-crafted prose and did not signal poetry to the earliest readers or commentators.[58] Similarly, introductory formulas and the beginning of a passage with a relative pronoun are features of nonhymnic passages as well. Regarding cultic milieu, Peppard explains that there are too few examples to be able to identify this with any certainty. Finally, he explains, the major hymns in this discussion (Colossians and Philippians) do not show some of these features. In short, for Peppard, "the method does not supply results repeatable by different readers."[59] Again, why this is a problem is not explained. Differing interpretations of texts, even by scholars using similar methodologies, is a common feature of the discipline of biblical studies and is not a problem that is unique to these passages.

By outlining these issues and explaining them to the extent that he does, Peppard, like Fowl and Brucker, raises some important points. Peppard goes too far, however, in revealing what he believes is in the mind of earlier scholars who have written about these passages. For example, he claims, "Most scholars, when they use the term 'hymn,' do not provide evidence in their publications that they know what they are talking about."[60] Peppard goes on to describe what these scholars are and are not envisioning:

> They are not imagining the sort of hymnody that likely was practiced in Philippi—a hymn newly created and sung by one person to a god as a public display of piety and a showcase of epideictic rhetoric. Rather, most scholars have imagined a hymn more like a modern Christian assembly—an old favorite sung by a limited group of people as a private experience of worship.[61]

He warns: "The guild of biblical scholarship would do well to be careful when we choose our anachronisms to describe the past."[62] While his caution about the importance of recognizing the vast difference between contemporary Christian song and first-century hymnody is on target, it is also important to note that the concept of a hymn is not an anachronism at all. As we will see,

---

[58]In this he anticipates the findings of Strawbridge and Edsall, whose contribution to the discussion is an analysis of the reception of these passages in the early Fathers. Their findings will be discussed below.

[59]Peppard, "Poetry," 326.

[60]Ibid., 338. It is unclear what would constitute sufficient evidence that interpreters know what they are talking about.

[61]Ibid.

[62]Ibid.

hymnody was a prominent feature within ancient Greco-Roman and Jewish culture. In fact, Peppard cites with approval the work of Adela Yarbro Collins, who reads Colossians 1:15-20 as a prose *hymn*.

Peppard's analysis anticipates the contribution of Jennifer Strawbridge and Benjamin Edsall, who, after reviewing a number of the problems already identified by the scholars noted above, ultimately suggest that the term *hymn* should be avoided altogether. In this they repeat the thesis of Brucker and recommend the German term *Christuslob*, praise of Christ.[63] An important contribution of their analysis is that they consider the reception of Philippians 2:6-11 and Colossians 1:15-20 by early readers and look for any evidence that these passages were considered hymnic or poetic. Their review of the reception history of both texts shows that they were extremely important in early Christianity and that they were cited more than any other New Testament texts.[64] However, importantly for these authors, the passages lack "reception in a collection of songs praising God."[65] Although they acknowledge that this is an argument from silence, Strawbridge and Edsall use this silence to support their claim that language of hymns should not be applied to these texts.[66]

Interestingly, one of their findings coheres with the findings of my study that these passages should be considered hymnic or poetic in nature. Strawbridge and Edsall note the very clear didactic function these passages play in early Christian writings. With regard to Colossians 1:15-20: "The high frequency of the use of this passage and its role in supporting early Christian writers in their Christological and theological arguments both point to the understanding that this pericope was a crucial text for formation in early Christianity—both in terms of formation of doctrine and formation of Christians themselves."[67] Of Colossians in particular, they note: "Amongst early Christian writers, this passage triggers different images and comparisons in a way that is more imagistic and poetical than argumentative, even though

---

[63]Edsall and Strawbridge, "Songs We Used to Sing," 306. Apart from "some subsequent textual discovery [that] will demonstrate conclusively that these passages were used as hymns in antiquity" they argue that "we should be content with the descriptor *Christuslob*" (306). Thus "the default position for analyzing these passages needs to be simply that they are heightened prose as part of a letter" (306).

[64]Ibid., 300-305.

[65]Ibid., 306.

[66]Ibid., 301, 306.

[67]Ibid., 303.

many of the references are found within apologetic works and treatises."[68] In evaluating their findings, I find that these extensive "imagistic and poetical" uses are not at all surprising since the value and impact of hymnic texts (whether poetry or prose) lies, in part, in their ability to evoke ideas and images in a mode that is not always simply rational or logical.[69] Though silence is notoriously difficult to interpret, the extensive use of these hymnic passages in the early church coheres with a claim that these fit the tradition of didactic hymnody. Their familiarity and extensive use by early writers may also suggest their use in communal gatherings of worship. That is certainly one plausible explanation for their widespread popularity in early Christian writings.

Our brief look at these methodological critiques shows that the list-of-criteria approach has come under fire. It is important to note, however, that the criticisms do not generally discount that the features are present in a given passage. Rather, the issue has to do with the significance of the recognition of those features. The presence of one or several features cannot automatically lead to the conclusion that a passage is a preexisting composition cited by the author in a new context. Nevertheless, in my view several of these features do at least point to the possibility that a passage may be preexisting material, even if these features are not conclusive in themselves.

In my view the following features could suggest that a particular passage may be preexisting material. First, disruption of the context and flow should be considered. This is similar to what Longenecker calls contextual dislocations, namely, "poetic material in a prose section or doctrinal material in an ethical section."[70] But beyond those contextual dislocations this also includes the change of person or address (i.e., from second person to third person and then back to second-person address). Second, content that goes beyond the concerns of the immediate context is a clue. Richard Longenecker similarly discusses the observation of "the continuance of a portion after its content has ceased to be relevant to its immediate context."[71] Third, recognizability of

---

[68]Ibid., 302.

[69]See Gary S. Selby, *Not with Wisdom of Words: Nonrational Persuasion in the New Testament* (Grand Rapids: Eerdmans, 2016), 13-16. Psalms and poems are known to have played a role in identity formation in early Judaism. For example, on the Hodayot of Qumran see Carol A. Newsom, *The Self as Symbolic Space: Constructing Identity and Community at Qumran*, STDJ 52 (Leiden: Brill, 2004).

[70]Longenecker, *New Wine*, 10-11.

[71]Ibid.

formal structural features could be an indicator. These factors, coupled with the other observable features noted above, while not decisive, make it reasonable to at least ask whether the passage under consideration could be traditional material of some kind.

Even so, it of course must be noted that in most cases the author does not indicate that he is citing some other source. This observation should not, however, be taken to mean that the author is not citing traditional material. We have examples both in and out of the New Testament where preexisting material is cited without explicit identification.[72]

Finally, there is evidence from within the New Testament and from the broader Greco-Roman world that hymn singing was an important feature of early Christian gatherings. This recognition does not prove that we have any such hymns recorded in the New Testament. However, it does point to the fact that such compositions existed at the time of the writing of letters of the New Testament. This means that their purported inclusion in the New Testament writings is, at the very least, not an anachronism.

In the discussion above I have made the case that the question of preexisting material in the New Testament and the question of hymns in the New Testament really should be considered as two separate issues. Though there are a number of criteria to which one can appeal in order to demonstrate plausibly that a passage may be drawing on preexisting material, the critiques of this approach caution against faulty logic that would imply that if features *a*, *b*, and *c* are found in a text then conclusion *d* naturally follows. Instead, the question that needs to be asked is, What explanation best accounts for the concentration of this high number of unique (within the context) features that are also shared by a selection of texts across the spectrum of New Testament writings? This question must be answered on a case-by-case basis. For now, it is safe to say that features in Philippians 2, Colossians 1, and John 1 have led many scholars to conclude that they represent preexisting material. However, even if they are not direct citations of preexisting compositions, there are good reasons for concluding that they were written in such a way that they draw on specific kinds of traditional material.

Moreover, when these passages are viewed individually and as a group in light of the conventions of ancient Jewish and Greco-Roman hymnody, it

---

[72]For example, citations of the Old Testament in the New are presented in a wide variety of ways.

becomes clear that the features of these passages justify calling them hymns. What *kind* of hymn each one might be is a different question altogether. It is an important one, however.

Additional concerns related to finding hymns in the New Testament. If there are hymns in the New Testament, is there any value in analyzing them as hymns? There can be. But there are also some dead ends. Fowl points out a major problem common in the analysis of New Testament christological hymns: the attempt to get behind the text as we have it and to reconstruct an original hymn is purely speculative. Three interrelated speculative moves are often made once a passage is identified as an early Christian hymn. First, it is often argued that the writer who is citing the hymn may have felt free to modify or adapt the hymn to some extent in order to highlight certain key concepts that were important to this writer in the context of the epistle. Two classic examples can be noted here briefly: (1) in Philippians 2:8c the phrase "even death on a cross" is often viewed by scholars as a Pauline interpretive gloss; (2) in Colossians 1:18a the clause "the church" is often viewed as an interpretive addition to the phrase "and he is the head of the body." In order to defend these theories, arguments are usually made on the grounds of style, form, and theological content. Fowl is correct to point out that such theories are problematic and that one should be very cautious in evaluating a part of a passage as a gloss. As we will see, there are good reasons to consider these "Pauline" elements as original and not editorial insertions.

Second, it is often assumed that the hymn is only cited in part, so that in most cases we do not have the entirety of the hymn. N. T. Wright cautions that if we allow that material has been added, then we must also acknowledge that material may also have been removed. An author may also be quoting only part of a source.[73] What is missing is most often considered to be the opening line. Theories as to what a hymn's opening line may have looked like are based on the stream of tradition in which the interpreter places the hymn as well as on the liturgical context for which the interpreter imagines the hymn was composed. For example, Colossians 1:15-20, as several other hymns do, begins in its context with the relative pronoun "who." A typical reconstruction of the beginning of the hymn is: Blessed be Jesus Christ, who.[74] This follows a typical

---

[73]Wright, "Poetry and Theology in Colossians 1:15-20," 445.
[74]Christian Stettler, *Der Kolosserhymnus: Untersuchungen zu Form, traditionsgeschichtlichem Hintergrund und Aussage von Kol 1, 15-20*, WUNT 2/131 (Tübingen: Mohr Siebeck, 2000), 92.

psalm pattern and makes sense on some level. Again, however, Fowl is correct to urge caution. The opening line would be much different if the traditional material being cited were a thanksgiving hymn, a didactic hymn, or a piece of catechetical instruction in poetic form. The conventions of psalm and hymn writing in the first century were fluid enough that it is nearly impossible to imagine what a missing line or phrase might have looked like. As a result, for Wright the task of reconstruction is "virtually impossible," amounting to "unprovable speculation."[75]

Third, an imagined original hymn is often arranged in lines and strophes. The addition or deletion of words and phrases often helps to create a more balanced and better structured passage than what one finds in the New Testament citation. The main problem here is the extent to which scholars should expect to find balance, symmetry, and perhaps even rhythm in a passage that does not immediately display such features. The basis for such stylistic standards is often very thin.

The three moves noted above are common in the analysis of hymnic passages in the New Testament. One additional move that has occasionally been made has been to posit an original hymn in a language other than Greek. Thus Hebrew and Aramaic originals have been proposed for the Colossian hymn and Philippian hymn respectively.[76] While potentially instructive on some level, the degree of speculation would seem to increase with each step away from the texts as we have them in the New Testament writings. If the conclusion that a passage was preexisting material can only be tentative, then the proposal that the original was composed in another language is another step (or more) removed from what can be demonstrated plausibly from the text as we have it.

Though there have been several surveys of New Testament hymns over the years, an influential approach that is illustrative of the kinds of concerns raised by Fowl, Brucker, and others is the work of Reinhard Deichgräber.[77] As I examine his approach I will bring it into conversation with Fowl's critiques as a way to advance the discussion. To begin with, it is important to note that Deichgräber's explicit focus is *form- und stilgeschichtliche Probleme* (form- and style-critical problems) in the texts. As a result of this approach he asks the following questions:

---

[75]Wright, "Poetry and Theology in Colossians 1:15-20," 445.
[76]See Peppard's comments on this maneuver in "Poetry," 326-27.
[77]Deichgräber, *Gotteshymnus und Christushymnus.*

1. Can we discern the construction and the strophic structure of the passage?

2. What was the original wording before it was adapted to its current context?

3. Does the linguistic peculiarity of the hymn allow conclusions about its origin?

4. What can be said about the *Sitz im Leben* of the original composition?

These are important questions, but as I have already suggested, there are more important questions that can and should be raised. His first two questions deal with recognizing hymnic material and then reconstructing the original hymn. Fowl has cautioned against the process since the likelihood of success is limited, and further, there is no way of verifying the results. However, the criteria that have been employed for this purpose do carry some weight in that there is a distinct set of observable features that serve to unite the passages in question and that justify their being called hymns. Further, additional criteria may be added, including rhetorical features, rhythm, and metrical analysis. At the very least, these features, which occur with a high degree of concentration in passages that offer a description of Christ and his accomplishments, need to be accounted for.

In reconstructing the original, Deichgräber has been lauded for his cautious and judicious application of method.[78] One must agree with Fowl, however, in that once one begins eliminating lines or phrases from the hymn, and proposes adding in other lines, the procedure becomes speculation built on speculation. One is on surest footing, then, when one can make sense of the text as is, with a minimum of proposed interpolations or hypothetical lines. This will be a fundamental assumption of my study. Appeals to interpretive glosses in order to remove phrases that seem to interrupt the hymn or do not fit for some reason must not be made hastily. When such an idea is proposed it must be with good reason and must draw support from the text itself, rather than simply from the fact that it does not fit with an external idea of what a supposed original hymn was really about. For example, in the Colossian hymn I identify an interpretive gloss in the

---

[78]Fowl himself recognizes Deichgräber's "rigor and cautious use of evidence." For his treatment of Deichgräber, see Stephen E. Fowl, *The Story of Christ in the Ethics of Paul: An Analysis of the Function of the Hymnic Material in the Pauline Corpus*, JSNTSup 36 (Sheffield: Sheffield Academic, 1990), 15-17.

hymn on the basis of the fact that one specific line is not composed in the same rhythmic manner that the remaining lines are composed. Recognizing the intrusion of this line into the hymn opens up the possibility that in this section of the hymn the author of the epistle is making his primary point and explaining an issue that may have been unclear for the recipients. Thus the proposed interpolation is not based on theology or perspective of the hymn, but on the appropriateness of the rhythm of the line compared with the rest of the passage. Nevertheless, such a conclusion must be recognized as provisional, and more elaborate theories of origin and liturgical use should not be drawn from such a provisional conclusion.

From this point in the method, Deichgräber goes down a more difficult path, as he attempts to draw conclusions about the origin of each hymn and its *Sitz im Leben*. Deichgräber's conclusions here are again restrained. He does not propose complex theories about baptismal liturgies and so forth. Still, Fowl's critique as to the value of such explorations must be considered. In light of such critiques, another path is proposed here, one that Fowl himself has taken to some extent. This path is the analysis of the function of the hymn in its current epistolary context.

By attending to the hymnic features and strophic structure of the passage, one can identify both the main emphases of the hymn and its distinctive theological perspective. With this information in view, one is then able to read the hymn in the context of the epistle in order to see how this hymn, with its unique emphases, is put to use in service of the rhetorical goals of the author. This is a dynamic process that is based less on speculation and the building of elaborate theories and more on examining the contents, themes, and concerns of the hymn in the context of the epistle's guiding purpose.

In view of the above criticisms and procedures, it is clear that scholars must proceed with caution in each step. Some, however, prefer to reject outright the idea of identifying and reconstructing an original hymn, preferring to deal with the text as is. While that approach seems like a safe place to start, the unique features of these passages require further explanation and in some cases do justify the claim that they are hymns of some kind. Therefore, it is not out of bounds to consider how the passages might at least be arranged to reflect more clearly their hymnic nature. That is the goal of the chapters that follow: to elucidate the hymnic nature of these passages to the extent that it is possible to do so.

WHAT THE NEW TESTAMENT CHRISTOLOGICAL HYMNS REVEAL ABOUT EARLY CHRISTIAN WORSHIP

What does such a procedure enable us to discover? Attending to the hymnic features and structure in the ways noted above ultimately yields a better appreciation of each passage individually. It also can result in a greater understanding of the primary emphases of each hymn. Further, it can facilitate comparison with other similar hymnic expressions from antiquity, thus allowing for a greater appreciation of a passage's features. This kind of analysis can also foster a more nuanced understanding of early Christian thought and reflection on the person and work of Christ more broadly. In some cases, it may also yield an appreciation of how traditional materials are used to undergird an author's overall argument and discussion. Taken together, my analyses of these hymnic passages in praise of Christ will yield some important conclusions about early Christian worship. This is not because all of these passages were preexisting hymns but rather because they likely reflect to some extent what was already common in early Christian praise of Jesus. I will spell out those conclusions here and then demonstrate and elaborate on them throughout the volume.

Early Christian worship exhibited the following characteristics:

▶ It was Christocentric. At the very least, we can say that the early Christian milieu was generative of passages that offer praise to Christ or hymnic declarations about Christ in elevated or poetic style.

▶ It invited participants to embrace a particular view of reality centered in the events surrounding the life, death, and resurrection of Jesus.

▶ It was deeply rooted in a Jewish conception of the divine.

▶ It was creatively and critically engaged with the Jewish Scriptures.

▶ It was closely connected to the Jewish psalm tradition.

▶ It was connected to a living tradition of psalm composition and religious poetry that had a long tradition of engaging culture and resisting easy answers.

▶ It appropriated aspects of Greek and Roman culture.

▶ It represented a fusion of Jewish and Greco-Roman literary conventions and styles.

▶ It was conscious of its imperial context.

▸ It provided its participants with resources to resist Roman imperial ideology and pagan religious beliefs as the overarching forces controlling their lives.

▸ It was much more than doctrinal or cognitive; it also had an affective dimension and an allusive quality. Accordingly, early Christian worship offered imagery and language that had an allusive power capable of engaging the emotions of its participants.

We will see that these features are represented to varying degrees in the passages under consideration in this volume. When the hymnic passages are considered as a whole, they point to early Christian worship as a phenomenon that was dynamic and complex. They also point to the reality of worship of Jesus as a central component of early Christian thought and practice. Expanding on the quotation of Ralph Martin that opened this chapter, we may conclude this introduction by agreeing with John Anthony McGuckin's claim that "the Christian community was embryonically formed within the womb of worship."[79] If this is so, then it is not too much to claim that this survey will take us close to the very origins of the Christian faith.

I will discuss the collective impact of my survey of these passages and the significance of these findings in the concluding chapter. In addition to summarizing my claims about the nature of early Christian worship, I will also point to some ways that these hymnic passages can be a resource for helping contemporary Christian worshipers reflect deeply about their own worship, practices. It may be that a deeper appreciation for the genius of these hymnic compositions in praise of Christ will lead to new insights that have relevance not just for those studying ancient texts but also for those intending to follow Jesus today.

---

[79]McGuckin, *Path of Christianity*, 815.

– Two –

THE CULTURAL MATRICES OF EARLY CHRISTIAN WORSHIP

To appreciate more fully the ways in which early Christians utilized the medium of hymnody within their communal gatherings and within their compositions, it is vital that we understand the role of hymns in Greco-Roman and Jewish culture. When we see the extent to which hymns, psalms, and related kinds of praise poetry were a feature of life in the first century CE, we will be in a better position to consider the ways in which early Christian hymns participated in this broader cultural practice. To facilitate such an understanding I provide in this chapter an overview of the ways that hymnody permeated Greco-Roman culture and Jewish culture, with a particular emphasis on ancient hymns that show a degree of comparability to New Testament hymns, through their subject matter, themes, background, provenance, or likely functions for their authors and the communities that preserved them. When it comes to examining the specifics of the New Testament christological hymns in the chapters that follow, we will be better positioned to be able to appreciate both continuity with first-century practices as well as innovations unique to the early Christians. I begin with hymnody in the Greco-Roman world and then move on to psalms and hymns within early Judaism.[1]

---

[1]Even while making such a distinction for the sake of analysis, it is important to recognize that the categories are problematic in that both are already exceptionally broad and both overlap

PART 1: HYMNS IN THE GRECO-ROMAN WORLD

Hymns and hymn singing were important features of Greek and Roman public life. Hymns were composed in praise of gods in connection with several aspects of society, including the cultic offering of sacrifice, public thanks and praise, large public festivals, and more intimate banquets known as symposia. Accordingly, they played important roles not only for religious rituals but also in shaping culture, teaching values, and promoting particular ways of viewing the world. As William D. Furley and Jan Maarten Bremer observe, "In every hymn there is always the internal communication addressed by the worshipping mortal(s) to the god. But in many cases there is also *external* communication between the poet and/or the performers and the audience."[2] It is this fusion of communication to the gods as well as communication to the human audience that is suggestive for our study.

To see that hymns played a prominent role in the Hellenistic world, we need look no further than the *Iliad*. In book one readers immediately encounter a priest and a diviner, see sacrifice and divination, and witness prayer, both individual and communal. Chryses, for example, prays in a loud voice with uplifted arms. In addition to Chryses, everyone else prayed as well. For our purposes it is notable that, in addition to prayers, singing of hymns to the gods accompanied all of the feasting (lines 472-74):

> So the whole day long they sought to appease the god with song, singing the beautiful paean, the sons of the Achaeans, hymning the god that worketh afar; and his heart was glad as he heard.[3]

While not a religious text in the sense of a sacred text belonging to a particular sect, nor in the sense of being a theological or literary reflection on the nature or practice of religion, the *Iliad* nonetheless provides a fascinating window onto the religious practices and worldview perspectives that shaped life in ancient Greece. And though not describing any real or historical events as a firsthand witness, the accounts of prayers, hymns, sacrifices, oaths, meals, and other religious ritual practices reflect the kinds of

---

considerably since Jewish psalms and hymns of the Second Temple period already indicate a great deal of interaction with hymnody from the wider Greco-Roman culture.

[2]William D. Furley and Jan Maarten Bremer, *Greek Hymns: Selected Cult Songs from the Archaic to the Hellenistic Period*, STAC 9-10 (Tübingen: Mohr Siebeck, 2001), 1:59.

[3]Homer, *Iliad*, trans. A. T. Murray and William F. Wyatt, LCL 170-71 (Cambridge, MA: Harvard University Press, 1999).

practices that were a customary part of the lives of readers; these were not strange descriptions of exotic ancient customs but rather the same kinds of practices that were common in Greek cities.[4] We know this from archaeology, history, epigraphy, and other literary accounts that have enabled scholars to paint a picture of ancient religious life among the Greeks and Romans. The fact that each of these practices is mentioned in passing suggests the extent to which these were commonplace features of ancient life for the readers.[5] In the same vein Virgil's *Aeneid* likewise affirms the place of songs of praise in the Roman world. As King Evander describes to Aeneas the annual rites in honor of Hercules, readers are treated to an elaborate description of worship involving a procession, feasting, dancing, choirs, and songs of praise (*Aeneid* 8.268-305).

Aside from literary depictions of hymn singing, we know from inscriptions and other evidence that ancient Greek festivals of many kinds were accompanied by hymns.[6] Hymns were performed with a chorus encircling the altar or during a long procession. Special choruses were formed for the singing of hymns, a practice that continued well into the Roman era.[7] Individuals were given special titles of *hymnōdoi* and *hymnētiai*.[8] Bremer notes that in the Hellenistic and Roman periods, "It seems to have been normal for city authorities everywhere to take much care of religious traditions and more in particular of hymnody."[9] He explains that within choral societies individuals "were trained to sing the hymns properly and they performed them in honour of gods or deified men on the festival days according to the religious calendar."[10] Examples provided by Bremer show hymns being sung during processions, during the opening of temple doors, and in some cases with elaborate

---

[4]The *Odyssey* likewise attests to the place of hymns in the ancient world with an explicit mention of the term *hymnos* in 8.429. For further discussion of hymnody in Homer see Michael Lattke, *Hymnus: Materialen zu einer Geschichte der antiken Hymnologie*, NTOA 19 (Göttingen: Vandenhoeck & Ruprecht, 1991), 13-15.

[5]In his chapter on the development of Christian hymnography, John McGuckin writes, "Hymn singing was, of course, the ancient bedrock of ancient Greek religion." John Anthony McGuckin, *The Path of Christianity: The First Thousand Years* (Downers Grove, IL: IVP Academic, 2017), 819. For the entire discussion, see 815-59.

[6]Jan Maarten Bremer, "Greek Hymns," in *Faith, Hope and Worship: Aspects of Religious Mentality in the Ancient World*, ed. H. S. Versnel, Studies in Greek and Roman Religion 2 (Leiden: Brill, 1981), 193-215, here 197-99.

[7]Ibid., 199. In addition, Lucian satirizes this practice in his *Alexander the False Prophet* 41.

[8]Ibid. Bremer cites Pollux, *Onomasticon* 1.35.

[9]Ibid., 200.

[10]Ibid. As we observed in *Aeneid* 8.

instructions for the size of the chorus, its gender, its clothing, and other details of performance.[11] Hymns were also sung at meals. In some cases, new hymns were sung, while in others preexisting, prescribed hymns were used.[12] From these kinds of descriptions alone, found in both literary and nonliterary sources, we can gain a general sense of the widespread importance of hymnody within Greco-Roman culture.

In addition to this general understanding, we also have knowledge about specific hymns in antiquity from a variety of different kinds of sources.[13] First, individual freestanding hymns are preserved through inscriptions that record the words of hymns. Second, many hymns are preserved through other means, including being found in collections of hymns. Third, hymns are found embedded within other genres. Whether these represent actual sung hymns is open to question so that the extent to which hymns embedded in other genres are indicative of general hymnic practice is something we will need to consider. Fourth, lengthy discussions about hymns are found in a number of ancient writers. Of particular interest are comments found in rhetorical handbooks and treatises about the nature of ancient hymns in light of other kinds of praise in the ancient world. Taken together, these sources have a lot to tell us about the roles that hymns played in ancient life, and we will explore each in turn below.

Hymns in literature and philosophy. In an earlier volume, I explored the plurality of ways that ancient Greek and Roman hymns served as vehicles of instruction for the human audiences that sung, heard, or read them.[14] Going back as far as the hymns, prayers, and related texts in the body of works associated with Homer and Hesiod, we can see that hymns played an important role in cultural formation. The Homeric Hymns in particular, through their inclusion of direct claims about the gods, as well as narratives about the founding of cult centers, passed on traditions and clear teaching about the ways in which the divine and human worlds interacted.[15] For example, the Hymn to Demeter not only instructs readers about the

---

[11]Ibid., 200-203.
[12]Ibid., 207-8.
[13]Furley and Bremer, *Greek Hymns*. See the discussion in Frances Hickson Hahn, "Performing the Sacred: Prayers and Hymns," in *A Companion to Roman Religion*, ed. Jörge Rüpke (Malden, MA: Blackwell, 2007), 235-48.
[14]Matthew E. Gordley, *Teaching Through Song in Antiquity: Didactic Hymnody Among Greeks, Romans, Jews and Christians*, WUNT 2/331 (Tübingen: Mohr Siebeck, 2011).
[15]Ibid., 30-54.

goddesses Demeter and Persephone but also provides insight into the origins of the Eleusinian mysteries and the founding of the cult.[16] In a similar way, Hesiod's hymnic preludes to his *Theogony* and *Works and Days* provide a picture of a world in which Zeus reigned and in which poets were divinely authorized to speak forth.[17] Thus the surviving hymns from these influential writers show us quite clearly that hymns had an important role to play in the ancient world. In addition to what these hymns taught and communicated for their audiences, they also served as models that later poets and writers would emulate, adapt, and utilize to address the needs and concerns of later eras.

Indeed, later writers, particularly philosophers, would utilize the genre of *hymnos* to put their teaching into memorable and meaningful forms.[18] In this way hymns not only were vehicles of instruction but also conveyed to their readers a sense of grandeur and profound significance as their ideas were shown to be valuable both in the human world and in the divine realm. One of the most well-known instances of this kind of philosophical hymnody is Cleanthes's *Hymn to Zeus*. But other examples abounded in antiquity, including compositions like the hymn to Zeus at the beginning of Aratus's *Phaenomena*, Aristotle's *Hymn to Virtue*, and the hymns embedded at key junctures in Lucretius's *On the Nature of the Universe*. Hymns like these show quite clearly just how the influential hymns of Homer and Hesiod provided a model for later poets, writers, and philosophers to adapt in order to express their understanding of ultimate reality, and to invite their readers to encounter this reality in both a cognitive and an affective way.

Performance hymns. Apart from literary hymns and philosophical hymns, many examples survive of the kinds of hymns that would have actually been performed at sacrifices, banquets, and festivals in honor of gods. These show a very close affinity to the pattern of the literary hymns, suggesting both that literary hymns were formed on the model of "real," sung hymns, and also that the literary hymns likewise influenced the tradition over time.

One deity whose worship was particularly connected with hymnody was the healing god, Asclepius. The cult of Asclepius was popular from the late

---

[16]See, for example, Helene P. Foley, *The Homeric Hymn to Demeter: Translation, Commentary, and Interpretive Essays* (Princeton, NJ: Princeton University Press, 1994), 84.
[17]See Hesiod, *Works and Days* 1-10 and *Theogony* 1-115.
[18]Gordley, *Teaching Through Song in Antiquity*, 68-99.

classical period well into the Roman era. A number of hymns to Asclepius have been preserved, many as inscriptions in sanctuaries devoted to the god.[19] As Emma Edelstein and Ludwig Edelstein explain,

> In all the ceremonies, be they daily exercises or solemn festivals, one feature recurs: the singing of hymns. They were recited in the temples morning and night; they were chanted during processions; they were accompaniment for sacrifices. The song characteristic of the Asclepius worship was the paean, a choral hymn with no music other than that of the cithara.[20]

Based on the testimonies of healing, the cult's popularity, and the role of hymns in the worship of Asclepius, some scholars have sought to make connections with the worship of Jesus.[21] These comparisons are not just a recent scholarly creation, however. They can be traced back as early as the second century CE to the writings of Justin Martyr.[22]

Similarly, surviving inscriptions and hymns to Isis demonstrate the popularity of this cult and the role of hymnody within it.[23] Isis aretalogies, first-person pronouncements in which the goddess describes herself and her benefits to humanity, have been found in numerous cities and suggest the widespread influence of the Isis cult throughout the ancient Mediterranean world. In inscriptions, papyri, and literary works, compositions in praise of Isis have been found from the first century BCE through the third century CE in both prose and metrical verse. Praises of Isis were often composed in a unique first-person aretalogy style, but were also written at times in the second- and third-person style, which was more common among ancient hymns in general. Isis is often praised as a universal goddess, identified with other gods in the new places in which she is worshiped, and is praised for both her benefactions to humanity as a whole and her saving acts for individuals. As with the praises of Asclepius, these instances of praise of a

---

[19]Furley and Bremer, *Greek Hymns*, 1:201-14.
[20]Emma J. Edelstein and Ludwig Edelstein, *Asclepius: Collection and Interpretation of the Testimonies* (Baltimore: Johns Hopkins University Press, 1998), 199.
[21]Ibid., 206 n. 28; Maureen W. Yeung, *Faith in Jesus and Paul: A Comparison with Special Reference to "Faith That Can Remove Mountains" and "Your Faith Has Healed/Saved You,"* WUNT 2/147 (Tübingen: Mohr Siebeck, 2002), 83-97.
[22]See M. David Litwa, *Iesus Deus: The Early Christian Depiction of Jesus as a Mediterranean God* (Minneapolis: Fortress, 2014), 2-3.
[23]See my discussion of these sources in Matthew E. Gordley, *The Colossian Hymn in Context: An Exegesis in Light of Jewish and Greco-Roman Hymnic and Epistolary Conventions*, WUNT 2/228 (Tübingen: Mohr Siebeck, 2007), 147-55.

universal savior likewise invite comparison with the worship of Jesus among the early Christians.[24]

One intriguing example of a Greek hymn from the second century BCE is Melinno's *Hymn to Rome*.[25] This five-stanza hymn treats Rome (Roma) as an actual goddess, giving her all the kinds of attributes and hymnic praise that were attributed to Greek deities. This hymn illustrates several of the features of ancient hymnody in the Greco-Roman world both by its adherence to convention as well as the way in which it provides a vehicle for innovation and addressing current issues. First, this hymn to Rome shows many of the formal features that were common to ancient hymns. For example, with respect to its contents, the hymn begins in a typical manner, with a salutation to the god ("hail!") followed by the goddess's name (line 1). This greeting is followed by a mention of the goddess's family origin, epithets ("war-loving queen"), and dwelling place (lines 1-4). Her specific powers are described next, with a particular emphasis on the power to rule and lead (lines 5-8). This theme is then developed further in the final three stanzas, where her sovereign rule is described, noting her ability to "safely steer the cities" of her people (lines 9-12), to maintain a rule that is unchanged by time (lines 13-16), and to bear the most powerful warriors (lines 17-20).

Second, this hymn indicates an effort by the author to incorporate a new deity, Roma, within the scope of ancient gods and goddesses. The providing of a lineage (Roma is the daughter of Ares), the specific form of a Greek hymn, the use of Sapphic meter, and the kinds of classical Greek imagery used all work together to lend the appearance of ancient and divine origins to this new world power.

Third, by the preceding features, this hymn thus plays a role not only in praise but also in shaping hearers' perceptions about the goddess. Whatever Greeks may have thought of Rome, perhaps with fear or some trepidation, this hymn enables them to welcome the power of Rome as a natural outgrowth of their own worldview.

---

[24]Bruce W. Longenecker, *The Crosses of Pompeii: Jesus-Devotion in a Vesuvian Town* (Minneapolis: Fortress, 2016), 108-15.
[25]See the discussion in Ronald Mellor, ΘΕΑ ΡΩΜΗ: *The Worship of the Goddess Roma in the Greek World*, Hypomnemata: Untersuchungen zur Antike und zu ihrer Nachleben (Göttingen: Vandenhoeck & Ruprecht, 1975), 119-24; C. M. Bowra, "Melinno's Hymn to Rome," *JRS* 47 (1957): 21-28. An English translation is available in I. M. Plant, *Women Writers of Ancient Greece and Rome: An Anthology* (Norman: University of Oklahoma Press, 2004), 99-100.

Finally, this hymn demonstrates the difficulty of identifying a specific occasion that prompted the composition of the hymn. Due to the limited information surrounding its history, scholars debate whether it was composed on the commission of a wealthy patron, or for use in religious ritual, or perhaps both. In favor of the hymn's having a role in an actual religious ritual, C. M. Bowra points out the popularity of the worship of Dea Roma and the evidence for festivals in honor of Rome throughout the Greek world. He also notes that, although the hymn is composed in Sapphic style, the five stanzas each end with full stops, as opposed to the running of lines across stanzas, which was more typical of literary or festival hymns. This unique feature suggests that each stanza was intended to be recited at a particular location or particular moment within a ritual.[26]

Although the precise circumstances of this hymn are lost, the broader context of the worship of the goddess Roma is instructive. For the Greeks, the worship of Roma seems to have derived from the Hellenistic ruler cults, which provided an imaginal space in which rulers of kingdoms were associated with the divine. Though not itself a ruler cult, the worship of Roma seems to have provided a conceptual framework that eventually opened the door to the development of the Roman imperial cult.[27] Ronald Mellor summarizes: "This little poem impressively encapsulates the themes of Roman rule found in later Latin poetry: Roma's domination over the world, the religious and national aspects of her rule, and Roma's transcendence of physical and temporal boundaries. Only the divine, eternal ruler is missing."[28] Mellor goes on to explain that, from the personification and deification of the state itself, "it is only a short step to the poetic treatment of the emperors."[29] This notion brings us to another dimension of ancient Greco-Roman hymnody: the hymnic praise of rulers and other men.

Hymns and the imperial cult. Studies of hymns in the context of the Roman Empire show that hymns played a role in promoting the overall message of imperial benefits and blessings to the conquered peoples of the empire. Given the widespread use of hymnody in religious rituals in honor of both gods and deified men, it is not surprising that hymnody would also come

---

[26]Bowra, "Melinno's Hymn to Rome."
[27]See the discussion in Mellor, ΘΕΑ ΡΩΜΗ, 20-26.
[28]Ibid., 124.
[29]Ibid.

to play a role in the imperial cult.[30] Certainly the most influential study of the imperial cult has been that of S. R. F. Price.[31] In addition to demonstrating the ubiquity of imperial imagery associating the emperor with the divine, Price also argues that the imperial cult is best understood as part of a worldview system that helped cities and individuals in the Roman world to make sense of Roman power and find their places within it.[32] Without using the term *worldview*, Price nevertheless explains that he wishes "to develop the idea that imperial rituals too were a way of conceptualizing the world."[33] In this way of thinking, rituals surrounding the imperial cult should be viewed not merely as "a series of 'honours' addressed to the emperor but as a system whose structure defines the position of the emperor."[34] Price thus talks about what I have already referred to as aspects of worldview, particularly when he writes of the "interpretation of ritual as a cognitive system."[35] In this context, Price draws on the idea of symbolic knowledge to understand the impact of ritual as he considers "the evocative power of ritual and symbolism."[36] Thus Price argues that the imperial cult derived from an existing worldview and also helped to change that worldview into one in which the unconquerable power of Rome could have a place.

Though focused on the imperial cult as a whole and not on ancient hymnody specifically, Price nevertheless provides a number of references to the role of hymnody in the imperial cult.[37] In addition to the building of temples, the creation of statues, the offering of sacrifices, and the celebration of festivals and banquets on days devoted to the emperor, the provinces also honored the emperor through the creation of special choirs that were dedicated to singing hymns in praise of Augustus, much like the choruses noted above that were created to sing praises to the gods.[38] Taken together, all of

[30]Angelos Chaniotis, "Der Kaiserkult im Osten des Römischen Reiches im Kontext der zeitgenössischen Ritualpraxis," in *Die Praxis der Herrscherverehrung in Rom und seinen Provinzen*, ed. Hubert Cancik and Konrad Hitzl (Tübingen: Mohr Siebeck, 2003), 3-28, esp. 12-14.
[31]S. R. F. Price, *Rituals and Power: The Roman Imperial Cult in Asia Minor* (Cambridge: Cambridge University Press, 1986).
[32]For a helpful analysis of Roman imperial religion with attention to matters of worldview, see N. T. Wright, *Paul and the Faithfulness of God* (Minneapolis: Fortress, 2013), 311-43.
[33]Price, *Rituals and Power*, 7.
[34]Ibid., 8.
[35]Ibid.
[36]Ibid., 9.
[37]See, for example, ibid., 118, 209.
[38]Ibid., 88.

these activities had connections with tradition, but also represented innovation as they combined around the person of the emperor. Within this constellation of activities, the singing of hymns obviously had a rich and ancient
pedigree, and by engaging in hymn singing, these associations helped to reinforce a particular view of the stature of the Roman emperor and the power
of Rome.

Inscriptional evidence of these associations of hymn singers is collected by
Philip Harland, who reviews a number of inscriptions from Asia Minor from
the first and second centuries CE.[39] These inscriptions provide clear evidence
of associations of hymn singers whose function was, primarily, to compose
and sing hymns in honor of Augustus. One inscription from Pergamon was
dedicated by "the hymnsingers (*hymnodoi*) of god Augustus and goddess
Roma" (lines 3-4).[40] Another inscription from Ephesus, dating to the reign of
Claudius, explains how the various associations would join together for a pro-
vincial celebration on the birthday of Augustus. The inscription reveals
that among their activities were "singing hymns to the Augustan household,
accomplishing . . . sacrifices to the Augustan gods, leading festivals . . . [and]
banquets."[41] Yet another inscription from Pergamon includes the rare term
hymnodidaskaloi, referring to "hymn instructors."[42] Thus it seems that the
entire cultural mechanism that was already in place to praise the gods was now
also employed in service of the hymnic praise of the emperors.

While the specifics of most of these hymns are lost, enough examples
remain to show us the nature of the scope and contents of these hymns. Horace's *Odes*, for instance, give us a clear picture of the kind of praise that was
rendered to the Roman rulers, with several *Odes* offering explicit praise to
Augustus.[43] In *Odes* 4.5, for example, Horace extols many of the benefits of the
reign of Augustus as the ode opens by addressing Augustus directly as "De-
scendant of the kindly gods" and comparing his presence among the people

---

[39]Philip A. Harland, *Greco-Roman Associations: Texts, Translations, and Commentary*, vol. 2, *North Coast of the Black Sea, Asia Minor*, BZNW 204 (Berlin: de Gruyter, 2011), 128-40.

[40]*IPergamon* 374, trans. Harland, 128.

[41]*IEph* 3801, trans. Harland, 137.

[42]*IPergamon* 485, line 6, trans. Harland, 118-20.

[43]See Gordley, *Teaching Through Song in Antiquity*, 126-33. My analysis is informed by the extended discussion in Timothy S. Johnson, *A Symposion of Praise: Horace Returns to Lyric in Odes IV*, Wisconsin Studies in Classics (Madison: University of Wisconsin Press, 2004), 114-33, 198-213. See also Michael C. J. Putnam, *Artifices of Eternity: Horace's Fourth Book of Odes* (Ithaca, NY: Cornell University Press, 1986).

as the sun that brightens their days.[44] Safety, peace, prosperity, virtue, and the
rule of law are among the blessings that Augustus has bestowed (lines 17-30).
Of particular interest in this ode is a vivid picture at the end, where the rural
farmer includes the worship of Augustus within the traditional worship practices. After working in his vineyard all day,

> He returns happily to his wine and requests your divine presence at the
>   second course.
> He honours you with many a prayer, pouring libations from the dish,
> and combines your worship with that of the household gods,
> as Greece does when remembering Castor and mighty Hercules. (lines 31-36)

With this verbal picture Horace uses a traditional image to present a recent
innovation as having ancient precedent. The implication is clear: as the Greeks
remember such heroes as Castor and Hercules as true offspring of the gods,
so do the Romans consider their ruler, Augustus. Not surprisingly, the themes
of the hymnic praise of Augustus found in Horace mirror those found in the
wider scope of Roman imperial ideology: the emperor as a gift of the gods to
humanity, a bringer of universal peace, a restorer of virtue, and a civilizing
force toward the barbarians.[45]

Given that poems, songs, and hymns in praise of the divine ruler were
common in antiquity, it is valuable to pause here to note the ways in which early
Christian praises of Jesus align with those practices, and also the ways in which
they diverge from them. As we will see, some of the early Christians' use of
hymnody tapped directly into those dynamics as Jesus is praised for his divine
origin, exceptional accomplishments, and divine honors.[46] But rather than recounting the blessings of empire, early Christian hymns took a different approach: from a worldview perspective we can observe that they may have provided a kind of resistance to the imperial messages on display through hymns
and a variety of other means. Neil Elliott, while not explicitly looking at hymns,
examines Paul's epistle to the Romans and provides a good framework for appreciating the ways in which Paul engaged with concepts of empire in subtle

---

[44]Horace, *Odes and Epodes*, trans. Niall Rudd, LCL 33 (Cambridge, MA: Harvard University Press, 2004).
[45]See also *Odes* 4.15 and Horace's *Carmen Saeculare*.
[46]See the discussion of this in relation to Phil 2:6-11, Adela Yarbro Collins, "The Worship of Jesus and the Imperial Cult," in *The Jewish Roots of Christological Monotheism: Papers from the St. Andrews Conference on the Historical Origins of the Worship of Jesus*, ed. Carey C. Newman, James R. Davila, and Gladys S. Lewis (Leiden: Brill, 1999), 234-57.

ways.[47] For example, Paul regularly uses Roman imperial terms for his own purposes such that Elliott can claim that that "aspects of Paul's theology echo the poetry and propaganda of the Augustan and Neronian eras."[48] Elliott also notes that, in addition to providing some conceptual background to Paul's thought, Roman practices and rituals provided Paul with a set of practices for performing his own work as an apostle: "The ritual medium for the dissemination of imperial values, so thoroughly described by Simon Price, allows us to recognize the performative character of Paul's apostolic presence and proclamation. . . . Paul understood his apostolic praxis as the manifestation of divine power on the public landscape."[49] Undoubtedly, one dimension of the performative features of Paul's apostolic praxis was the utilization of hymnic expressions of praise. Just as the emperor had his composers of hymns and encomia, so Jesus had his own and Paul may have seen himself in just this light.[50] Thus not only did the content of hymns convey meaning, but in a culture and context rich with hymnic traditions and practices the very fact of the composing, singing, and preserving of hymns had meaning in and of itself. The fact that an individual had hymns written in his honor said something significant and unmistakable about the status of that person.

Rhetoric about hymns and the rhetoric of hymns. In addition to the above kinds of evidence of literary hymns, performance hymns, and inscriptional and narrative evidence about hymns, there are other important sources for our understanding of ancient hymnody. In fact, there exists a considerable body of writings from the ancient world that explicitly discusses the nature, scope, contents, and style of hymns. I refer here to the rhetorical handbooks, progymnasmata, and other ancient discussions about epideictic and poetics. While it would go well beyond the scope of this volume to provide detailed analyses of these ancient understandings of hymns, several of these sources are of particular interest to our project of seeking to understand early Christian hymns within their ancient context.

---

[47]Neil Elliott, "Paul and the Politics of Empire: Problems and Prospects," in *Paul and Politics: Ekklesia, Israel, Imperium, Interpretation; Essays in Honor of Krister Stendahl*, ed. Richard A. Horsley (Harrisburg, PA: Trinity Press International, 2000), 17-39.

[48]This can be seen in Paul's use of terms such as *euangelion*, son of God, *parousia*, "peace and security" (1 Thess 5:3), *kyrios*, an *oikoumene* of nations; being led in triumph; making a spectacle in the arena; and "carrying about" the dying of Jesus (2 Cor 4:10). Ibid., 24-26.

[49]Ibid., 25.

[50]Cf. esp. p. 372 of Adela Yarbro Collins, "Psalms, Philippians 2:6-11, and the Origins of Christology," *BibInt* 11 (2002): 361-72.

Rhetorical handbooks and progymnasmata. Within recent decades, New Testament scholars have given increased attention to what the ancient rhetorical handbooks and progymnasmata (collections of school composition exercises) reveal about ancient conceptions of hymnody.[51] This increased attention to what well-known writers like Aristotle, Quintilian, and Cicero have said about hymns as well as what lesser-known authors such as Menander Rhetor, Alexander Numenius, and Theon have written has raised awareness of several important issues. While space does not permit a full analysis of ancient Greek rhetorical theory here, we can note five important considerations that should be taken into account when looking at New Testament passages that may be hymns.

First, the basic notion of a hymn as a song in praise of the gods was common in antiquity. This idea is deeply rooted (cf. Plato, *Rep.* 10.706a) and reflected in many surviving examples of ancient hymnody.[52] However, as we will see, this simplistic idea does not account for the complexity of the evidence of ancient hymnic practices. Nevertheless, this idea does provide a starting point for thinking about ancient hymnody. Hymns involve praise of gods through song.

Second, the tradition indicates a widespread understanding of hymnody as an aspect of epideictic rhetoric, one of the three branches of rhetoric. Within the rhetorical handbooks there is thus discussion about the appropriate contents of hymnic praise of gods and what the standard topoi are (cf. Quintilian, *Inst.* 3.7.7-9).[53] These are found to be mirrored in practice as well.[54] This recognition suggests a need for a closer look at the nature of epideictic rhetoric, a topic I will take up below.

Third, within the broad scope of epideictic rhetoric, hymn and *encomion* (a speech of praise) are sometimes distinguished from one another, and sometimes not. For example, Plato and others made a distinction between *encomion* and *hymnos* based on whether the subject being praised was human or divine.[55] However, apart from the nature of the individual who

---

[51]See my analysis in Gordley, *Colossian Hymn in Context*, 112-24. More recently, see the survey of similar texts in Michael Wade Martin and Bryan A. Nash, "Philippians 2:6-11 as Subversive *Hymnos*: A Study in the Light of Ancient Rhetorical Theory," *JTS* 66 (2015): 90-138.

[52]Furley and Bremer, *Greek Hymns*, 1:8-14.

[53]See Heinrich Lausberg, *Handbook of Literary Rhetoric: A Foundation for Literary Study*, trans. Matthew T. Bliss, Annemiek Jansen, and David E. Orton (Leiden: Brill, 1998), 105-6.

[54]Furley and Bremer, *Greek Hymns*, 1:50-63.

[55]Alexander Numenius distinguishes *epainos* and *encomium* (lines 1-7, 14-15).

is the subject of the praise, rhetoricians note that the approach to praise is essentially identical.[56]

Fourth, according to the rhetorical handbook tradition, as well as from examples, the typical parts of an ancient hymn are fairly standard. Hymns often follow a tripartite structure, beginning with an invocation (calling on the deity to hear, in a variety of standard ways), followed by the body of the hymn, which is typically a praise section (*eulogia*), and concluding with a prayer or request.[57] The body is the longest part of a hymn, generally speaking, and can contain a number of different topoi, including "predication of powers through relative clauses or participles," "repeated (anaphoric) addresses," *hypomneseis*, which are reminders of earlier benefits of the deity, *ekphraseis* (vivid descriptions), and narratives.[58] Compared to traditional performance hymns, encomia are works that tend to be longer and more carefully structured, while *epainos* (praise) can be a shorter, discrete unit. In view of this distinction, Brucker prefers to refer to short segments of praise in other genres as epideictic passages, but not necessarily as hymns.[59] Accordingly, readers should look for these kinds of structural features in order to shed light on our understanding of texts that may be hymnic in nature.

Fifth, according to both ancient theory and practice, a text actually need not be sung and need not be written in meter in order to be considered a hymn. There is a rich tradition of prose hymnody in the ancient world, represented especially well by the prose hymns of Aelius Aristides.[60] In addition, as Quintilian notes, hymnic praise can be included in other prose genres of speeches (Quintilian, *Inst.* 3.7.2). Thus, taking into account the full picture of ancient rhetorical theory and practice we rightly need to expand on the initial observation noted above that a hymn is merely, or only, a song in praise of a

---

[56]See the review and discussion of the sources in Gordley, *Colossian Hymn in Context*, 112-24. Cf. Martin and Nash, "Subversive *Hymnos*," 93-109.

[57]Furley and Bremer, *Greek Hymns*, 1:50-63.

[58]See the discussion of these typical parts of hymns in William H. Race, "Aspects of Rhetoric and Form in Greek Hymns," *GRBS* 23, no. 1 (1982): 5-14; William H. Race, *Style and Rhetoric in Pindar's Odes* (Atlanta: Scholars Press, 1990), 85-118.

[59]Ralph Brucker, "'Songs,' 'Hymns,' and 'Encomia' in the New Testament?," in *Literature or Liturgy? Early Christian Hymns and Prayers in Their Literary and Liturgical Context in Antiquity*, ed. Clemens Leonhard and Hermut Löhr, WUNT 2/363 (Tübingen: Mohr Siebeck, 2014), 1-14, here 5-7.

[60]See my overview of this material in Gordley, *Colossian Hymn in Context*, 142-47. See also Edgar Krentz, "Epideiktik and Hymnody: The New Testament and Its World," *BR* 40 (1995): 50-97; D. A. Russell, "Aristides and the Prose Hymn," in *Antonine Literature*, ed. D. A. Russell (Oxford: Clarendon, 1990), 199-216.

god. While that narrow definition was a good starting point for this discussion, it is evident that hymnody in antiquity was a much broader phenomenon.

An understanding of these dynamics helps in this study of early Christian hymns as we seek to understand arguments in favor of or against a particular passage being identified as a hymn. To begin with when we understand that the ancient category of hymn was quite broad, including both prose and poetry, freestanding song and literary praise of gods embedded in other genres, we can avoid the mistake of too quickly dismissing a New Testament passage as a hymn because it does not fit one particular aspect of ancient conceptions of hymnody. For example, meter is not a necessary feature of an ancient hymn, and therefore it would be premature to disqualify a particular passage as a candidate for hymnody simply because it does not have poetic meter. Furthermore, the fact that a passage is carefully woven into another literary context does not mean that it cannot be considered a hymn.

Here we may pause to ask ourselves what is gained by identifying a New Testament passage as a hymn or claiming it has hymnic features. To begin with, it is important to recognize that such an identification does not necessarily lead to a corresponding conclusion that a passage was preexistent and perhaps known to the recipients of a particular New Testament letter. As we saw in chapter one, Stephen Fowl is correct that, given our very limited knowledge, we simply cannot know this about the prehistory of any text. Instead, identification of a passage as a hymn leads to a recognition of the ways in which a passage participates in broader cultural conventions of praise of the divine, which communicated to the recipients not merely in a logical, rational way but also in an affective, suprarational way. This recognition can enable a more informed appreciation for the role that passage may be playing in its literary context by understanding the meaningful cultural norms, core values, and cherished heritage on which it is drawing. With the New Testament christo-logical hymns we can examine the way the hymnist has composed the hymn utilizing certain features, and we can consider how those features work to-gether to invite, as other hymns do, a human listener into an experience of the imaginal world of the hymn.

Hymns as epideictic rhetoric. Recognition of the diversity of kinds of texts that could be called hymns or, more broadly, hymnic suggests a need to step back and consider some broader categories within which these kinds of texts fall. Here we will look briefly at two concepts: epideictic and poetics. We have already noted that epideictic rhetoric is the branch of rhetorical theory that includes hymns. In addition, beyond the strictly rhetorical categories noted in the handbooks are the ancient concepts of style and poetics that can also shed light on the dynamics occurring within ancient hymns of many kinds, whether poetry or prose hymns.

Epideictic rhetoric, the rhetoric of praise and blame, is commonly understood as the rhetoric of display (from the Greek *epideixis*). In this sense it either puts on display the abilities of the rhetor or puts on display the qualities of the subject that is being praised or blamed. Often epideictic is defined in contrast to genres that have a more explicit persuasive purpose. In this approach epideictic speeches are those that are *not* intended to persuade a jury or judge (judicial rhetoric) and are *not* intended to persuade an assembly to adopt a certain course of action (deliberative rhetoric). This approach is clearest in Aristotle's definitions of the types of rhetoric based on the action and disposition of the listener. For epideictic rhetoric, the listener is merely a spectator.[61]

As commonplace as this understanding is, it does not fully account for the persuasive impact of epideictic rhetoric. Epideictic rhetoric has a persuasive power of its own, even if this dimension was not widely discussed by ancient rhetorical theorists. As a speaker utilizes the medium of words to bring a vivid picture before an audience, that speaker also shapes the perceptions of that audience, either favorably or unfavorably, about the subject he or she is describing. Jeffrey Walker explains this dynamic:

> "Epideictic" appears as that which shapes and cultivates the basic codes of value and belief by which a society or culture lives; it shapes the ideologies and imageries with which, and by which, the individual members of a community identify themselves; and, perhaps most significantly, it shapes the fundamental grounds, the "deep" commitments and presuppositions, that will underlie and ultimately determine decision and debate in particular pragmatic forums.[62]

By focusing on the values that are promoted through epideictic discourse, Walker is able to suggest that epideictic can serve several purposes. While on the one hand it can reinforce existing values and beliefs, on the other hand it can also be used to promote new values or to transform existing ones. It is

---

[61]See Aristotle, *On Rhetoric* 1.3.1-3, in George Alexander Kennedy, *Aristotle: On Rhetoric* (New York: Oxford University Press, 1991), 47-48.
[62]Jeffrey Walker, *Rhetoric and Poetics in Antiquity* (New York: Oxford University Press, 2000), 9.

along these lines that we can appreciate the ways in which hymns draw on this dynamic and may serve to reinforce, promote, or transform the values of a community of listeners.

Basing his approach on ethnographic research, Walker explains why epideictic discourse is so powerful, particularly in oral societies. Three strands of Walker's theory about epideictic are useful here. First, he suggests that epideictic discourse is memorable, and hence repeatable, and therefore much more permanent than less formal forms of ordinary discourse.[63] Second, epideictic discourse is persuasive. Because of its memorable and archaic quality, things uttered in an epideictic mode convey their meaning on a deeper level than the speech of everyday life. Walker explains, "This power derives, in part, from its felt authority as 'permanent' or 'timeless' discourse embodying ancient, ancestral wisdom."[64] Epideictic speech thus draws on the perceived stature of the community's shared wisdom. Third, the rhythmic eloquence and vivid imagery of epideictic speech heightens receptivity among the listeners. In other words, the fact that epideictic speech is pleasing to the ear makes the listener more readily disposed to receive it as true. The combination of these three features—memorability, persuasiveness tied to depth, and pleasing style—lend to epideictic discourse a unique power that is not necessarily present in other more mundane genres. It is this power that is inherent in hymns and hymn-like passages from the ancient world to today.

As we have seen already, ancient rhetoricians like Quintilian saw the value of utilizing epideictic features or passages in other genres. Based on his ethnographic studies, Walker similarly envisions a spectrum of pragmatic and epideictic discourse in which even pragmatic speech (deliberative and judicial speeches) may utilize epideictic elements for effect. Walker notes:

> The pragmatic and epideictic discourse genres of oral/archaic cultures fall into a sort of spectrum, with the casual business talk of everyday life at one extreme, and the highly formalized song and chant of religious ritual at the other. Between these extremes, we find a heterogeneous collection of epideictic and formalized pragmatic genres, ranging from song and intoned or spoken "recitative" to oratorical declamation and plain speech—but a plain speech, if it is skilled, that will be punctuated and pervaded by sententious flights of wisdom-invoking eloquence, and often a general sense of rhythmic composition as well, derived

---

[63]Ibid., 11-12.
[64]Ibid., 12.

from epideictic registers. Speakers and singers learn their eloquence and wisdom, and audiences learn what counts as eloquence and wisdom, from the models embodied and preserved in epideictic discourse.[65]

Walker's analysis enables us to appreciate the ways in which eloquence and wisdom can be included in many types of speech. At the same time, this recognition does not necessarily help us if we simply want to classify one particular passage as a hymn proper or not. Instead, Walker enables us to be attuned to the fact that hymnic features may be present in a passage that may not itself be a hymn.[66] Walker also provides us another way of seeing that hymnic praise, wherever it falls on the spectrum of ancient discourse, is well-suited for promoting a view of reality that inscribes values, beliefs, and cherished practices that are normative for a community. Thus, in reading a hymn or hearing a passage with hymnic features, we can be attuned to the fact that more is going on than just praise.

Poetics and ancient writers. As an extension of this brief look at ancient discussions about epideictic rhetoric and the rhetoric of hymns, one more dimension of ancient discourse also deserves to be considered here. Awareness of this further dimension will enhance our ability to perceive the subtle dynamics occurring in ancient hymnic texts. This dimension is a consideration of poetics, an aspect of discourse that ancient writers treated separately from rhetoric. By poetics, we refer to the ways in which poetic texts were written in such a way that they influenced the reader not simply in a cognitive way but in an affective one as well. If rhetoric is aimed at listeners who are rational judges, poetry is aimed at listeners who will have an emotional response to the verbal picture of reality that the poet has created. Accordingly, poetry and epideictic are closely related, though not necessarily identical since epideictic tends to refer to prose speeches, even if they make use of poetic features.

Gary Selby has argued recently that a closer consideration of poetics in the New Testament is needed since the New Testament writers were not writing simply about facts and ideas; rather, they aimed to foster faith in their listeners, an aim that is different from cognitive modes of discourse.[67]

---

[65]Ibid., 14.

[66]To anticipate some of the findings of our study, we will see this dynamic at play in passages such as Heb 1:1-4 and 1 Pet 3:18-22, which are not necessarily hymns but do have hymnic features. See the discussion of these passages in chap. 6.

[67]Gary S. Selby, *Not with Wisdom of Words: Nonrational Persuasion in the New Testament* (Grand Rapids: Eerdmans, 2016).

Poetics are thus important in helping us appreciate the ways in which poetic features contribute to the shaping of meaning for the poet and the listener.[68] Selby writes,

> The art of poetry reflected a fundamentally different understanding of how dis-course influences its hearers from that of rhetoric. That understanding . . . was far better suited than that of rhetoric to religious communication, which took place not in a courtroom or the legislative assembly, but in the church, and which had as its end not judgment, but faith.[69]

It is this consideration of how poetic texts promote a response of not just reasoned judgment but of faith that is significant for our purposes.

One of the principal dynamics of poetic discourse is its use of mimesis. Mimesis "places an audience in a position where they imaginatively experience states of consciousness that normally would only be experienced by other natural means."[70] Selby explains, "Poetic discourse . . . achieves its end not by marshalling evidence in support of a thesis, but by using language to create a mimetic performance in which hearers are transported into an imaginative consciousness of the discourse's content."[71] Though outside the scope of Selby's study, such a dynamic can be well illustrated by some of the hymns from the Dead Sea Scrolls in which the Qumran community understands itself to be participating in heavenly worship in the presence of angelic beings.[72] In any case, the language used is intended to create an experience for the listener.

In ancient rhetorical theory and in poetics, the creation of this experience was made possible through the concept of *phantasia*, imagination. A concept discussed by Aristotle and also by later rhetoricians, *phantasia* had to do with bringing before the mind objects, people, or events not literally in view, with the attendant emotional response to seeing or experiencing such things. Quintilian helps us understand this concept and its place in rhetoric:

> There are certain experiences which the Greeks call *phantasiai*, and the Romans *visiones*, whereby things absent are presented to our imaginations with such

---

[68]See Selby's discussion of how this works in light of Aristotle's *Rhetoric* and *Poetics* and the works of other ancient writers (ibid., 20-29).
[69]Ibid., 24.
[70]Ibid., 27.
[71]Ibid., 28.
[72]See, for example, the Songs of the Sabbath Sacrifice.

extreme vividness that they seem actually to be before our very eyes. From such impressions arises that *enargeia* which Cicero calls illumination and actuality, which makes us seem not so much to narrate as to exhibit the actual scene. (*Inst.* 6.2.29, 32)[73]

While the understanding of *phantasia* is present to some degree in the rhetorical tradition, Longinus in his *On the Sublime* provides a rhetorico-poetic approach that integrates the notion of imaginative transport with reason to create a compelling discourse.[74] In Longinus's words:

> The effect of genius is not to persuade the audience but rather to transport them out of themselves. Invariably what inspires wonder, with its power of amazing us, always prevails over what is merely convincing and pleasing. For our persuasions are usually under our control, while these things exercise an irresistible power and mastery, and get the better of every listener. Again, experience in invention and the due disposal and marshaling of facts [i.e., the tools of rhetoric] do not show themselves in one or two touches but emerge gradually from the whole tissue of the composition, while, on the other hand, a well-timed flash of sublimity shatters everything like a bolt of lightning and reveals the full power of the speaker at a single stroke. (*Subl.* 1.4)[75]

Without denying the power of rhetoric, Longinus attributes much more power to this experience of transport, *ekstasis*. Ultimately Longinus proposes that both reason and imagination be engaged. He writes, "Visualization (*phantasia*) when combined with factual arguments . . . not only convinces the audience, it positively masters them" (*Subl.* 15.9).[76] Selby claims that this approach was the approach of the New Testament writers who, with the conversion experiences of their audiences in view, "used poetic form and language to create and recreate those experiences in the present."[77] Hearing or reading a poetic text was thus not merely an exercise in thinking but also one of experiencing an event.[78] As we examine the poetic passages of the New Testament, we will need to be attuned to ways in which the poets were seeking

---

[73]Adapted from Selby, *Not with Wisdom of Words*, 32.
[74]Ibid., 29-36.
[75]Adapted from ibid., 34.
[76]Ibid., 36.
[77]Ibid., 38.
[78]Selby explains, "The NT writers hoped their hearers would do more than recall an ecstatic occurrence from the past; rather, it would be as if they were subjectively encountering that reality in their present experience" (ibid., 38).

not only to convey information but also to create such an experience of reality for their readers and hearers.

We have now looked briefly at the power of poetry, the force of epideictic rhetoric, and the conventions for hymnic expression in antiquity. To complete this discussion of the rhetoric of hymns, we can conclude that the praxis of hymnody in the ancient world demonstrates a unique set of rhetorical conventions that go beyond the theoretical discussions of the rhetoricians and the poets. Instead of one discrete genre, ancient hymnic praise may be more fruitfully considered as an aspect of communication that incorporated a number of features from other genres just as constellations comprise many stars, not all of which are unique to that constellation. Here we may follow Laurent Pernot, who, going beyond just what the rhetoricians and theorists discussed, is able to speak of a "rhetorical language of religious experience that was common to both pagan and Christian texts."[79] Pernot argues that pagan observers would have found the Christian usage of hymns and prayers quite within their frame of reference, largely due to "elements of a common language in praise of God" found throughout the Greco-Roman world.[80] As we have now seen, this common language includes the following elements:

▶ Hymns as epideictic rhetoric that, by incorporating structural elements and topoi that are readily recognizable, invite the listener into a consideration of divine realities.

▶ Hymns as poetic expression that, through imagery and expressive language, invite the listener into an affective encounter with the subject.

▶ Hymns as a cultural practice that, by giving honor to a deity or exemplary human in recognized ways, create a shared sense of communal identity as it elevates its subject.

Taken together, these perspectives allow us to understand hymnody in antiquity as having rhetorical dimensions, poetic dimensions, and practical dimensions.

Conclusion about hymns in the Greco-Roman world. Hymns, prayers, and religious poetry, we have seen, played a number of important roles within the larger sphere of ancient Greek and Roman worship. First, as hymns outlined the deeds, accomplishments, and characteristics of the gods in poetic or

---

[79]Laurent Pernot, "The Rhetoric of Religion," *Rhetorica* 24 (2006): 235-54.
[80]Ibid., 245.

elevated style, they invited the listener or worshiper to embrace a particular view of how the divine and the human worlds engage one another. They thus played a role in passing on values and in teaching, even as they offered praise of the divine. Second, this passing on of values, teaching, and other worldview dimensions was not simply a rational, cognitive process, but also an emotional, affective one. Through painting a picture of reality, and inviting listeners into the imaginal world of the hymn, listeners not only heard content but also were ushered into an experience of the numinous. Third, and related, hymns carried a particular weight and authority of their own, as hymn writers often claimed (or sought) divine inspiration for their work and also drew on established traditions in their compositions. These conventions conveyed a sense of grandeur and conferred intrinsic authority on a hymn in a way that differed from other genres such as narrative or epistle. There was a conventionally accepted way to compose a hymn, and when done right a hymn conveyed something that other genres could not. Finally, hymns often addressed not only spiritual or religious matters but also issues of political importance, including human rulers and authorities. In this way hymns both carried on the tradition and served as vehicles for innovation. The visions of the divine conjured up by poets included within their scope the god-ordained rulers of the Roman Empire: this was an innovation, but one that was fully backed by the revered tradition of hymnic praxis.

When we turn to the hymns of the early Christians, I will argue that they should be understood as in some sense participating in each of these trajectories. Early Christian hymns instruct as much as they praise, and thus we can consider their instruction in comparison to the kinds of instruction offered in other hymns that use poetic language and vivid imagery to portray divine realities to the listeners. But this instruction goes beyond rational argument or logical persuasion; rather, it taps into the power of poetry and elevated speech to draw an audience into participation in the realities it describes. Further, as hymns utilize ancient conventions and styles that carry their own weight, early Christian hymns tap into registers that convey their teaching in authoritative ways—ways that differ from the authority of other kinds of teaching. And finally, early hymns have their sights not just on God as ruler of all, but on the world as well, and thus have important implications for empires that have likewise made claims about divine rulership of various kinds. Looking at early Christian hymns in these ways, we will be able to see just how revolutionary the confluence of ideas and worship practices around the person of Jesus may have been.

It should now be clear that the comparative approach followed here is quite different from an examination of specific Greek or Latin hymns for evidence of borrowed phrases, imitated forms, and other close linkages. On the one hand, that kind of approach would work better in terms of finding linkages with the Jewish psalm tradition, the Jewish Scriptures, and other Jewish writings of the Second Temple period, since the christological hymns of the New Testament do draw more explicitly on those traditions. However, even there, I advocate for an approach that reads these hymns in light of the ways in which psalms, hymns, and prayers were likely to have functioned for their authors and audiences. On the other hand, while there may be some verbal and formal connections with Jewish psalms and prayers, and possibly some connections with specific Greek hymns, the real value in comparing hymns across these traditions with the New Testament hymns is to consider how they participate in the kinds of communicative work that other ancient hymns were doing. Awareness of this broad landscape allows our interpretive imaginations to move beyond just word-for-word quotations or other similar parallels, and to appreciate why these hymns were written and why they were included within these other writings within the New Testament. We now turn to the early Jewish practices of composing psalms and hymns in order to further broaden our appreciation of the dynamics of hymnody in the ancient world.

PART 2: PSALMS AND HYMNS IN EARLY JUDAISM

Psalms and hymns make up a significant portion of the Jewish texts that survive from the Second Temple period.[81] The existence of these texts and the variety they demonstrate suggest the importance of psalmody and poetry for

---

[81]For the literature of this period, see Michael E. Stone, *Jewish Writings of the Second Temple Period: Apocrypha, Pseudepigrapha, Qumran, Sectarian Writings, Philo, Josephus*, CRINT, section 2, LJP-STT 2 (Assen, Netherlands: Van Gorcum; Philadelphia: Fortress, 1984). For an overview of hymns and psalms, see Daniel Falk, "Psalms and Prayers," in *Justification and Variegated Nomism*, vol. 1, *The Complexities of Second Temple Judaism*, ed. D. A. Carson, Peter T. O'Brien, and Mark A. Seifrid (Grand Rapids: Baker Academic, 2001), 7-56; James H. Charlesworth, "Jewish Hymns, Odes, and Prayers (ca 167 BCE–135 CE)," in *Early Judaism and Its Modern Interpreters* (Philadelphia: Fortress, 1986), 411-36. More recently, see the collection of essays in Jeremy Penner, Ken M. Penner, and Cecilia Wassen, eds., *Prayer and Poetry in the Dead Sea Scrolls and Related Literature: Essays in Honor of Eileen Schuller on the Occasion of Her 65th Birthday*, STDJ (Leiden: Brill, 2012).

early Jewish groups. Moreover, the rich content, significant themes, and wide-ranging subject matter of these hymns provide a window into the beliefs, values, and practices of some early Jewish groups. These surviving texts are an important resource for understanding the theological and cultural matrices in which the earliest Christian hymns were composed. In fact, it is fair to say that the importance of Jewish psalms and hymns from the Second Temple period for the purposes of this study cannot be overstated. As Dead Sea Scrolls scholar George Brooke has noted, "The texts that reflect the prayer and worship of a community and its members are a, probably *the*, key indication of what the community thought particularly important."[82] Thus a careful look at early Jewish psalms and hymns will help us get to the heart of some of the most important aspects of early Jewish communities, and will be a good pointer to some of the traditions and values inherited by the earliest Christians, many of whom were themselves part of Jewish communities.

It is important to clarify at the outset that the relationship of these early Jewish psalms and hymnic texts to the christological hymns of the New Testament is not simply one of borrowing phrases and concepts. If it were, then analysis of early Christian hymns would primarily be the task of tracing ideas and phrases to their Jewish roots, and exploring similarities, differences, and developments. The relationship is more complex. Early Christian hymns do not necessarily allude to early Jewish psalms and hymns as much as they derive from the same milieu and share many of the same dynamics. Early Christian hymns are less connected to Jewish psalm *contents* and more deeply connected to the living *practice* of psalm composition. Thus the purposes and the use of psalms in early Judaism are important to consider. Far more than simple expressions of praise to God, or even the expression of theological beliefs in verse form, psalms and hymns manifestly inscribe key values of the authors and their communities, providing a vehicle for deep reflection about the traditions of the community and how these are to be understood in light of the community's current circumstances. These kinds of considerations are then shared with the community through the medium of psalmody in ways that facilitate both an acceptance of these ideas (they are put forward in a way that connects with the head/intellect and the heart/emotions) and a collective sense of

---

[82]George Brooke, "Aspects of the Theological Significance of Prayer and Worship in the Qumran Scrolls," in Penner, Penner, and Wassen, *Prayer and Poetry*, 54 (italics original).

perspective that helps to shape the community's understanding of itself in light of this particular interpretation of the tradition.

By recognizing the ways in which psalms and hymns are carriers of tradition, translators of tradition, and transformers of tradition for the needs of a new generation, we can be better prepared to see these kinds of dynamics at work in similar ways in early Christian hymns. It is this kind of approach to early Jewish psalms and hymns that will be most helpful in looking at early Christian hymns and understanding their role in the earliest Christian communities. In this section, following a brief discussion of our sources for understanding the nature of psalms and hymns within early Judaism, we discuss several features of Jewish psalmody that are of immediate relevance for the study of New Testament hymns. We will then look at three examples of early Jewish hymns that illustrate these features and have direct relevance for this study of the New Testament christological hymns: Ben Sira's praise of the ancestors (Sir 44:1–50:24), Wisdom of Solomon's praise of Sophia (Wis 10), and an instance of resistance poetry from Psalms of Solomon (Pss. Sol. 17).

Sources for the study of Second Temple-period Jewish psalms and hymns. Naturally, the Hebrew Bible is a primary source for hymns and psalms that, though composed much earlier, were still valued, treasured, and widely read in the Second Temple period. The most obvious starting point for understanding Jewish psalmody is the canonical book of Psalms, a collection of individual compositions from a variety of time periods and a variety of authors. Their titles, opening lines, and other textual indicators give the reader some sense of how these psalms may have been used at a point in time in Israel's history.[83] That their use changed and developed over time is also evident, particularly as the original settings were lost and psalms were collected and used in new contexts. Their value to the early Christians is seen most readily in the extent to which the Psalms are cited or alluded to in the New Testament as well as in their inclusion in early Christian worship.[84] In addition to that influential collection, numerous individual psalms are also embedded in the historical narratives of the Hebrew Bible and Septuagint. In these contexts

---

[83]Sigmund Mowinckel, *The Psalms in Israel's Worship*, trans. D. R. Ap-Thomas, 2 vols. (Grand Rapids: Eerdmans, 2004).

[84]According to the list of citations and allusions in NA28, the Psalter is cited in the New Testament more than any other biblical or extrabiblical text. For the use of biblical psalms in early Christian worship, see Larry W. Hurtado, *At the Origins of Christian Worship: The Context and Character of Earliest Christian Devotion* (Grand Rapids: Eerdmans, 2000), 88-89.

they play a role in helping the reader understand the narrative, and often provide a theological commentary on the narrative.[85] In addition, psalms are embedded in other genres including Wisdom literature and apocalyptic writings.[86] These psalms that stood on their own, were curated in collections, or were embedded in other genres were an important theological and cultural resource for Jews of the Second Temple period.

Just as important as their content, the psalms of the Hebrew Bible also served as models that could be imitated and that could enable Jews in later time periods to connect their present circumstances with the traditions they inherited. Thus, rather than being a relic of the religious life of Israelites in the past, the composition of psalms and hymns (and of course, prayers) was a living tradition in the Second Temple period. In the same way that there were both freestanding psalms and hymns and collections of psalms and hymns within the Hebrew Bible, so there were new compositions and collections in the Second Temple period.[87] And just as psalms and hymns were embedded within other genres in the Hebrew Bible, so too in the period of the Second Temple they were included within many different kinds of writings. Wisdom writings (e.g., Sirach), narratives (e.g., the Song of the Three Young Men in the Greek additions to Daniel), and apocalyptic literature (e.g., 2 Baruch) all contain psalms, hymns, and prayers styled after earlier examples.

Apart from these many surviving examples of psalmody that illustrate the vitality of the psalm tradition, further evidence of this practice comes to us through Philo of Alexandria. In his treatise *De vita contemplativa* (On the contemplative life) Philo provides an elaborate description of hymn composition and hymn singing among a group known as the Therapeutae.[88] Though he does not use the specific Greek term *psalmos*, from Philo we learn that the

---

[85]See, for example, James W. Watts, *Psalm and Story: Inset Hymns in Hebrew Narrative*, JSOTSup 139 (Sheffield: JSOT Press, 1992); Terry Giles and William Doan, *Twice Used Songs: Performance Criticism of the Songs of Ancient Israel* (Peabody, MA: Hendrickson, 2009).

[86]Gordley, *Teaching Through Song in Antiquity*, 158-83.

[87]Among many examples we could cite, two important hymn collections from the first centuries BCE are Psalms of Solomon and the Hodayot from Qumran. Later collections include the Hellenistic Synagogal Prayers and the Odes of Solomon.

[88]See especially Philo, *Contempl.* 25, 29, 80-88, for specific mention of hymns and hymn singing. For further discussion see Jutta Leonhard, *Jewish Worship in Philo of Alexandria*, TSAJ 84 (Tübingen: Mohr Siebeck, 2001), 156-72; Gordley, *Colossian Hymn in Context*, 105-8. See also Peter Jeffery, "Philo's Impact on Christian Psalmody," in *Psalms in Community: Jewish and Christian Textual, Liturgical, and Artistic Traditions*, ed. Harold W. Attridge and Margot E. Fassler (Atlanta: Society of Biblical Literature, 2003), 147-87.

men and women who belonged to this community studied ancient hymns along with other sacred writings, composed their own new hymns, and recited them together as a community. Philo explains, "So they do not only contemplate, but also compose songs and hymns to God in all kinds of meters and tunes, which they inscribe necessarily by more reverent rhythms" (*Contempl.* 29). His description of their hymn singing includes references to newly composed and ancient hymns sung by individuals with the assembly joining in on the closing lines or refrains (*Contempl.* 80), hymns sung by a male choir and a female choir antiphonally or together (*Contempl.* 83-84), and hymns sung by one combined choir following the model of the Song of Moses and Miriam at the Red Sea (*Contempl.* 85-88).[89] While we cannot necessarily extend Philo's description as being representative of widespread Jewish practice during this period, Philo's description demonstrates that the composition of hymns within a particular community was a living tradition in the first century CE. Further, Philo's description shows the extent to which Jewish practices could be described in ways that resonated with Greek and Roman practices.

Key features of early Jewish psalmody. The psalms, hymns, and prayers of the Second Temple period have been cataloged and their various provenances and contents described elsewhere.[90] For our purposes, it will be important here to note some of the key features of early Jewish psalmody. These general features and themes are what provide a thicker description of the Jewish context of the New Testament christological hymns.

Issues of form and style. In contrast to Greek and Latin poetry, Hebrew poetry was marked not by any special meter, but rather by its construction. Specifically, Hebrew poems use parallelism of a variety of kinds, as well as grammatical constructions and vocabulary that show that they are elevated in style. Naturally, these elements occur to some extent in other genres as well, an observation that has led some to question whether it is even valid to make a sharp distinction between poetry and prose. Nevertheless, many scholars are comfortable recognizing that a high concentration of these features is a

---

[89]On the significance of the Song of Moses and Miriam for Philo and its implications about gender roles in Jewish worship at this time, see Joan E. Taylor, *Jewish Women Philosophers of First-Century Alexandria: Philo's "Therapeutae" Reconsidered* (Oxford: Oxford University Press, 2003), 322-34.

[90]David Flusser, "Psalms, Hymns, and Prayers," in *Jewish Writings of the Second Temple Period: Apocrypha, Pseudepigrapha, Qumran Sectarian Writings, Philo, Josephus,* ed. Michael E. Stone (Philadelphia: Fortress, 1984), 551-77; Charlesworth, "Jewish Hymns."

clear indication that one is dealing with a Hebrew poem, particularly in the case of the psalms.[91]

Form critics have sought to classify ancient Hebrew poetry according to various categories such as individual lament, communal lament, wisdom psalm, historical psalm, hymns, thanksgiving psalms, and royal psalms. While these classifications cannot always be rigidly applied, it is clear that certain psalms share features that enable them to be profitably compared. Within the psalmody of the Second Temple period, scholars note a continued use of earlier forms, though there does not appear to be a rigid adherence to the earlier exemplars.[92] For instance, in the example below from Wisdom of Solomon 10, we will note a close connection to earlier psalms that review history (e.g., Ps 105), but also see that the form of Wisdom of Solomon 10 differs from canonical psalms and shows the influence of other genres such as Wisdom writings and Hellenistic hymns.

Deep connection to earlier traditions. Among its central qualities, early Jewish psalmody demonstrates deep connections with earlier traditions.[93] As we will see below in Ben Sira's "Hymn in Honor of Our Ancestors" and in the "Ode to Wisdom's Saving Role in History" in Wisdom of Solomon 10, the psalms and poems of the Second Temple period show a particular connection to the wisdom tradition.[94] But the psalms of the Second Temple period also engage with prophetic traditions as well. Psalms of Solomon, for example, is modeled on a psalm style utilizing titles, ascriptions, and calls to praise that are reminiscent of the canonical psalms, even as the psalms themselves convey their own distinct message relating to a Deuteronomic theology.[95] Even when we know that a particular community has adopted theological or other kinds of innovations, and these innovations are reflected in their psalmody, there is

---

[91]Robert Alter, *The Art of Biblical Poetry* (Edinburgh: T&T Clark, 1990). See also the influential work by James L. Kugel, *The Idea of Biblical Poetry: Parallelism and Its History* (New Haven, CT: Yale University Press, 1981).

[92]See the discussion of what Mowinckel calls "learned psalmography" during the Second Temple period: Mowinckel, *Psalms in Israel's Worship*, 2:104-25.

[93]On the many ways in which the poetry of the Hebrew Bible was already creatively drawing on and reflecting earlier tradition, see the analyses of selected poems in Hugh R. Page Jr., *Israel's Poetry of Resistance: Africana Perspectives on Early Hebrew Verse* (Minneapolis: Fortress, 2013).

[94]Sigmund Mowinckel, "Psalms and Wisdom," in *Wisdom in Israel and in the Ancient Near East*, ed. M. Noth and D. Winton Thomas, VTSup (Leiden: Brill, 1955), 205-24.

[95]Brad Embry, "Some Thoughts on and Implications from Genre Categorization in the *Psalms of Solomon*," in *The Psalms of Solomon: Language, History, Theology*, ed. Eberhard Bons and Patrick Pouchelle, EJL 40 (Atlanta: SBL Press, 2015), 59-78.

still a clear debt to earlier psalm and prayer traditions. As but one example of how Second Temple Jewish hymnic texts drew on earlier traditions, we can note that the Hodayot of Qumran utilize several features of penitential prayer in service of their distinctly sectarian message.[96] These include adaptation of the motif of the proclamation of divine justice, as well as inclusion of other extrabiblical developments in prayer and praise. Esther Chazon explains, "Not only in their use of blessing formulae but also in their proclamations of divine justice, Teacher and Community hymns exhibit a familiarity with contemporary liturgical practice and reflect the combination of stability and fluidity that is typical of the intermediate stage of Jewish liturgical development, between biblical prayer and the rabbinic institutionalization of Jewish liturgy begun in the second century CE."[97] The notions of stability and fluidity capture well the dynamics of psalmody in the Second Temple period and are features we can attend to in the christological hymns of the New Testament.

Innovations. As already noted above, like its biblical precedents, Second Temple–period psalmody not only followed earlier traditions but also demonstrated clear signs of change and innovation. We can see this clearly in some of the new and adapted forms that appear in this period, as well as the mixture of psalm styles that earlier generations of scholars considered a degeneration from more "pure" forms.[98] We can also note some development and change in terms of the focus of Second Temple psalmody. For example, an increased emphasis on agents of God is observable. These included figures such as Sophia (Wisdom), a messiah, and other exemplary persons of faith, as we will see in the examples below. Finally, we can note some new elements that come to the foreground in some communities. For example, in the Hodayot and the Songs of the Sabbath Sacrifice there are some quite revolutionary understandings of the ways in which earthly and heavenly worship correspond. The Hodayot, for example, can be understood as fostering an "experiential sense in the group that its worship was incorporation into the worship of heaven."[99] While reflecting some earlier traditions (e.g., the Isaianic vision of worship around the heavenly throne), such a perspective goes well beyond anything explicitly promoted within the Hebrew Bible. Innovations like this, rooted in

---

[96]Esther G. Chazon, "Tradition and Innovation in Sectarian Religious Poetry," in Penner, Penner, and Wassen, *Prayer and Poetry in the Dead Sea Scrolls*, 55-67.

[97]Ibid., 64.

[98]Mowinckel, "Psalms and Wisdom," 213.

[99]Brooke, "Aspects of the Theological Significance of Prayer," 54.

tradition but meeting the needs of the community in the present, find in psalmody a medium that is well-suited for the new idea to be incorporated and accepted.

Didactic functions aligned to the present circumstances of the community. Early Jewish psalms and hymns often indicate that they have a didactic function in addition to, or even more so than, merely communicating praise or petition to God. Didactic function, in this context, refers to the ways in which the psalm addresses the human audience, in addition to the divine, and offers a way of viewing the world, a way of understanding the community's present circumstances, and at times, a desirable set of responses to those circumstances. Didactic functions were certainly in view in ancient Israelite psalmody, particularly in what have been called Wisdom psalms and Wisdom poetry. However, didactic emphases addressing particular historical circumstances appear to be a more significant feature of the psalmody of early Judaism.[100] Although many psalms and hymns have a style and tone that allow them to have broad appeal and applicability, it is still possible to see that psalms are a locus in which a particular community can address issues that the community is facing. A number of psalms from Qumran (e.g., the teacher and community hymns of the Hodayot; some of the Barkhi Nafshi hymns), as well as the examples from the Psalms of Solomon and Wisdom of Solomon (below), provide clear indicators that they are intended to address issues of concern in the authors' communities.

Resistance poetry. Some early Jewish hymns, like their predecessors in the Hebrew Bible, show an implicit, and at times explicit, concern for resistance to other grand narratives about reality that may have a claim on the lives of the community members.[101] In these instances, the concerns of the community are dire and poets cast a vision that often includes a concern for history (the history of violence and oppression they have endured), for identity (clear expressions of who "we" are in contrast to the oppressors), and for articulating hope for the future (some kind of deliverance or a return to a golden age). Scribal resistance, as it has been called, has often taken the form of apocalyptic literature, which casts the struggle in dramatic and vivid imagery.[102] Anathea

---

[100]Gordley, *Teaching Through Song in Antiquity*, 186-201.

[101]For the prominence of this tradition within the Hebrew Bible see Page, *Israel's Poetry of Resistance.*

[102]See Anathea Portier-Young, "Jewish Apocalyptic Literature as Resistance Literature," in *The Oxford Handbook of Apocalyptic Literature*, ed. John J. Collins (Oxford: Oxford University Press,

Portier-Young argues that the historical apocalypses, for example, "articulated a resistant counterdiscourse to the discourse and project of empire. They also envisioned, advocated, and empowered resistant action."[103] In a similar way, poetry also provided a powerful medium for articulating a grand vision of reality in the midst of circumstances and imperial realities that claim their own totalizing view of the world.[104] Even if it did not advocate resistant action, such poetry offered a vision of the world in which God ruled and in which spiritual practices embodied faithful resistance to imperial ideologies on the one hand, and despair on the other hand.

Three examples of psalms and hymns in Second Temple Judaism. We will now survey three examples of Jewish hymnody in the Second Temple period. These examples are drawn from the Wisdom of Ben Sira, Wisdom of Solomon, and the Psalms of Solomon. Each hymnic passage illustrates the dynamics noted above as well as introduces some of the challenges attending the analysis of hymnic passages.

Ben Sira's praise of the ancestors. The inclusion of psalms and hymns of praise within the Wisdom of Ben Sira is a notable feature that illustrates the close connection between the wisdom tradition and Jewish psalmody. This feature also showcases the importance of hymnody within the Second Temple period. Among the numerous psalm-like passages within Ben Sira one can find a first-person psalm in which Sophia sings her own praises and saving qualities (Sir 24), a third-person psalm in which the author praises God for God's power over all things (Sir 39), and a first-person psalm in which the author praises God for God's deliverance in a time of trouble (Sir 51).[105] Each of these passages can be shown to have a close connection with earlier traditions of Jewish psalmody as well as to include innovations or departures from earlier models.[106] They likewise all appear to have a clear didactic purpose,

---

2014), 135-62; Anathea Portier-Young, *Apocalypse Against Empire: Theologies of Resistance in Early Judaism* (Grand Rapids: Eerdmans, 2011).

[103]Portier-Young, *Apocalypse Against Empire*, 383.

[104]Richard A. Horsley, *Revolt of the Scribes: Resistance and Apocalyptic Origins* (Minneapolis: Fortress, 2010), 143-58.

[105]Di Lella identified the following as hymns in praise of God: Sir 1:1-10; 18:1-7; 39:12-35; 42:15–43:33; 50:22-24; 51:1-12. Patrick W. Skehan and Alexander A. Di Lella, *The Wisdom of Ben Sira: A New Translation with Notes and Commentary*, AB 39 (New York: Doubleday, 1987), 27.

[106]For an entry point into the discussion of psalmody in Ben Sira, see Jan Liesen, "A Common Background of Ben Sira and the Psalter: The Concept of תּוֹרָה in Sira 32:14–33:3 and the Torah Psalms," in *The Wisdom of Ben Sira: Studies on Tradition, Redaction, and Theology*, ed. Angelo Passaro and Giuseppe Bellia, DCLS 1 (Berlin: de Gruyter, 2008).

situated as they are within a wisdom context that is explicitly instructional in nature (Sir 51:22-28).[107]

While we could examine profitably any one of Ben Sira's hymnic passages, a brief look at Sirach 44:1–50:24, the "Hymn in Honor of Our Ancestors" (labeled so according to the Greek text), will be useful. This passage is unique in its length, the corresponding wide scope of its coverage of Israelite history, as well as the detail that is included about specific historical figures.[108] After a brief summary of its contents, I will note several features of this composition that have significance for this study of New Testament hymns.

The hymn opens in a manner not unlike many ancient hymns, with a call to sing the praises of the hymn's subject: "Let us now sing the praises of famous men, our ancestors in their generations" (Sir 44:1).[109] From there the hymn advances to a short section of praise of those who are praiseworthy but forgotten (Sir 44:3-15), and then moves on to praise important figures in Israelite history including Enoch, Noah, Abraham, Isaac, Jacob, Moses, Aaron, Phinehas, Joshua, Caleb, Samuel, Nathan, David, Solomon, Rehoboam, Jeroboam, Elijah, Elisha, Hezekiah, Isaiah, Josiah, and others, concluding with Simon who was the high priest in the days of Ben Sira. The description of Simon is noteworthy in that it culminates in an account of the Israelites' worshiping the Lord under the leadership and direction of Simon, including actions such as offering prayers (Sir 50:19), bowing in worship (Sir 50:17, 21), singers' offering songs of praise (Sir 50:18), and Simon's raising of his hands and pronouncing a blessing (Sir 50:20). The passage then concludes with a short blessing:

> And now bless the God of all, who everywhere works great wonders,
>   who fosters our growth from birth, and deals with us according to his mercy.
>   May he give us gladness of heart,
>   and may there be peace in our days in Israel, as in the days of old.
>   May he entrust to us his mercy, and may he deliver us in our days!
>   (Sir 50:22-24)

---

[107]For an analysis of these passages with regard to their didactic emphases, see Gordley, *Teaching Through Song in Antiquity*, 208-14.

[108]For further discussion of this passage, see Maurice Gilbert, "The Review of History in Ben Sira 44-50 and Wisdom 10-19," in *Rewriting Biblical History: Essays on Chronicles and Ben Sira in Honour of Pancratius C. Beentjes de Gruyter*, ed. Jeremy Corley and Harm van Grol, DCLS 7 (Berlin: de Gruyter, 2011), 319-34; and Burton L. Mack, *Wisdom and the Hebrew Epic: Ben Sira's Hymn in Praise of the Fathers*, CSHJ (Chicago: University of Chicago Press, 1985).

[109]All translations from the Wisdom of Ben Sira and Wisdom of Solomon are from the NRSV.

This blessing may be read quite naturally as the conclusion of the hymn itself. For our purposes, three observations are important.

First, not surprisingly, this passage shows a very close engagement with earlier traditions, particularly those found in the Hebrew Bible. We can readily see a close connection between this hymnic review of history and canonical exemplars of psalms that do the same, such as Psalms 78, 105, and 106. Such psalms are rightly associated with wisdom traditions and provide examples of how different generations have sought to explore the work of God in the past as a way of making sense of the ways of God in the present.[110] Reviewing historical events and personages is a standard feature of ancient Jewish poetry as well as Jewish instructional texts.

Second, while drawing on the events of the past and the exemplars of the past, the passage also demonstrates innovation within the tradition. On the one hand, no Jewish Wisdom author before Ben Sira had so explicitly recalled the history of Israel.[111] On the other hand, this passage exhibits very close connections with Greco-Roman encomia, much more so than other instances of hymnic reviews of history. Whether the passage as a whole should be considered an encomium, or if it is more of an epic poem with encomiastic traits, it is clear that the passage reflects Hellenistic conventions of praise.[112] This way of praising individuals allows the passage to focus not only on God's saving work in Israel's history but also on the notion that God used individuals as God's agents of blessing. In this way the passage further manifests its clear didactic function in that it espouses the values and priorities that the teacher wished to inculcate among his students and readers. To the extent that individuals are praised for their good qualities, these are the kinds of qualities that the song promotes. Likewise, the song identifies sins and bad qualities that have led to God's judgment and that are to be avoided. For example, the folly of Solomon in contrast to the wisdom of his youth (Sir 47:14) is a warning to the listeners, as is the example of the Israelites who would not repent and were thus carried off into exile (Sir 48:15-16).

Third, with its encomiastic features this passage demonstrates a dual focus both on God and on God's agents. As for God's actions, God exalts people and

---

[110]See Brevard S. Childs, *Memory and Tradition in Israel* (Naperville, IL: Allenson, 1962), 88-89; Mowinckel, "Psalms and Wisdom," 214.
[111]Gilbert, "Review of History," 329.
[112]Ibid., 321-22.

glorifies them. For example, this is the case with Aaron (Sir 45:6) and David (Sir 47:6). God also exalted Moses, and "made him equal in glory to the holy ones, / and made him great, to the terror of his enemies" (Sir 45:2). While these are God's actions, the hymn's focus is just as much, if not more, on God's agents, a feature that appears with greater frequency in the psalms of the Second Temple period than in earlier Jewish psalmody. Even so, while the subjects of this hymn receive high praise from Ben Sira, it is clear that there is no confusion about whether they should be identified directly with God in any way. The result of their actions as human beings was the praise and glory of God. Although the people glorified David (*edoxasan auton*, 47:6), the resulting glory was reflected to God: "In all that he did he gave thanks / to the Holy One, the Most High, proclaiming his glory" (Sir 47:8).

Taken together, these features—engagement with tradition, poetic innovation with a didactic edge, increased focus on the agents of God resulting in praise of God—indicate that the composition of this psalm was part of a living tradition in which the teachings and exemplars of the past provided a treasure trove of resources that a sage could draw on in a new age for purposes of instructing his students in the ways of God.

Wisdom of Solomon's praise of Sophia. Many of the points we have just observed with regard to Ben Sira's "Hymn in Honor of Our Ancestors" are relevant for another instructional poem from the Second Temple period, the "Ode to Wisdom's Saving Role in History" found in Wisdom of Solomon 10.[113] This ode is central to Wisdom of Solomon, both in terms of its placement within the larger composition and in terms of its themes. A Jewish composition written in Greek, Wisdom of Solomon was concerned with encouraging Alexandrian Jews to remain committed to their Jewish heritage and with showing them that the traditions of their forefathers were still capable of standing in the marketplace of ideas in Egypt in the first century BCE.[114] Supporting this perspective, Wisdom of Solomon is commonly viewed as a *logos protreptikos*, a kind of ancient philosophical writing that was intended to urge its readers to continue to embrace a particular path of philosophy while

---

[113]The title to this passage is that given by David Winston in his *The Wisdom of Solomon: A New Translation with Introduction and Commentary*, AB (Garden City, NY: Doubleday, 1979), 210. See my analysis of the passage in Gordley, *Teaching Through Song in Antiquity*, 201-8.

[114]On its provenance and date, a debated topic, see Hans Hübner, *Die Weisheit Salomons*, ATDA 4 (Göttingen: Vandenhoeck & Ruprecht, 1999), 14-19; Winston, *Wisdom of Solomon*, 20-23.

warning them to avoid the errors of other paths.[115] This type of writing includes elements of all three branches of rhetoric—deliberative, forensic, and
epideictic—such that the inclusion of an epideictic passage such as a hymn is
fitting and serves to support the overall purpose.

The hymn in Wisdom of Solomon 10:1-21 provides a review of history from
Adam to the exodus, and showcases key moments in the lives of individuals
in which Sophia (Wisdom) played a saving role for the righteous. While none
of the individuals are identified by name (a stylistic feature of this passage that
adds to the sense of its universal applicability), the level of details provided
would have indicated to the informed Jewish reader that the praiseworthy
models who benefited from the saving power of wisdom were Adam (Wis
10:1-2), Noah (Wis 10:4), Abraham (Wis 10:5), Lot (Wis 10:6), Jacob (Wis
10:9-12), Joseph (Wis 10:13-14), and Moses and the Israelites (Wis 10:15-21). By
contrast the hymn also includes instances of individuals who turned from
Wisdom and were therefore lost. In this vein we can note Cain (Wis 10:3), the
inhabitants of Sodom and Gomorrah (Wis 10:6-8), and the Egyptians who
oppressed the Israelites (Wis 10:19). By highlighting both good and bad examples the poem takes on an explicitly didactic role, as what is praised among
the human subjects of the hymn becomes a model to be imitated. In the same
way, the examples of those who perished are negative examples of behaviors
and attitudes to be avoided. These features are not surprising, as they embody
the primary purpose of a *logos protreptikos*, namely, to encourage the reader
to continue to follow a specific form of teaching.

A close reading of the hymn provides examples of the features of Second
Temple Jewish hymnody that we noted above. As for its close engagement
with the tradition, scholars have long noted this passage's connections with
Israelite historical narratives as well as with the book of Psalms.[116] Psalm
105 is an interesting point of comparison as it likewise provides a review of
history with mention of many of the same events in a way that both praises
God and instructs the audience that is reciting or listening to the psalm.[117]
A close comparison of the two shows that, while the author of Wisdom of
Solomon may be informed by some of the content of Psalm 105, he is not

---

[115]Hübner, *Die Weisheit Salomons*, 26-27.
[116]Patrick W. Skehan, "Borrowings from the Psalms in the Book of Wisdom," *CBQ* 10, no. 4 (1948):
    384-97.
[117]Gordley, *Teaching Through Song in Antiquity*, 156-58.

simply copying the pattern or form. The author of Wisdom of Solomon makes mention of additional historical figures such as Adam, Cain, Noah, Lot, and Jacob, who are not included in Psalm 105. In addition, the author of Wisdom of Solomon often uses different Greek terms and expressions than those found in the LXX of Psalm 105.[118] In these ways, the use of tradition is not merely imitation but rather an engagement that is likely intended to bring the tradition into conversation with the needs of the author's present day. It is this living interpretation of tradition that creates the opportunity for innovation.

We can observe innovation within Wisdom of Solomon 10 as we note that the emphasis of the hymn is on an agent of God, namely, Sophia. Further, the specific actions that are attributed to Sophia go beyond those described in earlier biblical accounts such as Proverbs 8:22-31 or Job 28:12-28. She is described as having protected, delivered, guided, rescued, preserved, saved, and stood by those who were righteous, while those who departed from Wisdom or abandoned her are shown to have perished. These actions attributed to Sophia are remarkably similar to the kinds of actions that are attributed to Isis in the aretalogies preserved from antiquity.[119] Isis aretalogies and inscriptions frequently identify Isis as a savior who rescues, guides, and delivers those in need. The connections are quite striking, especially with the thematic emphasis in Wisdom of Solomon 10 on Sophia's saving role in the lives of the righteous.[120] Given the author's aim to persuade his readers to embrace their Jewish heritage and to resist the religious and philosophical currents of their Alexandrian environment, it is clear that such allusions are aimed at addressing the author's audience in language that would resonate with their cultural context.[121]

The hymn is also noteworthy in that while it is focused on the actions of an agent of God it also makes explicit mention of the praise of God, a feature that we saw above in Ben Sira. In Wisdom of Solomon 10:20-21 we learn of the singing of hymns inspired by Sophia:

---

[118]Ibid., 206.
[119]See the discussions in John S. Kloppenborg, "Isis and Sophia in the Book of Wisdom," *HTR* 75 (1982): 57-84; James M. Reese, *Hellenistic Influence on the Book of Wisdom and Its Consequences*, AnBib 41 (Rome: Biblical Institute Press, 1970), 43-50.
[120]Gordley, *Teaching Through Song in Antiquity*, 202-4.
[121]We will observe a similar deployment and development of existing wisdom themes in Col 1:15-20 and Jn 1:1-18.

they sang hymns, O Lord, to your holy name,
and praised with one accord your defending hand;
for wisdom opened the mouths of those who were mute,
and made the tongues of infants speak clearly.

The praise to which the hymn refers is the praise that occurred after the exodus, a part of the history that is in view (cf. Ex 15:1-21). But it also suggests the ongoing importance of praise for those who are beneficiaries of Wisdom's saving power. In this way the hymn points to praise in the past as an exemplary response while at the same time modeling for the reader what that praise looks like in the writer's own day.

In this brief look at this rich passage, we have seen that a hymnic passage of praise embedded within a larger composition has provided a compelling vision of reality for an audience that needed not only to hear of God's sovereignty but also to know that the saving wisdom of God that had worked on behalf of God's people in the past was also available to them in the troubles and challenges of the present. While ancient Jewish tradition provided much of the content, Hellenistic patterns and themes also provided the author with a contemporary form of expression that went beyond mere assertion and utilized the dynamics of poetry to connect with his audience in a deep way.

Psalms of Solomon 17 as resistance poetry. Psalms of Solomon 17 has long been a point of interest for New Testament scholars since it provides an elaborate description of Jewish hopes for the person and work of the messiah.[122] More than that, however, the entire collection of the Psalms of Solomon provides firsthand testimony to how a group of Jews in Jerusalem in the first century BCE sought to make sense of the Hasmonean and Roman conquest of their people in light of their faith in God's promises to Israel. Through recounting God's deeds in the past, affirming God's justice, and turning to God in devotion and trust in spite of God's judgments against them, the authors of the Psalms of Solomon provide a clear path forward in the midst of a time of great political and social upheaval. The collection as a whole thus provides another illustration of the fact that psalm composition was a living tradition in the Second Temple period, and one that provided a means for the community not merely to praise God but to articulate its understanding of itself

---

[122]For a recent entry point into the literature, see Joseph L. Trafton, "What Would David Do? Messianic Expectation and Surprise in Ps. Sol. 17," in Bons and Pouchelle, *Psalms of Solomon*, 155-74.

in relation to its current circumstances and the traditional Jewish beliefs it had inherited.[123] As we will see, this sense of communal identity ultimately amounts to a manifesto of resistance to the prevailing messages offered by the conquering Romans, Herod the Great, and those benefiting from their rule.

It has long been clear that the authors of the Psalms of Solomon were deeply concerned with the traumatic events surrounding the conquests of Jerusalem in the first century BCE. Though no individuals are named directly, many scholars accept that the description of the siege of Jerusalem fits the Roman invasion of Pompey.[124] Further, it appears that Herod the Great is in view in some cases, and that the emphasis on a messiah (Pss. Sol. 17:32) who is the Son of David (Pss. Sol. 17:21) may have been put forward in direct contrast to Herod's own claims to be a legitimate Jewish ruler in the tradition of David and who had even eclipsed the grandeur of Solomon.[125] It also seems likely that the pseudonymous attribution to Solomon, along with the lack of any explicit designation of current historical personages, may have been part of a strategy of protecting the community from accusations by the suspicious and wrathful Herod. Within such a complex historical context, we can consider Psalms of Solomon 17 with an eye toward how it embodies the salient features of early Jewish psalmody.

First, this psalm engages directly with Jewish tradition. It begins and ends with a strong emphasis on the kingship of God. From verse 1, "O Lord, you yourself are our king for ever and ever," to verse 46, "The Lord himself is our king forevermore," the emphasis is on the divine reign of God.[126] Kingship themes also pervade this psalm as it describes the selection of David as king (v. 4), the establishment of the Davidic covenant (v. 4), and the coming arrival of the messiah, the new "son of David." Verse 21, central to the psalm, reads, "Look, O Lord, and raise up for them their king, a son of David, to rule over your servant Israel." We may hear in these thematic phrases not only biblical echoes but also an implicit challenge to the one who claimed the kingship during the time of the authors.

---

[123]On this dynamic see Matthew E. Gordley, "Creating Meaning in the Present by Reviewing the Past: Communal Memory in the *Psalms of Solomon*," *JAJ* 5 (2014): 368–92.

[124]Kenneth Atkinson, *I Cried to the Lord: A Study of the Psalms of Solomon's Historical Background and Social Setting*, JSJSup 84 (Leiden: Brill, 2004), 5.

[125]Matthew E. Gordley, "*Psalms of Solomon* as Solomonic Discourse: The Nature and Function of Attribution to Solomon in a Pseudonymous Psalm Collection," *JSP* 25 (2015): 52–88.

[126]English translation of the Psalms of Solomon is from Robert B. Wright, *The Psalms of Solomon: A Critical Edition of the Greek Text*, JCTCRS (New York: T&T Clark, 2007).

Jewish traditions are evident also in the Deuteronomic theology of the
covenant blessings and curses that the author draws on to justify God's past
judgments and to provide hope for God's future blessings. The fall of Jerusalem to its enemies, graphically described in verses 11-20, was because of the
sins of the Israelites (vv. 5, 15, 19b-20). In further engagement with earlier
traditions, the blessings that the messiah will inaugurate (vv. 26-44) sound
very much like the blessings outlined by the prophets, as well as like the ideal
king according to the law of Moses (cf. Deut 17:14-20). In particular, the
messiah will inaugurate a return from exile and a restoration of Jerusalem (vv.
30-31). The psalm adopts the language and style of prophetic recounting of
history and of psalms that recount history. The tradition provides both theological resources and a model of expression to the psalmist.

Second, Psalms of Solomon 17 boasts a number of innovations. Joseph
Trafton has recently outlined seven surprises in the way that the Davidic
messiah is portrayed in the Psalms of Solomon, ways of describing the actions
and character of the messiah that go beyond the biblical descriptions of David
and his legacy.[127] These examples include the messiah's disposition toward
Gentiles, his disciplining of the people, and his gathering in the exiles, among
others. What is most noteworthy is not that these actions were unanticipated
in the divine plan. Rather, in the Hebrew Bible each of these actions was to
have been attributed directly to God, not to a messiah figure. Thus we see in
this psalm some very clear evidence of innovation within the context of the
biblical tradition.

Third, as with the other Jewish psalms we examined above, this psalm
likewise shows a dual focus on both God and God's agent. The agent here is
the messiah, the son of David. It is evident that with such an emphasis the
content of Psalms of Solomon 17 addresses the challenges facing the community in which this psalm was written. They have not yet seen the awaited
deliverance but are looking forward to it from the perspective of those who
are still under the oppression of their enemies (see v. 45). Their confidence is
in God to deliver them by means of his unique agent.

More so here than in the other psalms, this psalm includes many of the key
features of resistance poetry.[128] It shows a concern for remembering events

---

[127]Trafton, "What Would David Do?," esp. 166-71.
[128]See my forthcoming article, Matthew E. Gordley, "Psalms of Solomon as Resistance Poetry,"
     JAJ (forthcoming 2018). For an in-depth analysis of the scholarly study of resistance literature

and atrocities of the past; it addresses issues of the identity of the community as well as the identity of the oppressors, through language that characterizes each group in a distinct way; it articulates a vision of hope for the future. Though the psalm does not explicitly advocate active uprising or action against the ruling powers, it certainly empowers a spirituality of resistance among the community that enables them to maintain their faith, their identity, and their hope even when confronted by the possibilities of exile, suffering, or death.[129]

All of these features are facets of the complex ways in which Psalms of Solomon 17 not only addresses God but also speaks directly to the needs and concerns of the present community, by drawing on tradition, and by drawing on other elements to present the tradition afresh to the needs of the day. It is noteworthy that the genre of psalmody is used as a medium for this kind of formative communal reflection. The idea of singing praise to God is explicitly mentioned throughout the Psalms of Solomon, and it seems likely that the performative power of song reinforced the formation of communal identity intended by the authors of these psalms.[130]

The three examples above of psalms and hymns from early Jewish writings—and many others that could be examined—provide a window into the importance of psalmody and hymnody for Jews in the era of the New Testament. While engaging very deeply with historical and theological tradition, these hymns likewise show themselves to be products of a Hellenistic age both in terms of their style and content, which engages the present realities of the communities in which they were written and preserved.

CONCLUSION

From Homeric Hymns to Solomonic psalms, from Greek poems to Jewish Wisdom texts, from the praise of gods to the praise of divine agents, it is evident that hymns provided ancient poets a way of expressing their understanding of ultimate, unseen realities and the significance of those realities for the lives of their hearers or readers. In addition to simply praising the divine, hymns were

---

and resistance poetry see, for example, Carolyn Forché, *Against Forgetting: Twentieth-Century Poetry of Witness* (New York: W. W. Norton, 1993); Barbara Harlow, *Resistance Literature* (New York: Methuen, 1987).

[129]On the Psalms of Solomon as an instance of scribal resistance, see Horsley, *Revolt of the Scribes*, 143-57.

[130]Rodney A. Werline, "The Experience of God's *Paideia* in the Psalms of Solomon," in *Experientia*, vol. 2, *Linking Text and Experience*, ed. Colleen Shantz and Rodney A. Werline (Atlanta: Society of Biblical Literature, 2012), 17-44.

a powerful medium of instruction, promotion of values, and shaping of world-views for the human audiences that encountered them. As we turn to the christological hymns of the New Testament, our awareness of the inherent complexity and the far-reaching influence of ancient hymnody, in both Jewish and non-Jewish circles, will enable us to pursue a fuller understanding of the dynamics of hymnody in written contexts as well as in worship settings.

– Three –

THE PHILIPPIAN HYMN

Philippians 2:6-11 is a striking passage that is rich in content, full of biblical allusions, and demonstrates a number of the most moving features of hymns and psalms. The brevity of the poem and its unique vocabulary, combined with its cosmic scope and grand subject matter, along with its placement in a Pauline epistle, together with its coming out of a period in which little is known about early Christian worship practices, have meant that the passage is practically inexhaustible in terms of the ways it can be approached and the ways it can be interpreted. Also because of these qualities, it is difficult to draw conclusions about the passage that lead to any kind of a consensus among scholars. Judging by the amount that has been written on it and the ways it has been used throughout church history, readers have always been captivated by this short composition. And readers continue to be. The vistas that this passage opens up for those who take the time to ponder it are limited only by the extent to which they are able and willing to engage with the text and with the wider biblical, historical, and cultural contexts of the passage.

In this chapter I have three agendas. First of all, as the first major New Testament hymn that we will explore it will be important to provide a sense of the key lines of discussion in the history of scholarship on this passage. I will take care of that in summary fashion, looking at the influential works of Ernst Lohmeyer, Ernst Käsemann, and Ralph Martin, and then summarizing a number of more recent studies that enhance our understanding of the cultural background of this passage. Second, I wish to point to some of those vistas that can open before us if we take the necessary steps to trace the foot-prints of the poet in order to understand what this poem meant in a first-century Jewish and Greco-Roman context. Third, I will step back from those breathtaking views to consider how this poem sheds light on the worship practices of the early Christians. So I will proceed through a review of schol-arship, to my own analysis, then to a synthesis and reflection on the signifi-cance of these findings.

As we work through the material in this chapter we will see that the de-velopments of scholarship in the last century and in recent decades have shed light on many different facets of this passage: the thought-world of the passage, the Jewish motifs behind it, the intertextual allusions, the rhetoric of the passage, the ways in which it interfaces with its Roman imperial context, its variety of poetic features, the way in which it fits its epistolary context, and for what purpose it is included in the letter. What is needed now is the collecting of the key advances together in order to gain the deepest appreciation possible for the artistry and impact of this passage. When we do that, we will see that the Philippian hymn is (1) a carefully constructed poem in the Jewish psalm style, which (2) explicitly drew on certain key Jewish and Greco-Roman motifs, to (3) tell the story of Jesus in sparse but explosive form, (4) for a community that needed help in shaping its identity, (5) amid a variety of complex challenges facing it from within and from without.

Using our informed imagination, we are in a position to imagine the cog-nitive, affective, social, and communal dimensions of how this poem con-tributed to a community in this context. Such an approach will then allow us to appreciate the contributions of this poem to theology as well as to consider what a poem like this can contribute to individuals and communities today who regard it as inspired.

SCHOLARSHIP ON THE PHILIPPIAN HYMN

Scholarly work on the Philippian hymn covers a wide range of issues with—no surprise—little consensus. Ralph Martin cleverly refers to this passage as one of those that "provoke and baffle study,"[1] while Susan Eastman observes that "few passages in the New Testament have sparked as many debates as this

---

[1]Ralph P. Martin, *A Hymn of Christ: Philippians 2:5-11 in Recent Interpretation and in the Setting of Early Christian Worship* (Downers Grove, IL: InterVarsity Press, 1997), vii.

one."[2] It is now commonplace to refer to the massive amount of scholarship that has been produced on these six verses as "almost unmanageable"[3] and even "virtually infinite."[4] In his Philippians commentary John Reumann refers to the passage as "the Mt. Everest of Philippians study."[5] Thus a metaphor of climbing to view breathtaking vistas may be apt.

Common topics in the scholarship on this hymn include exegetical analysis of key phrases and terms, theological analysis, the origin of the hymn, authorship, structure, its role in the letter, the possibility of its use in liturgical settings, its Jewish background, its Greco-Roman background, and the ways in which it can be understood within the social context of social and class structure in Philippi.[6] As we will see, these topics are interrelated so that taking a position on one topic may lead toward reaching certain conclusions on another topic.

The interrelated nature of these topics and the conclusions one draws about them are quite natural. However, there is also a danger that one can end up with a circular argument in which assumptions about one issue support a particular view about another issue, and so on, which comes around to support the assumption about the first issue.[7] I will seek to guard against that dynamic and to note it where possible. However, as we saw earlier, scholarly research in this kind of material does not lead to repeatable processes that can be verified according to precise rules of science. This has been one of the spurious critiques of the analysis of hymnic material in the New Testament.[8]

---

[2]Susan Grove Eastman, "Philippians 2:6-11: Incarnation as Mimetic Participation," *Journal for the Study of Paul and His Letters* 1 (2010): 1-22.

[3]Joseph H. Hellerman, "The Humiliation of Christ in the Social World of Roman Philippi, Part 1," *BibSac* 160 (2003): 321-36.

[4]Thomas Tobin, "The World of Thought in the Philippians Hymn (Philippians 2:6-11)," in *The New Testament and Early Christian Literature in Greco-Roman Context: Studies in Honor of David E. Aune*, ed. John Fotopoulos (Leiden: Brill, 2006), 91.

[5]John Reumann, *Philippians: A New Translation with Introduction and Commentary*, AYB 33B (New Haven, CT: Yale University Press, 2008), 333.

[6]For an accessible overview of many of these issues see ibid., 333-39, 360-65, and now Gregory P. Fewster, "The Philippians 'Christ Hymn': Trends in Critical Scholarship," *CurBR* 13 (2015): 191-206.

[7]Sergio Rosell Nebreda points out a good example of this in *Christ Identity: A Social-Scientific Reading of Philippians 2.5-11*, FRLANT (Göttingen: Vandenhoeck & Ruprecht, 2011), 291.

[8]Raised, for example, by Michael Peppard, "'Poetry,' 'Hymns' and 'Traditional Material' in New Testament Epistles or How to Do Things with Indentations," *JSNT* 30 (2008): 319-42. In terms of "repeatability," Peppard expects that scholars who look at the same passage and use the same method should arrive at the same result in order for the result to even be considered as potentially valid (323 n. 5). He suggests that scholars working on the Dead Sea Scrolls have found such

Instead, any hypothesis offered (a certain conclusion or set of conclusions) should be evaluated by the extent to which it makes sense of the evidence available, using sound methodologies that are accepted within the discipline of biblical studies. The extent to which it does not account for some evidence or fails to utilize sound methodology (or fails to use a methodology appropriately) is the extent to which a proposal should be called into question.[9]

In this section I outline some of the key positions on the topics noted above. My own analysis below will touch on many of these issues. For detailed engagement with the positions noted here, readers are advised to consult the footnotes and bibliography.

Pioneering works. The thought-world of the Philippian hymn is rich, and scholars have sought to connect it with a variety of cultural, social, theological, and other backgrounds. Three scholars in particular have had a major influence on the development of the discussion of Philippians 2 as an early Christian hymn. The seminal work of Ernst Lohmeyer in his 1929 Philippians commentary and 1928 standalone treatment of Philippians 2:5-11 set the standard for treatments of the passage as an early Christian hymn. Ernst Käsemann's work went in some important new directions even as he built on the approach of Lohmeyer in his attempt to understand the background of the ideas within the passage and the significance of the passage for the community. Ralph Martin interacted at length with the works of both these scholars and produced the leading English treatment of the passage, with multiple new editions featuring a series of prefaces, which allowed for some continuing engagement with newer scholarship. For our purposes, it will be helpful to review the basic outline of each of their approaches before looking at some more recent and more narrowly focused studies.

Lohmeyer was the first to provide an arrangement of the hymn in strophes and then to draw conclusions from what he believed was an early Christian

---

a scientific approach to reading ancient texts, and that New Testament scholars could learn a few things from them. While it is certainly true that New Testament scholars can learn much from scholars of the Qumran writings, the ongoing debates about the scrolls suggest that Qumran scholars have not yet discovered the elusive key to repeatable results that Peppard describes.

[9]Naturally, to debate this issue goes well beyond the scope of this volume, and what counts as "sound methodology" is likewise open to question. See N. T. Wright's discussion of this issue in *The New Testament and the People of God* (Minneapolis: Fortress, 1992), 32-38. Much of the subsequent debate can be found in Samuel V. Adams, *The Reality of God and Historical Method: Apocalyptic Theology in Conversation with N. T. Wright*, New Explorations in Theology (Downers Grove, IL: IVP Academic, 2015), esp. 40-60.

psalm.[10] He dismissed the idea that the passage was rhetorical prose by Paul and argued instead that it was pre-Pauline, composed in Greek by a poet whose original language was Semitic, with a Pauline editorial addition in the phrase "even death on a cross" (Phil 2:8). Lohmeyer found the conceptual background to the hymn in the Psalms, the Servant Songs of Isaiah 53, and in the joining of the Old Testament concept of the name of God with the Danielic Son of Man. He thus favored a provenance that was closely tied to Jerusalem, without recourse to Hellenistic ideas or Greek philosophical motifs. He believed the song was used in liturgy and argued for a eucharistic context.[11] In addition, he made a case for what has been called the ethical reading of the passage with the humiliation of Christ being an act of will. Thus Lohmeyer argued that Philippians 2:5 was to be understood as the Philippians' having the mind that was the mind of Christ Jesus, with the story of Christ being provided as an illustration and example of that in Philippians 2:6-11.[12] Finally, he placed the christological ideas of the passage within the larger context of early christological hymns, comparing its conceptions to the Johannine prologue, Hebrews, and 1 Peter, as well as to Paul and the Synoptic Gospels. He concluded his study by noting that it is not at all surprising that this "Kyrioslied" became the locus classicus of early Christology since one finds in it the various lines of early Christian theology and piety.[13]

Käsemann offered a direct and weighty response to Lohmeyer and, while he agreed with Lohmeyer on a number of points that scholars still debate (i.e., that it was a hymn, that it could be arranged in six strophes, that it was pre-Pauline, that Paul added material to suit his emphases), he differed from him on two very important questions. These two points of difference are crucial to interpreting the hymn. First, rather than Christ's offering an ethical example to be imitated, Käsemann argued that the entire hymn as a whole was a revelation of Christ as the cosmic ruler. He explained, "The divine act at the enthronement of Christ shows that the action of him who was obedient on earth affects the whole world and is a salvation event; it shows that this obedience

---

[10]He refers to the passage variously as a Christ song ("ein carmen Christi"), a hymn ("Hymnus"), a psalm ("Psalm"), an early Christian chant ("urchristliche Chorals"), an early Christian psalm ("urchrisltlicher Psalm"), a song ("Lied"), a song to the Lord ("Kyrioslied"), and a jubilant prayer ("jubelndes Gebet"). See Ernst Lohmeyer, *Kyrios Jesus: Eine Untersuchung zu Phil. 2, 5-11*, SHAW, Philosophisch-Historische Klasse (Heidelberg: Winter, 1928), 7-13, 89.
[11]Ibid., 66-67.
[12]Ibid., 12-13.
[13]Ibid., 89.

was more than an ethical deed on the part of an individual, it was revelation."[14] Such an interpretation, Käsemann explained, made sense of the whole hymn and not merely the first half. This had been one important critique of the ethical view, namely, that the second half of the hymn does not provide an ethical example by any stretch of the imagination. Käsemann further supported his view by interpreting the phrase "in Christ Jesus" (Phil 2:5) not as the way of thinking that Christ Jesus himself had, but in the sense of the Philippians' thinking and conducting themselves "as is fitting in the realm of Christ."[15] Thus he understood the phrase according to the more general Pauline concept of being "in Christ."

Second, rather than this hymn deriving from a Palestinian Jewish context, Käsemann claimed that the world of thought behind the hymn was thoroughly Hellenistic in its outlook.[16] Specifically, he claimed that what lay behind the hymn was a Hellenistic Gnostic redeemer myth, a framework that he and others of his day believed was behind a number of New Testament concepts.[17] Accordingly, Käsemann could claim that the Hellenistic myths provided the early Christians a way of thinking about Jesus as savior that Jewish apocalypticism could not.[18]

Two of Käsemann's fundamental assumptions have since been challenged by scholars in the generations after him. On the one hand it is no longer valid to posit a sharp distinction between Palestinian Judaism and Hellenism (or Hellenistic Judaism).[19] On the other hand, it is no longer accepted that there was a well-established Hellenistic Gnostic redeemer myth in the first century on which the early Christian writers were drawing.[20] Removing those assumptions, we can still agree with Käsemann about some of the Hellenistic features of the Philippian hymn and some of the ways in which it reflects ideas popular within the Greco-Roman world, but we do not need to imagine that these came out of a non-Jewish setting. Rather, given the preponderance of

---

[14]Ernst Käsemann, "A Critical Analysis of Philippians 2:5-11," *JTC* 5 (1968): 45-88.

[15]Ibid., 84.

[16]Ibid., 67.

[17]Ibid., 73-74.

[18]Ibid., 85.

[19]Martin, *A Hymn of Christ*, 83-84. Though Martin raises this point with reference to Käsemann, the idea certainly has broad applicability with regard to the development of scholarly reconstructions of first-century Judaism.

[20]See the influential study by Carsten Colpe, *Die religionsgeschichtliche Schule: Darstellung und Kritik ihres Bildes vom gnostischen Erlösermythus*, FRLANT 60 (Göttingen: Vandenhoeck & Ruprecht, 1961).

Jewish motifs within the hymn, it is likely that the Hellenistic features represent Hellenistic ideas that were already available within Judaism to some degree.[21] We can also agree with Käsemann that the focus of the hymn is that "the obedient one is the cosmic ruler," but we do not need to imagine a Gnostic redeemer myth providing the schema or language for this.[22] Instead, we find that such claims fit well in light of claims within Judaism that sought to counter Roman and other imperial ideological formulations. Prominent developments within the psalmody of the Second Temple period included an emphasis on the universal kingship of God and a focus on praise of God's agents. We saw this illustrated in chapter two by examples in the Psalms of Solomon and Wisdom of Solomon. These dynamics are also seen to an extent in the apocalypses, giving rise to what has been called Jewish resistance literature. This is an avenue that opens up new horizons for understanding the thought-world of the Philippian hymn and that I will explore further in my own analysis of the hymn as incorporating features of resistance poetry.

Martin carried on the tradition of interpreting the Philippian hymn within a wide conceptual framework. Following both Lohmeyer and Käsemann, he accepted the hymn as a pre-Pauline composition of six stanzas, with Pauline additions and a liturgical *Sitz im Leben*. Martin's arrangement of the hymn differs from that of Lohmeyer, however, in two significant ways. First, Martin divided some of the strophes differently (e.g., Phil 2:7-8). Second, Martin accepted the identification of additional Pauline editorial additions in the phrases "in heaven, on earth, and under the earth" (Phil 2:10) and "to the glory of the God the father" (Phil 2:11).[23] Thus Martin's six strophes have a different center point and different emphases than those of Lohmeyer. Martin also followed Käsemann to a greater extent than he did Lohmeyer and thus rejected the ethical interpretation in favor of a view that the hymn presents Christ as *cosmocrator*. Along those lines, he interpreted the introductory phrase in

---

[21]This is part of a larger debate on the nature of the interaction between early Judaism, Hellenistic influences, and early Christianity. For a recent contribution to this topic see, for example, M. David Litwa, *Iesus Deus: The Early Christian Depiction of Jesus as a Mediterranean God* (Minneapolis: Fortress, 2014), 1-36. He claims, for example, that "Ancient Judaism was a living Mediterranean religion engaged in active conversation and negotiation with larger religious currents of its time" (19). As an example, he argues "*not* that early Christians *borrowed* their divine christology from Hellenistic theology, but that certain conceptions of deity were part of the 'preunderstanding' of Hellenistic culture—a culture in which Jews and Christians already participated" (20).

[22]Käsemann, "Critical Analysis," 83.

[23]Martin, *Hymn of Christ*, 36-37.

Philippians 2:5 the way that Käsemann did (describing the fitting way to think as those who are "in Christ Jesus"), rather than Lohmeyer (describing the way of thinking that was "in Christ Jesus").[24] And Martin found Philippians 2:11b as guiding the interpretation of the whole: "It is the lordship of Christ which gives us the right clue to an appreciation of the hymn as a whole. . . . The passage is an aretology in honour of Christ the Lord, which recounts His deeds and His ultimate triumph; and directs our thought to His present office and rank, as it proclaims Him worthy of all homage and worship."[25] Martin, however, rejected both the Gnostic redeemer myth and the sharp dichotomy between Judaism and Hellenism. Instead, he was able to imagine an author who was well-formed within Judaism but also had an eye toward the needs of the Hellenistic world. Someone like Stephen in the New Testament Acts of the Apostles, in fact.[26]

In Martin's view, as in Käsemann's, there remain very strong ethical implications that can be drawn from the hymn, despite their rejection of Lohmeyer's "ethical interpretation." However, these ethical implications do not derive from understanding the hymn as presenting an example to be imitated. Rather, they come as the Philippians recognize the era in which they live and come to grips with the lordship under which they live, and thus respond by living accordingly. Martin explained,

> The hymn is a solemn reminder to them that they have received in baptism the divine image and that they belong to this new Age in which the exalted Christ is the world-Ruler. All authority is committed to Him, and He exercises it in His Church visibly, even as He exercises world-dominion in the heavenly world. The Church, by the citation of this Christ-hymn, is summoned to live in that world as those who belong to the coming era, and to actualize in their relationship *hic et nunc* the quality of life which is the life of the Age to come in which the enthroned Christ is sovereign.[27]

In this way, the revelation of Jesus as Lord of all has very significant implications for Christian behavior. However, the specific behaviors of Jesus are not put on view primarily for the purpose of imitation. Martin sums up and restates his views in a final chapter.[28]

---

[24]Ibid., 289-91.
[25]Ibid., 295.
[26]Ibid., 304.
[27]Ibid., 294.
[28]Ibid., 287-311.

Though they were clearly not in agreement on every point, the legacy of these influential scholars has been an understanding of Philippians 2:6-11 as an early Christian hymn that Paul incorporated into Philippians with modification (or modifications) to suit his epistolary purposes. With this understanding in view, many other scholars have considered the further questions of the extent to which Paul edited or adapted the hymn, and therefore what the original form may have been. Identification of a supposed original form, in turn, has encouraged many scholars to consider the liturgical use to which such a hymn may have been put.

Scholars who see the hymn as preexisting and pre-Pauline find room for the hymn within the communal gatherings of the earliest Christians. If one can accept the liturgical background of the passage, that it was used in some kind of liturgical context, then a natural question is to consider what that context might have been. Since very little is known about the worship practices of the earliest Christians, and since what is known is limited to statements about practices in specific locations, we can already see that the attempt to extend a theory (this hymn *may* have existed previously) and to identify with specificity its original setting is problematic. Nevertheless, numerous scholars have attempted such identifications and offered support for their views, including the three Philippian hymn scholars I have discussed above. Lohmeyer advocated the setting of a eucharistic liturgy for the hymn.[29] Käsemann acknowledged that to decide this question with certainty was impossible, but he leaned toward a baptismal setting.[30] Jacob Jervell likewise argued against Lohmeyer and opted instead for a baptismal setting, a view that Martin later adopted.[31]

Reading the works of Lohmeyer, Käsemann, and Martin, one can get the impression that the hymnic nature of this passage is, for the most part, a given. However, as we saw in chapter one, it has become increasingly common for scholars to reject the hymnic designation in favor of seeing the passage as a Pauline excursus.[32] For my purposes, I have recognized fully the

---

[29]Lohmeyer, *Kyrios Jesus*, 66-67. See Martin's analysis and critique: Martin, *Hymn of Christ*, 94-95.

[30]Käsemann, "Critical Analysis," 88.

[31]See Martin, *Hymn of Christ*, 81-82, for his engagement with Jervell.

[32]See chap. 1. In this vein, I have noted especially the contributions of Fee, Fowl, Brucker, Peppard, Strawbridge, and Edsall. For an extended analysis of the passage that embraces the ethical reading and rejects the hymnic view, see Gordon D. Fee, *Pauline Christology: An Exegetical-Theological Study* (Peabody, MA: Hendrickson, 2007), 372-401.

methodological problems of identifying citations of preexisting christological hymns, especially when the separate issues of how to identify preexisting materials and what counts as a hymn are conflated. Here I treat Philippians 2:6-11 as a hymn since it is a passage marked by so many of the features associated with ancient hymnody. However, I remain agnostic with regard to whether Paul composed this on the spot or was citing a preformed tradition. In my view, the evidence available is not sufficient to allow anything more than an educated guess.

Recent investigations into cultural matrices. While the hymnic nature of the passage continues to be debated, there have been many worthwhile efforts to drill down into specific features of the passage and make connections with aspects of ancient culture in ways that extend some of the insights found in the earlier Philippians scholarship. The studies discussed below show particular promise for gaining a richer understanding of the Philippian hymn.

Thomas Tobin connects the hymn with its Hellenistic Jewish background in a unique way.[33] He suggests that the conceptual framework behind the Philippian hymn, with its preexistence, incarnation, and exaltation schema, is that of the tradition of Hellenistic Jewish speculation about the earthly man and the heavenly man. This tradition of interpretation, seen explicitly in Philo but also alluded to in the New Testament, makes a distinction between a "heavenly man" created in the first creation account (Gen 1:27) and an "earthly man" created in the second creation account (Gen 2:7). In early Jewish thought, traditions about the figure of the heavenly man and about the figure of the Logos became connected, as we see clearly also in Philo (esp. *Conf.* 41, 62-63, 146). Other New Testament christological hymns (e.g., Jn 1:1-18; Col 1:15-20; Heb 1:3-4), with their emphasis on the creating and sustaining work of Christ, who plays the role of God's intermediary, seem also to be drawing on some of the ideas from this tradition. Tobin suggests that the Philippian hymn, which includes preexistence and human-like characteristics but which lacks a cosmological role, is "drawing on a distinct strand of interpretation within that larger tradition."[34] So the Philippian hymn draws on the heavenly man tradition, without reference to the traits and actions associated with the Logos. Tobin writes, "Because Jesus was clearly a human being, the most obvious connection with this tradition of Hellenistic Jewish speculation would have

---

[33]Tobin, "World of Thought."
[34]Ibid., 103.

been through the figure of the heavenly man."[35] The conceptual framework provided by this tradition is thus what enabled the early Christians to come to consider a preexistent Christ. When we look at the other later hymns, we will consider Tobin's suggestion that the amalgamation of the figures of the heavenly man and the Logos within Hellenistic Jewish speculative traditions "would have offered an interpretive bridge by means of which the pre-existing reality of Christ found in Phil 2:6-11 could have taken on the much more cosmological role found in John 1:1-18; Col 1:15-20; and Heb 1:3-4."[36] We will also consider Tobin's recognition that the "more cosmological role became the dominant one as early Christianity developed."[37] At the point that the cosmological role became prominent through praise of Christ for his work in creation, the idea of preexistence no longer needed to be stated since it was already necessarily included by virtue of the nature of the cosmological role.

Connecting the hymn to its Greco-Roman context, Adela Yarbro Collins argues that, in addition to Jewish understandings informing the view of Christ put forth in the hymn, there are important aspects of Greek and Roman religion and culture that should be considered.[38] For example, she claims that in the three-stage interpretation of the hymn, the second stage (incarnation) and the third stage (exaltation) both find their closest parallels not in Jewish thought but in Greek and Roman ideas. Further, the worship of the emperor in poems and songs, among other things, provides a cultural practice that has close parallels. Earlier scholars had rejected such views, but that rejection seems to have been in response to claims for too strong of a connection to the practice.[39] However, even granting that the Philippian hymn is not formed in direct imitation of such practices, surely the recipients and readers of such a passage would have readily made the connections between the claims about Jesus and the claims made for the Roman emperor.[40] This is a subject to which we will return below.

---

[35]Ibid., 104.

[36]Ibid.

[37]Ibid.

[38]Adela Yarbro Collins, "The Worship of Jesus and the Imperial Cult," in *The Jewish Roots of Christological Monotheism: Papers from the St. Andrews Conference on the Historical Origins of the Worship of Jesus*, ed. Carey C. Newman, James R. Davila, and Gladys S. Lewis (Leiden: Brill, 1999), 234-57.

[39]Käsemann dismisses the connections based on the critique of Bornkamm. Käsemann, "Critical Analysis," 58.

[40]The claim here is not the same as the claims rejected by Lynn Cohick, who does not find direct anti-imperial elements in Philippians. See Lynn H. Cohick, "Philippians and Empire: Paul's

Extending this direct connection to the Greco-Roman context, David Litwa has argued that the conceptual background for the latter half of the Philippian hymn, Philippians 2:9-11, is the ancient practice of theonymy, the assigning of a divine name to an imperial ruler.[41] Acknowledging the importance of Isaiah 45:23 for this hymn, Litwa nevertheless suggests that the notion of bestowing a divine name is not found in Isaiah and is also foreign to Israelite and Jewish thought. Given the prevalence of theonymy in the ancient Mediterranean world (Litwa reviews examples of the practice in ancient Egypt, the Hellenistic era, and the Roman world), and its similarities to what we find in the Philippian hymn, viewing this practice as part of the larger context for the Philippian hymn seems appropriate. The implications are then that Jesus was understood in an analogous way as God's vice regent, just as ancient rulers were identified with Zeus or other supreme gods. But even here it should be noted that, although Litwa finds no evidence of the assigning of the divine name to the ruler in ancient Israelite religion or early Judaism, there is still a very close connection between the Davidic ruler and the God of Israel, so much so that the notion of the Davidic messiah as God's agent is explicit in Psalms of Solomon 17.21-46. The passage falls short of God's giving the divine name to the Davidic ruler, but Psalms of Solomon 17 nevertheless closely identifies the work of the Davidic king with the work of God, as is seen in various places of the Hebrew Bible and other early Jewish writings. Thus we can say that the explicit bestowal of the divine name on Jesus in Philippians 2:9-11 is unique in early Jewish writings, but the closely associated idea that a human would act as God's specially appointed agent is deeply rooted within the Israelite kingship traditions.

Recognizing the importance of honor and shame in the ancient world, and in Roman Philippi in particular, a number of scholars have pointed to ways in which the Philippian hymn subverts those values and puts forward a new vision. Joseph Hellerman has explored the evidence from Philippi which shows that the Philippians in particular placed great stock in public display of individual power and status.[42] At the same time, the status of a slave and the

---

Engagement with Imperialism and the Imperial Cult," in *Jesus Is Lord, Caesar Is Not: Evaluating Empire in New Testament Studies*, ed. Scot McKnight and Joseph B. Modica (Downers Grove, IL: IVP Academic, 2013), 166-82. Even Fee, who I have noted is dismissive of hymnic readings of the passage, nevertheless does see the connection between this passage and the claims made about the emperor. Fee, *Pauline Christology*, 383, 400-401.

[41]Litwa, *Iesus Deus*, 181-214.

[42]Hellerman, "Humiliation, Part 1."

ignominious death by crucifixion represented the lowest possible position of dishonor. By placing these as central themes within this hymn, Paul was putting forth a new paradigm.[43] Hellerman explains,

> Instead of rejecting the social realities of honor and shame, Paul and those who shared his sentiments sought to reconstruct their world by substituting, for those behaviors and attitudes deemed honorable by the dominant culture, a radically alternative set of behaviors and attitudes to be honored in the Christian Church. That God Himself had profoundly honored these very behaviors in Jesus assured Paul's readers that the alternative vision for social relations which he offered them is far superior to the public pomp and status-conscious world of Roman Philippi.[44]

Hellerman provides a thick description of the social context in which the Philippian hymn was composed and read. In this context the cosmic exaltation of a crucified individual identified as a slave (Phil 2:7) represents a shocking reversal of the dominant values.

Erik Heen makes a set of similar connections, although his emphasis is not so much on the shame associated with being a slave or being crucified as it is with an emphasis on the honors assigned to rulers within the imperial cult.[45] In particular, Heen argues that the phrase *to einai isa theo* (Phil 2:6c) strikes a chord that connects with and subverts the practice of giving divine honors to the emperor through the imperial cult. Using the notion of a "hidden transcript"—a message that would have been clear to insiders but not to those outside the group—the phrase alerts readers to the kind of resistance that the hymn is promoting within the community of insiders.[46] Heen writes,

> Phil 2:6-11 does appropriate for Jesus the honorific tradition of the ruler cult. The status claimed for the emperor (*to einai isa theo*) in the civic religions of the

---

[43]Joseph H. Hellerman, "The Humiliation of Christ in the Social World of Roman Philippi, Part 2," *BibSac* 160 (2003): 421-33.

[44]Ibid., 432. See also his further development of this notion in Joseph H. Hellerman, *Reconstructing Honor in Roman Philippi: Carmen Christi as Cursus Pudorum*, SNTSMS 132 (Cambridge: Cambridge University Press, 2005).

[45]Erik M. Heen, "Phil 2:6-11 and Resistance to Local Timocratic Rule: Isa theō and the Cult of the Emperor in the East," in *Paul and the Roman Imperial Order*, ed. Richard A. Horsley (Harrisburg, PA: Trinity Press International, 2004), 125-53.

[46]For a study that explores the notion of hidden transcripts in literature of the Second Temple period, see Adela Yarbro Collins, "The Second Temple and the Arts of Resistance," in *From Judaism to Christianity: Tradition and Transition*, ed. Patricia Walters, NovTSup 136 (Leiden: Brill, 2010), 115-29.

Greek cities of the East has been reassigned to Jesus in the early Christian hymn. The honor associated with the term in the public discourse is retained but redirected to one who is, from the perspective of the Pauline subaltern community, legitimately worthy of its claims.[47]

Not only does the hymn target the imperial cult, Heen claims, but by extension Philippians 2:6-11 makes the bold proclamation that the ruling elite, who honor the emperor and exercise his authority in Philippi, actually also fall under the authority of Christ.[48] Such a recognition creates room for the possibility of the creation of a new social reality, at least among those who embrace the worldview promoted by the hymn.[49] More recently, Rosell Nebreda has explored the notion of how such a countercultural picture of Christ supports a new kind of identity for the Philippians regardless of their background.[50]

Katherine Shaner has recently read the Philippian hymn with careful attention to the visual rhetoric that was prevalent in the first century CE.[51] Her major contribution lies in providing an example of how awareness of widespread imagery related to imperial victory themes can supplement our modern tendency to focus only on textual comparisons.[52] Shaner suggests that when attention is paid to the kinds of images used to depict the divine emperors' victories over conquered peoples, an enigmatic word in the Philippian hymn—*harpagmos*—gains new clarity, with the result that readers can understand the hymn's interpretive framework differently. Specifically, she claims that *harpagmos* should be translated as "rape and robbery" and should be understood as a term that captures the imperial violence against subjugated peoples as seen in ancient visual depictions such as the Sebasteios in Aphrodisias. By drawing on this imagery the hymn disavows such behaviors as befitting a divine conqueror and instead shows that Jesus, who took the form of the enslaved and subjugated, embodies the praiseworthy characteristics of the

---

[47]Ibid., 149.

[48]Heen explains: "From the perspective of the hymn, the exaltation of Jesus means that the *decurions* of the city find themselves subordinate to Jesus rather than the Princeps." Ibid., 151.

[49]Ibid., 153.

[50]Rosell Nebreda, *Christ Identity*. For the complexities that surround the scholarly construction of early Christian identity, see Maia Kotrosits, *Rethinking Early Christian Identity: Affect, Violence, Belonging* (Minneapolis: Fortress, 2015), esp. 26-45.

[51]Kathryn A. Shaner, "Seeing Rape and Robbery: ἁρπαγμός and the Philippians Christ Hymn (Phil. 2:5-11)," *BibInt* 25 (2017): 342-63.

[52]In this regard she extends the work of Laura Salah Nasrallah, *Christian Responses to Roman Art and Architecture: The Second-Century Church amid the Spaces of Empire* (Cambridge: Cambridge University Press, 2010).

true lord. In this way the hymn shows that Jesus is "a more worthy emperor" than the Roman emperors in the first century.[53]

Shaner's contribution to the study of the Philippian hymn is significant, and we can readily agree that the Roman emperor falls within the scope of this hymn and that the lordship of Jesus is portrayed in sharp contrast to the lordship of the emperor. However, while we may be open to Shaner's reading of the hymn as highlighting a critique of the blatant perversion of imperial power over the subjugated, her argument is not without problems. Shaner does make a very strong case for the prevalence of this imagery of subjugation throughout the Roman world and even in Philippi; however, she does not make a case that this visual rhetoric has any specific link with the term *harpagmos*. Nevertheless, while we may not accept her conclusion with regard to the specific term *harpagmos*, Shaner's analysis does suggest that this term, like others in the hymn, did in fact have broader cultural associations, potentially linking it to the visual rhetoric of imperial domination. At the very least, she reminds us of the importance of material culture and visual rhetoric in situating a text like the Philippian hymn in its ancient cultural context.[54]

Eastman has recently argued that the theatricality of the Roman Empire lies behind some of the terminology.[55] The term *schema* ("appearance," Phil 2:7), she argues, would have pointed first-century readers to the idea of visible display by an actor who takes on a role, and plays it fully, even to the point of death (as was quite possible given the Roman fascination with death). The language of theater also connects with philosophical notions of mimesis through the additional language of *homoioma* ("likeness," Phil 2:7), a key Pauline term. Both of these highly visual ideas connect also with the language of the theophanies of the Jewish Scriptures. The combination of these concepts allows Eastman then to argue for an ethical reading of the hymn that derives from the kerygmatic reading. Thus she does not advocate for the sharp dichotomy that some previous scholars had promoted. While I support her final claims as well as her impulse to attend with sensitivity to the cultural context of the passage, the connections between the hymn and theatricality are not strong enough for us to consider this a guiding motif for the composition. The background must be sought elsewhere.

---

[53]Shaner, "Seeing Rape and Robbery," 363.

[54]I will return to Shaner's analysis below when I consider the portrayal of Jesus in contrast to the portrayal of the Roman emperors.

[55]Eastman, "Mimetic Participation," 1-22.

Recently, Michael Wade Martin and Bryan A. Nash have argued cogently for understanding Philippians 2:6-11 in light of the ancient rhetorical understanding of *hymnos*.[56] Reviewing the primary sources on ancient rhetorical theory and practice that I and others have already explored, their study reaches similar conclusions.[57] First, ancient sources reveal "a fairly consistent theoretical understanding of *hymnos* and its essential features."[58] Second, the Philippian hymn fits that understanding very well. As they note, the Philippian hymn "is epideictic in content, it takes as its subject a divine being, it is in contrast to *epainos* a complete composition, and perhaps most importantly it is shaped beginning to end in both its form and content by epideictic topoi."[59] Third, they discuss the extent to which Greek meter, or lack thereof, is important for identifying a hymn. By considering the Jewish context as well as the Greco-Roman context, they consider this a poem or psalm. Finally, given the generic compatibility with *hymnos*, Martin and Nash then take a further step to note the ways that the content of Philippians turns conventional values on their head.

While none of the observations of Martin and Nash are new, their study does bring into focus several important factors. First, it is necessary to understand both the Jewish background and the Greco-Roman rhetorical background of this (and other) hymns. Second, a stronger grasp of the cultural context can allow contemporary readers to appreciate the ways in which early Christian hymns may be adapting and co-opting ancient forms for new purposes. While both of those are positive contributions, the third is a cautionary one. Portions of their study remind us that our assumptions need to be identified so that we do not inadvertently create a circular argument. A key part of their argument about the genre designation *hymnos* is that the subject of a hymn is a divine being. Their discussion of Christ as a divine being in the Philippian hymn is based on what they claim is a majority view.[60] They note, however, that even if the majority view is wrong, the notion still holds since

---

[56]Michael Wade Martin and Bryan A. Nash, "Philippians 2:6-11 as Subversive *Hymnos*: A Study in the Light of Ancient Rhetorical Theory," *JTS* 66 (2015): 90-138.

[57]See, for example, Matthew E. Gordley, *The Colossian Hymn in Context: An Exegesis in Light of Jewish and Greco-Roman Hymnic and Epistolary Conventions*, WUNT 2/228 (Tübingen: Mohr Siebeck, 2007), 111-24.

[58]Ibid., 92. See also my discussion of this issue above in chap. 2.

[59]Ibid., 135.

[60]Ibid., 111.

Christ is "at the very least a divinized human."[61] This point in itself should cause some concern since, as I observed in chapter two, praise of a divinized human may not earn a composition the generic designation *hymnos*, even though the manner of praising a mortal or a god is similar. But of greater concern is when the authors later explain that the chronological nature of the topoi of *hymnos* reinforces for them that the subject of the hymn is a pre-existent, and thus divine, Christ.[62] The logic is dangerously close to circular: Christ is a preexistent, divine figure, so we can refer to this passage in praise of him as a hymn; hymn topoi are chronological; therefore the temporal register of the opening line must be chronologically prior to the incarnation of the later lines; therefore the opening line can be taken as evidence of the preexistence of Christ, and thus his divine nature. But in this line of reasoning the divinity of Christ is primarily what has allowed for the generic identification of *hymnos* in the first place. For my part, I do not dispute the rhetorical designation here but just point out that if one does not see preexistence in the opening lines, then the argument works the other way and one would need to conclude that this was an encomium of an exalted human rather than a *hymnos*.[63] As noted in the introduction to this chapter, conclusions about one aspect or another of this passage have implications for how one interprets the passage as a whole.

More concerning than claims of circular reasoning, however, Jennifer Strawbridge and Benjamin Edsall have also recently reviewed the ancient, rhetorical discussions of hymns and reached a conclusion that is the opposite of Martin and Nash.[64] They argue that Philippians 2:6-11 does not fit the ancient category of hymn. Following Ralph Brucker, they opt for the designation of *Christuslob*. Even so, they do concede that if one were to take a wide enough view of the genre (which is what I and others have done), then the Philippians text could be considered a hymn. But rather than being concerned primarily with genre, the main concern of Strawbridge and Edsall is instead to caution that scholars should not draw from that conclusion about genre any further conclusions about the possible liturgical use of such a passage. They argue that

---

[61] Ibid.

[62] Ibid., 135.

[63] As Fewster rightly notes, the notion of preexistence in the passage is still contested. Fewster, "Philippians 'Christ Hymn,'" 203.

[64] Benjamin Edsall and Jennifer R. Strawbridge, "The Songs We Used to Sing? Hymn 'Traditions' and Reception in Pauline Letters," *JSNT* 37 (2015): 290-311.

such further conclusions go beyond what the evidence allows since we have no explicit evidence of liturgical use of this passage. While this cautionary note itself is not new within the conversation about New Testament hymns, the authors do add a new dimension by considering the reception of the Philippians passage (and of Col 1:15-20) within the early church. They find that, while these are two of the most widely cited Pauline texts, there is no explicit evidence that early Christian writers considered these to be hymns or to be liturgical in nature. These passages are cited by many early writers to support theological positions about the nature of Christ, but they are never collected together with other early hymns and are never referred to as hymns. Strawbridge and Edsall rightly note that theirs is an argument from silence and that this point does not prove that these texts were not considered liturgical. Yet they contend that this silence must be considered, since other New Testament hymnic passages clearly were considered liturgical and were preserved in collections of psalms and hymns.[65]

For my purposes, Strawbridge and Edsall's observations about the extent to which these passages provide a storehouse of theological resources for later writers are noteworthy. Indeed, this is something that poetic and hymnic texts are uniquely suited to do with their allusive language, compact forms of expression, and ability to tap into affective registers rather than just cognitive ones. While I agree with Strawbridge and Edsall that we cannot make much of the silence of early writers about the liturgical or hymnic reception of these passages, the facts of their disproportionate use and wide basis of appeal suggest a qualitative difference between these and other passages of the New Testament. They are more than just *Christusloben*, and my claim here will be that at the very least they function as didactic hymns and, to a certain extent, as resistance poetry.

ANALYSIS OF THE HYMN

With some of the important aspects of the history of scholarship in view, we are now in a position to set out the text and observe several features of the passage that are important for understanding its overall development and that are also critical for gaining a greater appreciation of its meaning. Not surprisingly, given the diversity of views about what is part of the original hymn and

---

[65]Ibid., 306. For example, the songs in Luke's infancy narrative were collected with other biblical psalms and included in the LXX Odes.

what is a Pauline gloss, there is likewise a wide variety of ways that scholars have identified the structure of the hymn. As noted in the introduction, this lack of agreement on the arrangement of the supposed original hymn, even among scholars who agree that the passage represents an early Christian hymn, is a common critique of the "hymn-hunting" enterprise.[66] However, that criticism is not a concern here. My purpose in arranging the hymn in a particular way is not to claim that this is the original, pure form of the hymn, but instead simply to highlight what is clearly present in the text in terms of how the lines relate to each other. For purposes of such an analysis, I have developed the following arrangement of the text:[67]

> Who, existing in the form of God,
> did not consider equality with God a thing to be seized,
>
> but emptied himself, taking the form of a slave,
> being born in human likeness.
>
> And being found in appearance as a human, he humbled himself,
> becoming obedient unto death—
> even death on a cross.
>
> Therefore God highly exalted him,
> and gave him the name that is above every name,
>
> that at the name of Jesus every knee should bow
> in heaven and on earth and under the earth,
>
> And every tongue confess
> that Jesus Christ is Lord
> to the glory of God the Father. (Phil 2:6-11)

This arrangement follows Lohmeyer's in identifying six stanzas, but differs in that Lohmeyer posited stanzas of three lines each, while I divide the stanzas into two lines (for one, two, four, and five) and three lines (for the climactic stanzas three and six). In addition, along with Otfried Hofius, I regard the phrase *thanatou de staurou* (death on a cross), of the third stanza, not as a

---

[66]This is just one of many aspects of Gordon Fee's critique in his "Philippians 2:5-11: Hymn or Exalted Pauline Prose," *BBR* 2 (1992): 29-46.

[67]This arrangement is only slightly modified from my 2011 volume, *Teaching Through Song in Antiquity: Didactic Hymnody Among Greeks, Romans, Jews and Christians*, WUNT 2/331 (Tübingen: Mohr Siebeck), 283. Here I have given the phase *thanatou de staurou* its own line both to highlight its centrality as well as to show the way in which it parallels the final line of the poem.

Pauline interpolation but as central to the original hymn.[68] However, regardless of whether this was a Pauline gloss or original to the hymn (or even not a hymn at all), scholars agree that, for Paul, this line is integral to the passage in its final form, and indeed that the anadiplosis provides a powerful climax to the first half of the passage.[69]

With the text in view and laid out this way, we can make nine general observations that will open up further avenues for exploration. These observations relate to (1) temporal development of the hymn through verbs; (2) focus on Jesus; (3) the expanding scope of the hymn from beginning to end; (4) significance of the emphasis on God throughout; (5) alignment with ancient strategies for encomiastic praise; (6) divergence from standard views of what is praiseworthy; (7) connections with Second Temple Jewish traditions and themes; (8) creative interplay between Jewish and Greco-Roman elements; and (9) explicit reference to worship practices.

First, as many have noted, the passage displays a clear temporal development through the verbs and participles. Each stanza in this arrangement has one main action verb, with the fourth stanza containing two. In the first three stanzas, Jesus' past actions are in view with aorist indicative verbs. He did not consider equality with God a thing to be seized; he emptied himself; and he humbled himself. In the fourth stanza it is God's past actions with regard to Jesus that are in view, also with aorist indicative verbs: God superexalted him and God gave him the name that is above every name. Finally, in the fifth and sixth stanzas the future actions of every created being with regard to Jesus are in view through the use of subjunctive forms: that every knee should bow and every tongue confess. Thus the temporal register of the hymn suggests that events of the past, both distant past (if preexistence is in view here) and recent past (in the events surrounding the life, death, and exaltation of Jesus), have results that are of both present and future importance.

---

[68]The standard rationale for seeing this phrase as a Pauline addition is that the cross is a central part of Paul's understanding of the gospel, whereas other emphases of the hymn are not necessarily so. Further, the addition seems to disrupt the pattern of line lengths that some interpreters expect. However, Hofius has shown that both the use of anadiplosis (here, the repetition of *thanatou* in this line) and the existence of uneven line lengths were common features of Second Temple Jewish and early Christian poetry. Otfried Hofius, *Der Christushymnus Philipper 2, 6-11: Untersuchungen zu Gestalt und Aussage eines urchristlichen Psalms*, WUNT 17 (Tübingen: Mohr, 1991), 9-12, 104-8.

[69]Markus N. A. Bockmuehl, *The Epistle to the Philippians*, BNTC (Peabody, MA: Hendrickson, 1998), 139-40. Bockmuehl rightly notes that the result is that the specific mention of the cross heightens the contrast between the shameful death of Christ and the honorable Greco-Roman value of dying a noble death for others.

Second, the passage follows a clear trajectory with regard to the figure of Jesus. The first three stanzas follow a downward trajectory from his somehow existing in the form of God, through a process of emptying himself and taking on human form, to the resulting obedience to death. By any reckoning, this low point—the death on the cross—is both the center point of the hymn and its turning point.[70] Because of these things (Greek: *dio kai*), an upward trajectory is initiated by God: highly exalting him, giving him the name that is above every name, and ultimately leading to universal worship of Jesus.

Third, as the hymn creates a trajectory with regard to the main subject, and as it expands its temporal register from distant past, to recent past, to future, it also expands its scope to include, apparently, all beings. Regardless of their involvement with God or Jesus Christ for the first two-thirds of the hymn, the final third focuses on the worship that all beings will accord to Jesus. As I will discuss below, there are exegetical questions aplenty in this observation: What beings are in view here? When are they taking these actions? And how are their actions to be understood?

Fourth, the passage is framed with references to God (Phil 2:6 and Phil 2:11c) highlighting for the reader the importance of God for this hymn. Not only so, but God is the performer of the action of reversal in the center of the hymn (Phil 2:9), the action that leads ultimately to the worship of Jesus. In the end, all that occurs—including the worship of Jesus—is done to the glory of God. This poem, though it is a poem in praise of Christ, is thus deeply concerned with God.[71] As Paul Minear aptly states, "Only after it is recognized as a *theo*logical hymn should this be called a *christo*logical one."[72]

Fifth, though a relatively short composition, this praise of Jesus follows the pattern for an encomium.[73] This is particularly true in that there is specific mention of his origins, his praiseworthy deeds, divine favor he has received, and honors he receives.[74] Such a pattern can be seen in rhetorical

---

[70]As already noted, whether original to the hymn or Pauline interpolation for emphasis, in the current form of the passage the cross is central to the development of the hymn.

[71]In this way, Phil 2:6-11 is similar to the worship of God and the Lamb in Rev 5. Cf. Richard Bauckham, *Jesus and the God of Israel: God Crucified and Other Studies on the New Testament's Christology of Divine Identity* (Grand Rapids: Eerdmans, 2009), 202.

[72]Paul S. Minear, "Singing and Suffering in Philippi," in *The Conversation Continues: Studies in Paul & John in Honor of J. Louis Martyn*, ed. J. Louis Martyn, Robert Tomson Fortna, and Beverly Roberts Gaventa (Nashville: Abingdon, 1990), 205 (emphasis original).

[73]This is the view taken by Reumann, *Philippians*, 364-65.

[74]For the general features of encomia in the ancient world, see Bruce J. Malina and Jerome H. Neyrey, *Portraits of Paul: An Archaeology of Ancient Personality* (Louisville, KY: Westminster John Knox, 1996), 19-63; Martin and Nash, "Subversive *Hymnos*," esp. 93-109.

handbooks, called progymnasmata, as well as in examples of encomia from the ancient world.

Sixth, in light of the clear connections with ancient encomia, it is noteworthy that the accomplishments of Jesus contrast sharply with those for which humans were commonly praised. In fact, the central accomplishment of Jesus, per the hymn, and for which God exalts him, is his death on the cross. As many scholars have pointed out in this vein, death by crucifixion in the Roman world would ordinarily be considered a source of shame.[75] Rather than glossing over it or downplaying it, this poem remembers Jesus precisely for this death in a central way. And in this, we can already observe a twist and an important point for considering the impact of such a hymn in its context. Remembering Jesus in this way turns conventional patterns of praiseworthy attributes and actions on their heads. This appropriation of Greco-Roman rhetorical practice, adapted or co-opted by early Jesus followers, will require further discussion below.

Seventh, there is a notable series of connections between the language of this hymn and several of the central concepts of Second Temple Judaism.[76] As we have seen, this is where a significant portion of the scholarly discussion of this hymn centers. Key concepts include the image of God (Phil 2:6), the servant (Phil 2:7), obedience (Phil 2:8), the divine name (Phil 2:9), and universal worship (Phil 2:10-11). Each of these in turn can be understood to tap into other networks of ideas. The image of God suggests creation imagery and may indicate that Jesus is to be understood in some sense as a new Adam who is able to accomplish what Adam was not.[77] The servant imagery suggests the Isaianic vision of the suffering servant and suggests that Jesus is to be understood in that light.[78] Obedience is a central covenantal theme for Israel, suggesting that Jesus fulfills what Israel was unable to achieve. The bestowal of the divine name is perhaps most important of all in that through this association what was suggested early in the hymn through allusions is confirmed: namely, that (1) Jesus is somehow to be identified with the God of Israel beside

---

[75]See especially Hellerman, who shows the connection between slavery and crucifixion. Hellerman, "Humiliation, Part 1." See also, Hellerman, Reconstructing Honor.
[76]Reumann, Philippians, 360-61; N. T. Wright, Paul and the Faithfulness of God (Minneapolis: Fortress, 2013), 680-89.
[77]For parallels between the Philippian hymn and Gen 1-3, see Minear, "Singing and Suffering," 210. For a critique of this view, however, see Fee, Pauline Christology, 375-76 and 390-93.
[78]Minear, "Singing and Suffering," 213-14.

whom is no other; and (2) this is accomplished through the resurrection and exaltation of Jesus.[79] This notion draws particularly on the connections between the Philippian hymn and Isaiah. Connections with the overall themes of Isaiah 40–55 and especially Isaiah 45:20-25 (e.g., that Phil 2:10 is a clear allusion to Is 40:23b) suggest that in Jesus the new age has been inaugurated.[80] Finally, universal worship is part of the prophetic vision of the new age, when Jew and Gentile alike are drawn into the worship of the God of Israel.[81]

To understand the significance of these kinds of connections, we might consider two perspectives. First, that of the author of the poem, whether Paul or someone else. Drawing consciously and unconsciously from his deep acquaintance with the Scriptures as well as with issues and concerns of Judaism in the Roman age, the presentation of Jesus in the hymn is in explicit conversation with key themes of Second Temple Jewish thought. Second, we could consider the community that would recite the poem (assuming we can have any degree of confidence that such a poem was recited) or at least have received and read it in their letter. While it is possible that both perspectives would be quite similar, it is more likely that the early Christian audience would appreciate only those themes for which they had some prior understanding. For example, Jewish Christians in Philippi would have recognized the Adamic and Isaianic echoes, while the Gentile Christians may not have, depending on their familiarity with Jewish traditions.[82] Likewise, Gentile Christians might have more readily picked up on echoes of the practices of hymnic praise directed at heroes, divinized rulers, and gods, all of which was a part of their cultural frame of reference as inhabitants of the Roman Empire and participants in its institutions.

Eighth, having noted the resonance with both Jewish and Greco-Roman ideas and practices, we are in a stronger position to notice the interplay between the two. In this regard, the Philippian hymn can be placed alongside other early Jewish texts that blend Hellenistic styles of praise with Jewish-themed content. Ben Sira's praise of the ancestors and the praises of Sophia in

---

[79]For extensive discussion of the assignment of the divine name and its significance for Christology, see Bauckham, *Jesus and the God of Israel*, 197-201. On the assignment of the divine name more broadly, see Litwa, *Iesus Deus*.

[80]See Wright, *Paul and the Faithfulness of God*, 680-89.

[81]N. T. Wright suggests that this passage is Paul's meditation on Is 52:7-10 and represents Paul's understanding of what it looks like when YHWH returns to Zion. Ibid.

[82]Minear, "Singing and Suffering," 213.

Wisdom of Solomon both offer fruitful material for comparison. As we have seen, texts like these show an increased focus on agents of God and do so in a manner that reflects the kinds of praise practices that are observable throughout the Greco-Roman world. We may consider that the picture of Jesus painted by this hymn places him on this spectrum of agents of God who are praised for their role in God's plans. We may also note that Jesus is set apart from the subjects of these other Jewish psalms in that he is identified with God and honored in unique ways both at the beginning and end of the hymn.

Finally, this praise poem about Jesus is noteworthy not only for what it says about Jesus, about God, and about their relationship. It is also noteworthy in that it explicitly and clearly describes worship practices from the first century. The two practices mentioned in Philippians 2:10-11 are bowing (a physical expression of worship) and confession (a verbal expression). From these references it is tempting to try to draw conclusions about the worship practices of the early Christians. Before attempting to do so, however, we must consider these phrases in their context. Not surprisingly, there are divergent strands of interpretation of this portion of the hymn, which, depending how we interpret them, will affect the conclusions we draw about early Christian worship.

Worship references in the Philippian hymn. The Philippian hymn concludes with a climactic vision of universal worship of Jesus. It is possible to see in these lines a direct reflection of the worship practices of the early Christians:

> that at the name of Jesus every knee should bow
> in heaven and on earth and under the earth,

> And every tongue confess
> that Jesus Christ is Lord
> to the glory of God the Father. (Phil 2:10-11)

Several basic questions are important here as we look at these lines. First, who is doing the bowing and confessing? Second, what is the nature of this bowing and confessing? Third, when are these actions occurring? The answers to these questions are closely related to one another.

Two major options have been posited for the answer to the "who" question: Either all humans or all beings everywhere, including especially the hostile spiritual forces referenced elsewhere as "the powers." With these options in view it is clear then that the answer to the "what" question, the kind of bowing and confessing, could be of two very different natures. On the one hand, all humanity might be coming before Jesus in a position of worship and praise, worshiping through physical posture and words. On the other hand, heretofore hostile powers might be surrendering in defeat, not worshiping as much as verbally acknowledging the lordship of Christ. Finally, then, the "when" question: Has this happened already (as with the death and exaltation), or is it still to come?

Two useful concepts in approaching these questions are the notions of deictic self-referentiality and the imaginal world of Greek hymns.[83] These concepts, familiar in ancient Greek hymnody, allow readers to distinguish between when the poet is providing liturgical instruction to the present audience reciting the hymn (things they would literally see around them; *deixis*) versus when the poet is describing a spiritual or otherworldly reality that can only be seen with the mind.[84] Charles Cosgrove's analysis of a late third-century Christian hymn with musical notation is helpful here since the hymn seems to include within its scope both the humans assembled for worship ("while we hymn," line 3) as well as heavenly powers who respond ("let all the powers answer, 'Amen, amen,'" line 4).[85] While the Philippians may actually be confessing that "Jesus Christ is Lord" in the moment that they are reciting the poem in the present, they are also proclaiming and imagining an otherworldly reality in which every creature participates in this universal worship. In this way, the hymn is a bridge between the two realities.

A similar dynamic can be observed in a composition in honor of Augustus that we briefly looked at in chapter two. Horace, in *Odes* 4.5, after outlining the benefits of the reign of Augustus, provides a powerful image of a landowner who, at the end of a day of working in his vineyard, pours a libation and offers worship and prayers to and for Augustus, along with his household gods. The practices of worshiping, pouring a libation, and praying were not new. In fact, these were traditional practices at a meal. The recitation of poetry, including songs and hymns, was also a part of such meals, so that Horace's song may itself have been recited in such a setting. But by including the emperor within the

[83]For an exploration of these concepts, see Charles H. Cosgrove, *An Ancient Christian Hymn with Musical Notation: Papyrus Oxyrhynchus 1786: Text and Commentary*, STAC (Tübingen: Mohr Siebeck, 2011), 73-81.
[84]*Deixis* of the eyes versus *deixis* of the mind. Ibid., 77-78.
[85]The full text of the hymn is found in ibid., 37.

worship of the gods, and including this imagery within his ode, Horace invites the readers not only to accept it but also to join in themselves.

One further consideration is whether these creatures in Philippians 2:10-11 are worshiping, like a scene of worship around the heavenly throne, similar to what we observe in Revelation 4–5, or whether they are bowing and confessing like a scene of the surrender of hostile forces to a conquering sovereign. The imagery of bowing and the language for confessing allows for both possibilities. And here is where a richer appreciation of the nature of poetry enables us to move forward. It is likely the allusive power of the language, the lack of specificity, that allows for these kinds of divergent interpretations. The ambiguity of expression allows for both cultic worship (all creatures bowing in worship of Jesus) and universal lordship (all creatures acknowledging the divine rule of Jesus) to be seen here. At the very least, neither is completely excluded from the scope of the hymn. Either way, the implication is clear: Christ uniquely participates in the divine sovereignty over all creation, and therefore is worthy of receiving the honor of all creatures.[86] Having made the observations above we are in a position to now consider the significance of these observations.

THE PHILIPPIAN HYMN AS RESISTANCE POETRY

What does a poem with these features, emphases, and themes, and with this kind of content, embedded in an ancient letter, tell us? As we have seen, a number of scholars see in the hymn elements of resistance to Roman imperial ideology or subversion of Roman values. For example, Charles Cousar notes that "this confession of Jesus as Lord places the Philippian readers in a subversive role in relation to their Roman context. To affirm that the name of power and authority belongs to Jesus and not Caesar is a dangerous commitment, one that stands in opposition to the imperial ideology of the day and in fact connects them with Paul."[87] Stephen Fowl makes a similar claim that the naming of Jesus Christ as Lord was "in direct competition with Caesar's claims."[88] He further claims that the hymn supports an alternative story of how

---

[86]Bauckham, *Jesus and the God of Israel*, 200-202.

[87]Charles B. Cousar, "The Function of the Christ-Hymn (2.6-11) in Philippians," in *The Impartial God: Essays in Biblical Studies in Honor of Jouette M. Bassler*, ed. Calvin J. Roetzel, Robert L. Foster, and Jouette M. Bassler (Sheffield: Sheffield Phoenix Press, 2007), 218.

[88]Stephen E. Fowl, *Philippians*, Two Horizons New Testament Commentary (Grand Rapids: Eerdmans 2005), 105. Even Fee recognizes this, though without acknowledging the hymnic overtones.

the world works: "It serves as a direct counter to the claims of the empire. These verses account for the nature and scope of Christ's dominion in ways that make it impossible for one also to acknowledge Caesar's claims to dominion. At the same time, these verses lay the foundation for the counter-politics that Paul desires the Philippians to embody in their common life."[89] Words like *subversive, competition, alternative, counterclaims,* and *counter-politics* suggest that the Philippian hymn plays a role that goes beyond simply praising Christ for his sacrificial death on the cross. The hymn may be empowering a kind of spirituality of resistance to alternative ways of viewing the world. That a hymn could be utilized to play this kind of role is not surprising, especially given the persuasive power of epideictic discourse and the affective impact of poetic expression.

We can extend this notion of a spirituality of resistance a little further by considering three common themes of resistance poetry in various epochs and cultures: a concern for history, an emphasis on identity, and a hope for the future.[90] In the Philippian hymn each of these themes takes center stage and finds poetic expression.

First, as resistance poetry, this passage manifests an explicit concern for history. It insists that the historical event of the death of Jesus by means of a powerful Roman imperial symbol of domination should be remembered. It will not do for this seemingly insignificant and shameful event to pass out of memory; it must be remembered. It is thus to be found as the poetic center and turning point of the hymn. Not only must Christ's death be remembered, but the fact that he willingly and in obedience to God chose the death of the cross must also be remembered. In this way God's power to overrule the plans of the Romans comes expressly into view. Fowl explains, "If Christ's life was freely offered up to God in obedience, then although Rome can take the life, Rome cannot make Christ its victim. Ironically, they

---

Fee, *Pauline Christology*, 400-401. As noted above, Cohick argues against any anti-imperial reading of Philippians as a whole. However, while she recognizes that the hymn has been a point of interest for anti-imperial readings, she neglects to provide any argument as to why it could not be the case that the Roman emperor is in view here. Cohick, "Philippians and Empire," 171-72. Shaner finds a "glimmer of liberation" in her reading of Phil 2:6 but with less of an emphasis on imperial resistance in the second half, where "the hymn re-inscribes Jesus as more imperial than the emperor." "Seeing Rape and Robbery," 362-63.

[89]Fowl, *Philippians*, 105.

[90]See my discussion of these features of resistance poetry in Matthew E. Gordley, "Psalms of Solomon as Resistance Poetry," *JAJ* (forthcoming 2018).

become unwitting agents in God's economy of salvation."[91] Here it is also noteworthy that the author has chosen an encomiastic poem as a means of recalling this history, rather than some other genre. As we have seen, this kind of discourse was directly associated with gods, emperors, and the ascription of honor to those to whom it was due. With this choice of hymnic genre, we can see that the author reflects Greco-Roman culture even as he resists the kinds of triumphalist interpretations of Roman rule that are commonplace in the ancient world.[92] The history that is remembered in the Philippian hymn does also have its ultimate triumph, but by means of a historical humiliation of the most disgraceful kind.

Second, as resistance poetry, this passage also shows a deep concern for issues of identity: the identity of Jesus is central. His is an identity grounded in God. It is also an identity marked by actions of submission, surrender, and death on the cross. Though utilizing the form and topoi of ancient encomia, the identity features that are highlighted contrast sharply with culturally prevalent notions about praiseworthy accomplishments. As Martin and Nash observe, "We see the hymnist meeting genre expectations [of *encomia*] at every turn, only in a subversive manner: nearly every generic feature attested by the theorists is taken up in a way that turns on end conventional, Greco-Roman notions of what is worthy of honour and status, and what is not."[93] In this way, not only the identity of Jesus but also the identity of the community from which this hymn emerged and in which it was preserved come into view.[94] Martin and Nash are helpful here as well in their observation that this passage "serves to establish for the Christian community a new way of evaluating what is and is not honourable and worthy of status. Topos by topos, Christ is praised because he divests himself of conventional status in service to others."[95] Jesus models the attitude that should mark the life of each member of the community: humble obedience. Thus the Philippian community is to be a community marked by the cross. The community celebrates Jesus' death on the cross, and the cross also provides a symbol of the identity of the community. The community's identity is "cruciform," to use Michael

---

[91]For more on this, see Fowl, *Philippians*, 99.
[92]For example, as found in the *Odes* of Horace in praise of Augustus.
[93]Martin and Nash, "Subversive *Hymnos*," 110.
[94]For a helpful summary of the ways in which the Philippian hymn contributes to the community's understanding of identity, see Rosell Nebreda, *Christ Identity*, 344-47.
[95]Martin and Nash, "Subversive *Hymnos*," 112.

Gorman's phrase.[96] As the hymn portrays, its values contrast sharply with those of the ruling powers.[97]

Third, as with other kinds of resistance poetry, there is concern not only for history and for identity but also for a sense of possibility. The brutal oppression of the past—which led to the killing of Jesus at the hands of Roman authorities—rather than being the final word, is a means to a new reality. In this new reality, Jesus is exalted by God and given the name above every name. The future possibility, then, is that all creatures will worship him, giving him the honor that is due to his name.[98] As with many examples of resistance poetry, this future does not seem to be guaranteed by anything that is in view at the moment. At the moment, the Roman emperors are the ones receiving universal homage. Perhaps "the powers" are also not yet fully subjected to Jesus: followers of the crucified Messiah, such as Paul, are currently in prison and suffering (Phil 1:29-30). Yet because of the cross and resurrection—understood as the fulfillment of some of the eschatological promises of Isaiah—the remainder of the promises will surely also be fulfilled. The death of the cross as the turning point of the hymn, and of history, provides meaning and hope for those, like Paul, who suffer for Christ. This hopeful assurance and sense of possibility also provides a motivation for readers of Paul's letter to embrace the cruciform way of life he advocates.

Such a vision of the exalted Jesus may indeed give hope that living as followers of Jesus in the present moment is aligned with ultimate reality in spite of what they see around them. This imaginal vision of the exalted Jesus supports and enables a countercultural way of living for those who find themselves under the rule of Rome but understand their true identity as part of the kingdom of God.

Having reached such a conclusion, we may also need to ask whether this vision of the victorious lord of all, while standing in contrast to Roman imperial ideology, is really all that far removed from its imperial parallels. To explore this dynamic we can return to the contribution of Shaner noted above. While I did not accept her assessment of the difficult term *harpagmos*, her

---

[96]Michael J. Gorman, *Inhabiting the Cruciform God: Kenosis, Justification, and Theosis in Paul's Narrative Soteriology* (Grand Rapids: Eerdmans, 2009).

[97]It is this set of values, then, that also is foundational to addressing the kinds of challenges that were facing the early Christian community in Philippi.

[98]For the view that this acknowledgment of Jesus is future and not something that has already happened, see Fee, *Pauline Christology*, 398.

impulse to understand the hymn in light of the Roman imperial context is on target. Particularly significant is her analysis of the extent to which the hymn offers a critique of and an alternative to Roman values related to power and authority. In short, Shaner suggests that, while the hymn promotes a savior who does not participate in the Roman practices of "rape and robbery," in the end the hymn does not offer any other critique of the prevailing Roman imperial power system. Jesus is exalted and given all power rather than the emperor, but the power system where one rules all remains in place. Such a portrayal of investiture of dominion over all things actually reinforces and reinscribes the Roman emphasis on "glory, victory, and imperial singularity as celebrated qualities of a god-human."[99] By the time Jesus is exalted and all creatures participate in venerating and confessing his lordship, Jesus has become "more imperial than the emperor" in Shaner's words.[100] Shaner's observation is intriguing and should lead us to consider what value system the hymn is promoting and whether it does indeed offer a critique of empire or just a new and improved replacement for it.

Is Shaner correct that the hymn actually reinscribes Roman values about power and domination rather than contesting them? If the final lines of the hymn were taken in isolation from the rest of the hymn, perhaps Shaner would be right. However, the picture is more complex. When the exaltation of Jesus is taken together with the humiliation and the death on the cross in the first half of the hymn, then Shaner's conclusion must be reconsidered. It is the paradoxical combination of humiliation and exaltation in which the meaning of the hymn and its potential for critique of empire is to be found. In this way, we must agree that the rhetoric of exaltation is used, but we might say instead that this rhetoric is co-opted by the hymnist and given a different sense. The language of imperial exaltation is shown, through allusions to the prophecies of Isaiah, to connect with God's ancient promises about the renewal and redemption of all things. This is ultimately, as we have seen, a hymn that is framed with references to God and God's working in the world. The power structure of the hymn is the power of the dominion of God, long ago promised to God's people, which precedes the power of Rome. Incredibly, the crucified/exalted Jesus is now understood to be central to God's dominion. Dominion *is* shown to be valued in the hymn—

---

[99]Shaner, "Seeing Rape and Robbery," 362-63.
[100]Ibid., 362.

Shaner is right about that. However, it is arguably a dominion that draws on a frame of reference that is broader than and markedly different from the dominion of Rome. The hymn's frame of reference is shaped by prophetic promises and by the centrality of the cross. These themes result in a power structure that may be seen as fundamentally different from the power of Rome, an empire in which the cross was a symbol and tool of brutal subjugation.

CONCLUSION

At this point we must circle back to where we began. We cannot be certain that this passage was a hymn that was chanted or sung in early Christian worship gatherings. Even if it was, we could not be certain whether this was a hymn that the Philippians already knew or if it was one that Paul was sharing with them for the first time. Regardless, the language, style, and content of the passage show multiple points of connection with ancient Greco-Roman and Jewish hymnic conventions. Based on these features we can conclude that this passage is reflective of the kinds of things that were included in the "psalms, hymns, and spiritual songs" (Col 3:16) advocated by Paul and that were part of early Christian worship. As we will see in the chapters that follow, while this hymn is unique, its emphases on the incarnation, the cross, and the exaltation of Jesus are not. We can conclude, then, that this passage very likely reflects the content and scope of early Christian hymns that were being used in worship. Moreover, we can also read it "as is" and consider the hymn's role in the letter, if not in a moment of communal song.

Ralph Martin captures well the way in which a hymn like this could have provided the Philippians a way of viewing their place in the world in light of both the present and future eschatological dimensions of the advent of Jesus:

> The Christ-hymn enables the Church to see beyond the present in which the Head of the Church reigns invisibly and powerfully—but known only to faith—to that full proof of his reign in the heavenly sphere in which all the powers are veritably subject to Him and His dominion is manifestly confessed.[101]

This poem, then, promotes a set of beliefs, values, and practices, as well as memories of historical events, that support a way of being that is quite different from the social and cultural values that were prominent within ancient

---

[101] Martin, *Hymn of Christ*, 270.

Greek or Roman cities. Whether intoned in communal worship or read aloud as part of Paul's letter, the hymn promotes a worldview that, while grounded in Jewish scriptural promises, directly confronted its Greco-Roman context with revolutionary claims about Jesus. That the hymn has the potential to play a similar role today is something I will consider in my final chapter.

– Four –

THE COLOSSIAN HYMN

A quick reading of the Colossian hymn compared to the Philippian hymn reveals a great deal of similarity between the two. One can note the similar length of each composition, the focus on Jesus with clear associations with the divine, the direct reference to the cross in each passage, and the prominence of allusions to Jewish scriptural themes.[1] The Colossian hymn also moves in some new directions and shows some striking differences from the Philippian hymn. Most notably, while the Philippian hymn may allude to some notion of preexistence, the Colossian hymn is unambiguous about the agency of Christ in the creation of all things. It also uses different titles and descriptors of Jesus and is explicit in naming the supernatural powers over which Christ is superior. Further, the Colossian hymn describes the redemptive work of Jesus as God's agent in the reconciliation of all things, in contrast to the Philippian hymn, which is silent on the issue of God's work of redemption. Finally, the structure and syntax of the Colossian hymn with its two distinct strophes and Asiatic rhetorical style create a different feeling than the more Semitic style of loosely parallel lines in the stanzas that make up the Philippian hymn.[2]

---

[1]The passages are also similar in that the issues within them continue to be widely debated. According to Sumney, "Nearly every statement in vv. 15-20 is fraught with difficulties." Jerry L. Sumney, *Colossians: A Commentary*, NTL (Louisville, KY: Westminster John Knox, 2008), 63. Wilson notes that the literature on the Colossian hymn is "almost infinite." R. McL. Wilson, *Colossians and Philemon: A Critical and Exegetical Commentary*, ICC (London: T&T Clark, 2005), 123.

[2]For recent scholarship on the Colossian hymn that explores these issues, see Matthew E. Gordley, *The Colossian Hymn in Context: An Exegesis in Light of Jewish and Greco-Roman Hymnic and*

These observations suggest that the Colossian hymn represents a further stage in the development of the tradition of christological hymns. In this chapter I explore the nature of these developments and show that the Colossian hymn can be read as a quasi-philosophical prose hymn that, for Paul, portrayed Jesus in exalted, cosmic terms. Aspects of the hymn resonate with Jewish traditions (particularly Wisdom, creation, and new creation) and arguably, but to a lesser degree, with Hellenistic philosophical discussions. At the same time, features of the hymn show some resonance with themes of Roman imperial propaganda. Throughout the remainder of the epistle to the Colossians Paul was able to draw on the rich ideas found in this hymn to help the readers as they confronted actual or potential challenges from a number of different angles. In the end, this passage amounts to an example of the "word about Christ" that was to dwell in them richly (Col 3:16). In this regard it is to be closely associated with the "psalms, hymns, and spiritual songs" that were a feature of the communal gatherings of the Colossian believers (Col 3:15-17). Such a hymn enabled them to live their lives in the light of the reality of the revelation of God through Christ and to resist the allure of other competing worldviews.

In order to explore these dimensions of the Colossian hymn, we will first examine the setting of the passage both within the epistle and within the cultural context of Colossae in Asia Minor. Second, we will review an arrangement of the hymn that highlights important features of the passage. Third, we will examine the hymn's employment of biblical motifs as well as philosophical ideas mediated through Hellenistic-Jewish thought. Fourth, we will consider the Roman context, and particularly Roman imperial ideology, as an important part of the conceptual world in which the Colossian hymn was written. With these pieces in place we will be in a position to consider the ways in which the Colossian hymn embodies a kind of counterdiscourse to the claims of empire as it provides a worldview framework for the Colossian believers. Within the context of their communal worship, such hymnic acclamations of Jesus as the agent of God in creation and redemption provided them the theological resources to be able to live their lives as citizens of the "kingdom of God's beloved son" (Col 1:13).

___

Epistolary Conventions, WUNT 2/228 (Tübingen: Mohr Siebeck, 2007). Note also Vincent A. Pizzuto, A Cosmic Leap of Faith: An Authorial, Structural, and Theological Investigation of the Cosmic Christology in Col. 1:15-20, CBET 41 (Leuven: Peeters, 2006); Christian Stettler, Der Kolosserhymnus: Untersuchungen zu Form, traditionsgeschichtlichem Hintergrund und Aussage von Kol 1, 15-20, WUNT 2/131 (Tübingen: Mohr Siebeck, 2000).

THE SETTING OF THE PASSAGE

Any interpretation of the Colossian hymn within its context must consider the authorship and circumstances that led to the composition of the epistle itself. As this is an issue that continues to be debated by biblical scholars, here I will simply provide the assumptions with which I am working, and point the reader to further resources for detailed discussion of the arguments.[3] When compared to the Pauline epistles that are agreed to have come directly from the hand of Paul, content and stylistic issues lead many scholars to conclude that Paul could not have written this particular letter.[4] Nevertheless, even those who reach that conclusion still admit a very close connection to Pauline themes, so much so that they must posit an individual in the Pauline tradition, someone with a very close relationship to Paul, as the author.[5] Given that the connections to Paul are so strong, it makes sense to me to consider either that Paul wrote it and the variations are appropriate to the subject he is addressing and his relationship with Colossae, or that someone very close to Paul wrote it as an expression of Paul's thinking. Either way the epistle can correctly be claimed to reflect a development of the Pauline tradition.[6] In the absence of definitive evidence one way or the other it seems unlikely that this would have been a completely fictional letter with fictional author and addressees, for the simple reason that Colossian believers and other associated individuals could easily have identified it as a forgery if it were not a letter actually received by them within the lifetime of Paul.[7] For our

---

[3]For recent extended discussions see Paul Foster, *Colossians*, BNTC (New York: Bloomsbury T&T Clark, 2016), 61-81; Ulrich Huttner, *Early Christianity in the Lycus Valley*, AJEC 85 (Leiden: Brill, 2013), 110-17. Vincent Pizzuto devotes four chapters to the issue in his published dissertation on the Colossian hymn: *Cosmic Leap of Faith*, 13-93. Earlier commentaries on Colossians also provide helpful summaries of the issues, and full-length monograph analyses are available by Mark Christopher Kiley, *Colossians as Pseudepigraphy*, BibSem (Sheffield: JSOT Press, 1986); Outi Leppä, *The Making of Colossians: A Study on the Formation and Purpose of a Deutero-Pauline Letter*, Publications of the Finnish Exegetical Society 86 (Göttingen: Vandenhoeck & Ruprecht, 2003).

[4]See, for example, Bart D. Ehrman, *Forgery and Counterforgery: The Use of Literary Deceit in Early Christian Polemics* (New York: Oxford University Press, 2013), 171-82. Witherington explains the stylistic features by recourse to the unique Asiatic style that the author employs in this epistle as a means of engaging this particular audience, as well as to the nature of the philosophy that the author was seeking to refute.

[5]This is the approach taken by Foster, *Colossians*, 80-81.

[6]Along this line of thought, Dunn considers Colossians a "bridge" letter. James D. G. Dunn, *The Epistles to the Colossians and to Philemon: A Commentary on the Greek Text*, NIGTC (Grand Rapids: Eerdmans, 1996), 19.

[7]As Huttner rightly notes. Huttner, *Early Christianity in the Lycus Valley*, 115-16. But this view persists, for example, in Ehrman, *Forgery and Counterforgery*, 182.

purposes I will consider that Colossians was written by Paul or one of his close associates and that it is a genuine letter in the sense that it was actually written to the believers in Colossae.

The letter as a whole tells us something of the author's expectation of the audience, particularly with regard to its use of earlier traditions. While the theology of Colossians draws heavily on Jewish motifs and ideas, Colossians is noteworthy in that not once does Paul actually cite a biblical passage. Instead, he alludes to a number of biblical traditions but without direct citation.[8] There are a number of ways that this feature can be explained. One likely explanation is that the Colossian Christians, whom Paul had not met personally, were Gentiles for whom the direct citation of the Jewish Scriptures would have had little significance. Even so, it is clear that the teaching of Colossians draws heavily on Jewish themes, which is not surprising given the Jewish matrix of early Christianity. Astute Jewish readers would likely have picked up on these many biblical allusions, but a Colossian reader who lacked such background would not seemingly have been hindered from understanding the message about the supremacy of Christ and life together "in him."[9] It is thus difficult to infer from the text alone whether the author expected a Jewish readership. Further, the extent to which Jewish opponents or an opposing message derived from Judaism may have been present in Colossae is hotly debated.[10] Taken together with the lack of conclusive historical and archaeological evidence about the presence of a Jewish community in Colossae it is difficult to say much more.[11]

As was the case in Philippi, the Roman context of Colossae should be considered significant. In Colossians Paul alludes to concepts and themes that would have been part of the experience of individuals living in a Roman city in Asia Minor.[12] Since some of these themes of Roman imperial ideology are pertinent to my investigation of the Colossian hymn, I will look at them

---

[8]See Foster, *Colossians*, 52-60; Jerry L. Sumney, "Writing 'In the Image' of Scripture: The Form and Function of References to Scripture in Colossians," in *Paul and Scripture: Extending the Conversation*, ed. Christopher D. Stanley, ECL 9 (Atlanta: Society of Biblical Literature, 2012), 185-229.
[9]Sumney, "Writing 'In the Image' of Scripture," 222-26.
[10]Wilson, *Colossians and Philemon*, 35-58.
[11]Foster, *Colossians*, 15.
[12]See Brian J. Walsh and Sylvia C. Keesmaat, *Colossians Remixed: Subverting the Empire* (Downers Grove, IL: IVP Academic, 2004); Harry O. Maier, "A Sly Civility: Colossians and Empire," *JSNT* 27 (2005): 323-49.

more closely below. For now, we may recall features of Roman imperial ideology and the way it was promoted throughout the empire. As for its features, Roman imperial ideology provided a worldview that included a divinely appointed Roman emperor who was understood to be the savior of the world, who brought peace and pacified hostile peoples, who was a source of benefactions to humanity, who renewed the moral character of Rome, and who was closely associated with the divine. These dimensions of Roman imperial propaganda were promoted through a wide variety of forms both verbal and nonverbal.[13] In terms of iconography, looking specifically at imperial art and sculpture in the Lycus valley, where Colossae was situated, Harry Maier explains,

> The imperial monuments that Roman authorities and civic elites erected to publish and promote Roman rule deployed a relatively narrow repertoire of images to celebrate and legitimate a rule of peace established through military power and skilful diplomacy. . . .
>
> . . . In multiple media, ranging from public monuments to household decoration, iconographers represented the pacification of once hostile and warring peoples. Often they depicted conquered peoples at the feet of emperors.[14]

Maier finds that the collective force of the images and claims about empire amount to what may be called a "realized eschatology of Roman imperial art," which communicated "the advent of an age of moral renewal, represented most forcefully by its development of neo-classicism." He goes on to explain, "This iconographical semiotic language was an important means for constructing an imperial worldview, and for helping to fashion social identity in the Roman Empire."[15] If this understanding is correct, then Paul's engagement with themes that were integral to this worldview takes on greater significance.

Without question, then, the reality of the Roman Empire was a feature of daily life in Colossae. That Paul was sensitive to this reality and could draw

---

[13]Harry O. Maier, "Reading Colossians in the Ruins: Roman Imperial Iconography, Moral Transformation, and the Construction of Christian Identity in the Lycus Valley," in *Colossae in Space and Time: Linking to an Ancient City*, ed. Alan H. Cadwallader and Michael Trainor, NTOA, SUNT 94 (Göttingen: Vandenhoeck & Ruprecht, 2011), 212-31; Huttner, *Early Christianity in the Lycus Valley*.

[14]Maier, "Reading Colossians in the Ruins," 217. He further notes, "Throughout the Julio-Claudian period imperial mints portrayed conquered subjects displaying submission to their rulers. This iconography rehearsed similar images spread across the Empire on victory monuments and imperial statues."

[15]Ibid., 221.

on aspects of it for his rhetorical purposes is clear from references throughout Colossians to imperial themes and imagery. Perhaps the clearest example is the image of an imperial triumph in Colossians 2:15. But there are other instances as well, including an expansive view of the whole world (Col 1:6), imagery of fruitfulness and growth (Col 1:6, 10), reference to the kingdom of the beloved son (Col 1:13; cf. Col 4:11), and the idea of the inclusion of even the furthest reaches of civilization (Col 1:23; 3:11).[16] Even the household code of Colossians 3:18–4:1 can be seen to tap into the Roman ideal of the well-ordered and virtuous home, which the Roman emperor had restored after a period of decline.[17]

While many scholars find that attention to the Roman context of Colossians and to allusions to Roman imperial ideology within Colossians are useful in interpreting this letter, not all are convinced that Roman concerns are present in these passages. Allan Bevere has argued strongly that Brian Walsh and Sylvia Keesmaat have overstated their case while ignoring other important themes within the letter.[18] For Bevere, Colossians is not primarily an "anti-imperial tract," and any kind of imperial critique is only "tangentially implied at best."[19] Instead he argues that Colossians can be read without reference to empire and in a way that links it to other concerns related primarily to a Jewish background. However, the recognition that an interpretation of the Colossian hymn can be offered without recourse to imperial ideology does not automatically lead to the conclusion that such background is not important in understanding the hymn. Given the realities of the Roman Empire it seems to me that Bevere's interpretation does not adequately take into account the imperial context. Colossians need not be an "anti-imperial tract" for the ideas and themes addressed in the letter to be tapping into the author's and recipients' experiences of empire. When it comes to the Colossian hymn we will see that the hymn most certainly does draw on some important ideas that were prominent in the imperial ideology, but for the purpose of showing the supremacy of Christ over all things. Given the extent to which hymnody

---

[16]Ibid., 215. Cf. Walsh and Keesmaat, *Colossians Remixed*, 72-81.

[17]See Deborah F. Sawyer, *God, Gender, and the Bible* (London: Routledge, 2002), 130-32. On the household code in the context of the Roman Empire, see Sumney, *Colossians*, 230-38.

[18]Allan R. Bevere, "Colossians and the Rhetoric of Empire: A New Battle Zone," in *Jesus Is Lord, Caesar Is Not: Evaluating Empire in New Testament Studies*, ed. Scot McKnight and Joseph B. Modica (Downers Grove, IL: IVP Academic, 2013), 183-96.

[19]Ibid., 193.

was a feature of the rituals that served to promote Roman imperial ideology and enhance the persona of the emperor, the inclusion of a hymn to Christ in Colossians takes on even greater significance.[20]

Before turning to the hymn, three other points about the epistle as a whole are important. First, the letter follows the pattern of philosophical paraenesis. That is, it offers encouragement to continue on with a particular view of the world, warns against being led astray by other philosophies, and urges readers to follow a particular way of life based on the teaching they have accepted.[21] In this regard it follows a pattern utilized by popular philosophers in antiquity as they wrote to their students and urged them to continue to adhere to the way of life advanced by their particular philosophy. Second, studies of Colossians have made much of the "Colossian heresy," which refers to the specific kind of teaching Paul was warning against in places like Colossians 2:8-23. Whether Paul was writing about one particular kind of teaching that was present in Colossae (over forty potential kinds have been posited) or just providing more general warnings based on his own experiences is a subject of vigorous debate.[22] Though a full examination of this issue would take us too far afield, my position is that whatever the nature of the threats to the Colossian community, it is certainly the case that the bulk of Paul's response is centered on the exalted vision of Christ portrayed in the hymn. Third, though I have already noted Jewish traditions and Roman cultural allusions, Colossians is also noteworthy for its use of other traditional material including the household code (Col 3:18–4:1) and lists of vices and virtues (Col 3:5, 8, 12), as well as the hymn (Col 1:15-20).[23] These features are best appreciated by reading Colossians as a philosophical paraenetic letter that utilizes earlier tradition to make its case to the readers to continue their way of life in Christ.

---

[20]Huttner, *Early Christianity in the Lycus Valley*, 59-66.

[21]For further explanation of this claim, see Gordley, *Colossian Hymn in Context*, 242-55; Walter T. Wilson, *The Hope of Glory: Education and Exhortation in the Epistle to the Colossians*, NovTSup 88 (Leiden: Brill, 1997), 229-55.

[22]For an overview, see Jerry L. Sumney, *"Servants of Satan," "False Brothers" and Other Opponents of Paul*, JSNTSup (Sheffield: Sheffield Academic, 1999), esp. chap. 6; B. J. Oropeza, *Jews, Gentiles, and the Opponents of Paul: Apostasy in the New Testament Communities*, Apostasy in the New Testament Communities (Eugene, OR: Cascade, 2012), esp. chap. 8. For an extended discussion see Wilson, *Colossians and Philemon*, 35-58.

[23]Sumney, "Writing 'In the Image' of Scripture," 225. Sumney explains, "While our reading suggests that Scripture had a basic authority for the author of Colossians and his readers and that their reading of Scripture derived from the church's tradition, it seems that the citation of tradition had a more immediate impact on the argument of this letter than its citation of Scripture. The church's tradition seems to have possessed a recognizable and direct authority" (225).

THE HYMNIC NATURE AND STRUCTURE
OF THE PASSAGE

In the late twentieth century, scholars like James Dunn and Peter O'Brien could claim that there was general agreement and that the weight of scholarly opinion favored seeing Colossians 1:15-20 as a preformed hymn.[24] Examinations of this passage by these and other scholars often included the necessary clarifications that the term *hymn* was to be broadly understood and certainly did not reflect the notion of ancient Greek hymn genres. Commentators would also acknowledge some dissenting views that were in the minority. At the present time the weight of scholarly opinion appears more evenly divided between the idea that this passage is a hymn and that it is simply the composition of the author at the time of writing.[25] It is not necessarily that new evidence has emerged, but rather that the same evidence within the text is being interpreted differently. Like the other New Testament christological hymns we are examining, the structure of an original hymn is not preserved for us either in the manuscript tradition or in unambiguous indicators from the context. However, a number of features within the text have pointed scholars toward the conclusion that this passage was a hymnic composition. These features mainly have to do with matters of elevated style and content.[26] And yet, even among those who accept the passage as a hymn, there is disagreement as to whether it represents something more akin to an early Jewish psalm, perhaps a mixed form of a *beraka* (blessing) and the Old Testament psalm *Gattung* hymn,[27] or something more along the lines of a prose hymn displaying features of epideictic rhetoric shaped by its Greco-Roman environment.[28]

Among some of the most recent commentators on the passage, Paul Foster still uses the terminology of *hymn* but focuses more on the passage's "lyrical quality" and "doxological language" rather than placing any significance on

[24]Dunn, *Epistles to the Colossians and to Philemon*, 86; Peter Thomas O'Brien, *Colossians, Philemon*, WBC 44 (Waco, TX: Word, 1982), 32.

[25]See, for example, Benjamin Edsall and Jennifer R. Strawbridge, "The Songs We Used to Sing? Hymn 'Traditions' and Reception in Pauline Letters," *JSNT* 37 (2015): 290-311.

[26]See Gordley, *Colossian Hymn in Context*, 176-87. For poetic and stylistic features see Luis Carlos-Reyes, "The Structure and Rhetoric of Colossians 1:15-20," *FN* 12, nos. 23-24 (1999): 139-54.

[27]Stettler, *Kolosserhymnus*, 84.

[28]Edgar Krentz, "Epideiktik and Hymnody: The New Testament and Its World," *BR* 40 (1995): 50-97. Kentz discusses the traditional hymnic topoi articulated by Seneca and that are found in Col 1:15-20, including nature in general, honor from descent, antiquity, individual powers, authority, superiority, immortal nature, immortality won by valor, relation to God, and discoveries for humans (89-90).

whether the passage may have been a preformed composition.[29] Michael Bird can say that it is "probably a Christian hymn or poem about Jesus Christ" with full awareness that "nearly everything about the passage is disputed."[30] Scholars who do not consider this passage to be a hymn also recognize the presence of these features. Jerry Sumney suggests that the passage is "poetic and liturgical," and could even have been recited antiphonally in Christian worship, but argues that it does not fit the ancient genre of hymn.[31] Further along the spectrum, Gordon Fee, N. T. Wright, and Ralph Brucker are among those most vocal in their assertion that this passage is *not* a hymn. They recognize the passage's unique qualities but conclude that these features point only to its being a very carefully constructed passage.[32] At present it is fair to say that many scholars accept the general idea that this passage is at least hymnic or poetic to some extent but most recognize the challenges inherent in the nomenclature.

For my part I have argued that the passage is a hymn when considered against the broad context of ancient Greco-Roman and Jewish conventions of praise.[33] However, as we saw in chapter one, the critics of "hymn-hunting" in the New Testament are right to point out that the quest to identify preexisting materials is problematic. We simply cannot know if Paul wrote this poetic passage himself or if he was citing something that already existed. In calling this passage a hymn and arranging it in strophes, my claim is not that this was necessarily a preexisting composition but that it is a passage which demonstrates many hymnic features. The strophic arrangement helps to bring those into view. For my part, I do think it is plausible that Paul is quoting earlier material here, and perhaps even adds in his own editorial expansion in a line or two. These points must simply be recognized as plausible but not provable. Below I present my own arrangement of the hymn in two strophes and an epode, and then point out the features of the passage that suggest this structure and point to its hymnic quality.

---

[29]Foster, *Colossians*, 31-33.

[30]Michael F. Bird, *Colossians and Philemon*, New Covenant Commentary (Havertown, UK: Lutterworth, 2011), 47-48.

[31]Sumney, *Colossians*, 61.

[32]Ralph Brucker, *"Christushymnen" oder "epideiktische Passagen"? Studien zum Stilwechsel im Neuen Testament und seiner Umwelt*, FRLANT 176 (Göttingen: Vandenhoeck & Ruprecht, 1997), 349-50. Cf. N. T. Wright, "Poetry and Theology in Colossians 1:15-20," *NTS* 36 (1990): 444-68; Gordon D. Fee, *Pauline Christology: An Exegetical-Theological Study* (Peabody, MA.: Hendrickson, 2007).

[33]Gordley, *Colossian Hymn in Context*, 269.

First Strophe (Col 1:15-18a)
He is the image of the invisible God,
the firstborn over all creation.
For by him all things were created:
things in heaven and on earth, visible and invisible,
    [whether thrones or powers or rulers or authorities.]
all things were created through him and for him.
And he is before all things,
And all things hold together in him.
And he is the head of the
body, the church.

Second Strophe (Col 1:18b-20a)
He is the beginning firstborn from among the dead,
so that in all things he might have the supremacy.
For he [God] was pleased
to have all his fullness dwell in him,
and through him to reconcile
all things to himself
making peace through the
blood of his cross—

Epode (Col 1:20b)
through him, whether things on earth
or things in heaven.

To begin with, the broader context of this passage in Colossians 1 is significant in supporting the view that this is a hymn. Colossians 1:15-20 interrupts
the flow of the passage as Paul moves from first- and second-person address to
third-person discourse beginning in Colossians 1:15. In Colossians 1:2-12 Paul
had been addressing the Colossians in the second person. In Colossians 1:13-14
he began speaking inclusively in the first-person plural. In Colossians 1:21-22
Paul resumes his second-person address, including himself again in Colossians
1:23 and following. Colossians 1:15-20 stands apart in that it makes no reference
to Paul or to the Colossians but is a third-person discourse about Christ.[34]

The view that this is a hymn is further supported by recognizing that the
beginnings of the two strophes are evident with their parallel use of the phrase

---

[34]Of course, this observation is not conclusive since this change of person can be considered simply
an instance of *stilwechsel* (i.e., change of style for rhetorical effect). See Brucker, *Christushymnen*, 349.

hos estin, which is followed immediately by a claim about Jesus using honorific titles. In addition, each instance of *hos estin* is followed shortly after by a *hoti* clause, which provides the justification for the claim. Furthermore, the rhythmic patterning of the Greek is identical for the first seven syllables of each strophe.[35]

The endings of the strophes are significant as well. A Greek metrical pattern consisting of a series of spondaic *metra* marks the ending of each strophe in the phrases "the body, the church" and "the blood of his cross." Spondees were long vowel patterns that were understood in antiquity to be a solemn and stately style of composition.[36] In addition, the spondee was noted for its use in Greek libation prayers.[37]

The two strophes that are indicated by these parallel phrases are reinforced by the inclusion of the honorific title "firstborn" (*prōtotokos*) in each as well as by the extensive use of prepositions relating to Christ: "by him," "through him," "for him," "in him." These kinds of parallels and repetitions support the notion of two strophes and are also a feature of the Asiatic style, which characterizes the letter as a whole but is even more prominent in the hymn than in the rest of the letter.[38]

This arrangement of the hymn in two strophes also helps us appreciate that there may be places where Paul has added editorial comments or expanded an earlier hymn in order to highlight important aspects. Attention to rhythmic patterning suggests that part of Colossians 1:16 is a later interpretive comment added to the hymn.[39] I have bracketed out the phrase "whether thrones or powers or rulers or authorities" in the arrangement above to indicate this possibility.

Finally, with the consideration of the use of an epode at the end (a feature of some ancient hymns), the symmetry of the strophes becomes clear, as does the overall thematic emphasis of the hymn. The first strophe describes the supremacy of Christ as God's agent in creation. The second strophe describes the supremacy of Christ as God's agent of reconciliation in initiating the new

---

[35]Gordley, *Colossian Hymn in Context*, 184-86.

[36]*Hermogenes' On Types of Style*, trans. Cecil W. Wooten (Chapel Hill: University of North Carolina Press, 1987), §252.

[37]M. L. West, *Ancient Greek Music* (Oxford: Clarendon, 1992), 155-56.

[38]Ben Witherington III, *The Letters to Philemon, the Colossians, and the Ephesians: A Socio-rhetorical Commentary on the Captivity Epistles* (Grand Rapids: Eerdmans, 2007), 132, cf. 102.

[39]Gordley, *Colossian Hymn in Context*, 176-96. Dunn also sees this as an editorial addition to an earlier hymn; Dunn, *Epistles to the Colossians and to Philemon*, 92.

creation. The epode summarizes the hymn with its emphasis on the agency of Christ in the creation and redemption of all things, both earthly and heavenly. Given the uncertainty of these kinds of reconstructions, if we grant that Paul added editorial explanations in places like Colossians 1:16, it may also be plausible that Colossians 1:20b is an explanatory addition rather than an epode.

Interestingly, Eduard Norden, who is generally acknowledged as the first to note the hymnic features of the passage, identified the beginning of the hymn in Colossians 1:12 rather than Colossians 1:15.[40] Ernst Lohmeyer and Ernst Käsemann, whose works were influential in the study of the Philippian hymn, both followed this approach. While they agreed in seeing the longer passage as hymnic, they disagreed in the thematic background and purpose. Lohmeyer saw the guiding idea as deriving from the Jewish Day of Atonement, with other concepts added in.[41] Käsemann, on the other hand, described the entire section as a "citation of the primitive Christian baptismal liturgy" that adapted and modified an earlier Gnostic hymn.[42] These specific proposals have not been widely accepted. More recently Reinhard Deichgräber has shown that the traditional material begins in Colossians 1:15, and this has become the consensus view.[43] It may be that Colossians 1:12-14 is part of another separate unit of traditional material, but scholars agree that Colossians 1:15-20 is distinct from those. The belief of earlier scholars of the *religionsgeschichtliche Schule* that Paul was adapting an earlier Gnostic hymn has also been set aside in favor of seeing this as a Christian composition, whether by Paul himself or another early believer.[44]

Many other arrangements besides mine are possible, each with its strengths and shortcomings. Proposals of anywhere from two to five strophes have been put forward.[45] The two-strophe arrangement appears to be the most popular,

---

[40]Eduard Norden, *Agnostos Theos: Untersuchungen zur Formengeschichte religiöser Rede* (Stuttgart: Teubner, 1956), 250-54.

[41]Ernst Lohmeyer, *Die Briefe an die Philipper, an die Kolosser und an Philemon*, KEK (Göttingen: Vandenhoeck & Ruprecht, 1954), 43.

[42]Ernst Käsemann, "A Primitive Christian Baptismal Liturgy," in *Essays on New Testament Themes*, Studies in Biblical Theology (Naperville, IL: Allenson, 1964), 149-68, esp. 164-65.

[43]Reinhard Deichgräber, *Gotteshymnus und Christushymnus in der frühen Christenheit*, SUNT 5 (Göttingen: Vandenhoeck & Ruprecht, 1967), 144-46.

[44]Dunn, *Epistles to the Colossians and to Philemon*, 86. See the discussion in Jack T. Sanders, *The New Testament Christological Hymns: Their Historical Religious Background*, SNTSMS 15 (Cambridge: Cambridge University Press, 1971), 75-87.

[45]Gordley, *Colossian Hymn in Context*, 5-16. Cf. Jean Noël Aletti, *Saint Paul Épitre aux Colossiens* (Paris: Éditions J. Gabalda, 1993), 90.

although even among two-strophe arrangements scholars disagree on what may have been original to the preexisting hymn and what may have been added by Paul.[46] Ralph Martin followed Eduard Schweizer in seeing a three-strophe structure, with the phrase "and he is before all things" in Colossians 1:17 beginning a new strophe of its own.[47] In addition to strophic structures, chiastic arrangements have also been proposed.[48] In spite of the variety of proposals, it is nevertheless fair to say that most scholars see some kind of two-part structure that focuses on the role of Christ in creation and redemption.

Given that readers can appreciate the content and development of this passage in two parts without calling it a hymn, we might pause to ask whether there is any value to be gained in considering this passage as a hymn. Foster suggests that there is not when he notes, "Whether this poetic section was a pre-existing unit, or whether it was a modified piece, or even a fresh composition, either from a Christian or pre-Christian context, is not only beyond conclusive proof, it is in many ways irrelevant."[49] While I can agree with Foster about the fact that these questions cannot be conclusively answered, I do find that there is relevance to the consideration of this passage's hymnic nature. First, if we find this passage is a hymn or at least hymn-like, then analysis of the passage allows us to compare claims about Christ with claims of others who were the subjects of hymns in the ancient world. This kind of analysis allows us to appreciate how this particular genre was creatively employed by early Christians, at least in their letters and, likely also, in their communal gatherings. Second, if this passage is a hymn then we can consider the text in light of the ways that other hymns functioned for their communities. This comparative approach can again allow us to consider how this hymn may be functioning in similar ways for this community. Third, if this passage is a hymn or even hymnic (i.e., using the conventions of ancient hymnody), the passage can be viewed as a window into the developing worship practices of the early Christians. We

---

[46]See, for example, the differing two-strophe arrangements by Jerome Murphy-O'Connor, *Paul: A Critical Life* (Oxford: Clarendon, 1996), 240-46; Christoph Burger, *Schöpfung und Versöhnung: Studien zum liturgischen Gut im Kolosser- und Epheserbrief*, WMANT 46 (Neukirchen-Vluyn: Neukirchener Verlag, 1975), 38.

[47]Ralph P. Martin, *Ephesians, Colossians, and Philemon*, IBC (Atlanta: John Knox Press, 1991), 105-6.

[48]See, for example, an ABBA proposal by Wright, "Poetry and Theology." An ABCBA proposal was put forward by Pizzuto, *Cosmic Leap of Faith*, 118-19.

[49]Foster, *Colossians*, 201.

do not have direct access to much information about early Christian worship practices, so even though not conclusive, consideration of the use of a hymn in an epistle can provide one small entry point into those dynamics. Finally, recognition of the hymnic genre of a passage like Colossians 1:15-20 allows a more nuanced interpretation of its claims not as a precise theological treatise but as the effusive language of praise.[50] As a hymn it not only tells but also shows as it paints a verbal portrait of Christ. In a context of worship it is not a stretch to imagine the way that this kind of special language invites the listener into an experience of the ultimate realities the hymn affirms.[51]

JEWISH TRADITIONS

The author of the hymn, whether Paul himself, a predecessor, or successor, made extensive use of biblical motifs and ideas as well as Jewish tradition. Each line of the hymn is rich with allusive power, and commentators have provided exceptionally good analyses of these links. It is clear that the author of the hymn draws on a number of biblical motifs and particularly those related to creation, new creation, and Wisdom. Some of the themes and ideas of the hymn can be seen in developments within Jewish thought within the Second Temple period as represented by writers like Philo of Alexandria. However, it is not clear that the portrayal of Christ in the hymn is indebted solely to one overriding concept. Robert McLachlan Wilson captures this well when he explains that it is

> difficult to be certain that our author is *directly* dependent on any one set of ideas, or that for example he was familiar with the works of Philo. It may rather be a question of ideas which were "in the air," in more or less general circulation, which could be drawn upon by an author to suit his own end.[52]

Rather than untangling the interplay of ideas that the author draws on, we will note a few of the biblical connections and then move to a discussion of connections with the wisdom tradition in general. Though not the only source for the ideas in the hymn, it is surely one of the most important aspects of the background of the hymn.

---

[50]Sumney, *Colossians*, 79.
[51]For more on this dynamic, see Gary S. Selby, *Not with Wisdom of Words: Nonrational Persuasion in the New Testament* (Grand Rapids: Eerdmans, 2016), 13-16.
[52]Wilson, *Colossians and Philemon*, 144.

Image of God (Col 1:15). The term *eikōn* (image) was used in a number of ways in the ancient world as well as in the Septuagint, New Testament, and other early Jewish writings. Accordingly, it is difficult to trace its significance to any one particular source. The concept of the image of God (*eikōn tou theou*) may draw on Genesis 1:26, 28.[53] In this regard it is possibly not far from the thought-world of the Philippian hymn with its "in the form of God" (*en morphē theou*) (Phil 2:6) and its Adamic allusions. Yet the term *eikōn* is not exhausted by allusions to creation; it certainly also alludes to Jewish discussions about Wisdom as the image of God, such as those represented in Philo and Wisdom of Solomon.[54]

Firstborn (Col 1:15, 18b). The term *prōtotokos* (firstborn) also had a wide range of uses in Judaism. Identifying Christ as the firstborn may allude to the use of this concept both in the Psalms and in Exodus (see Ps 89:27 [88:28 LXX]; Ex 4:22-23). Both Israel and the king were referred to as the firstborn. References to Christ as the firstborn may thus carry connotations of God's covenant promises to Israel now fulfilled in Christ, as well as Christ's kingship in line with Paul's comment in Colossians 1:13 about the kingdom of the beloved son. Further, like the term *eikōn*, *prōtotokos* has a rich pedigree that goes beyond the biblical references. Wisdom was also called God's firstborn in the Second Temple period.[55]

Agent of creation (Col 1:16). That all things were created "through him" taps into a wider discourse in antiquity. It certainly includes biblical creation accounts, but also alludes to other biblical and extrabiblical passages where Wisdom was the agent of God in creation. As Dunn explains, "We may deduce that the primary influence is the Jewish Wisdom tradition, within which such language had already been used of divine wisdom"[56] (e.g., Ps 104:24 [LXX 103:24]; Prov 3:19; Wis 8:5; as well as Philo, *Det.* 54 and *Fug.* 109).

Though not present in the Philippian hymn, this notion of Christ as agent of God in creation is something we will see again in John 1:3, 10, and Hebrews 1:2. It is also present in the short confession in 1 Corinthians 8:6. Greg Sterling has argued persuasively that the phrase "through him" is used in each case in

---

[53]Notably, Burney proposed that the whole hymn was an expansion of Gen 1:1 using the variety of possible meaning of the Hebrew term for "in the beginning" to show the supremacy of Christ. C. F. Burney, "Christ as the APXH of Creation," *JTS* 27 (1926): 160-77.

[54]Eduard Lohse, *A Commentary on the Epistles to the Colossians and to Philemon*, Hermeneia (Philadelphia: Fortress, 1971), 46-48.

[55]Cf. Philo, *Conf.* 62; Sumney, *Colossians*, 65. See also Sir 1:4; 24:9, and other references to Jewish speculation about Wisdom in Lohse, *Colossians*, 48-49.

[56]Dunn, *Epistles to the Colossians and to Philemon*, 91.

the sense of instrumental agency as popularized by Middle Platonism.[57] The concern with agency expressed through prepositions (e.g., "in him," "through him," "to him") was also part of a wider philosophical debate in antiquity. This philosophical debate extends well beyond the sophistication and scope of early Christian discussions about Jesus, so it is not likely that the early Christians were concerned about these philosophical issues. The use of these phrases was more likely mediated through Hellenistic Judaism represented by writers such as Philo.[58] Sterling explains, "Jewish understandings of God and Wisdom/Logos mediated the categories of Hellenistic philosophy to Christian theology. The case of prepositional metaphysics is but one example."[59]

This use of philosophical terminology can also be seen in the notion that "all things hold together in him" (Col 1:17). This phrase is noteworthy in that Paul attributes to Christ not only agency in creation but continued agency in maintaining all things. We will see a similar expression in Hebrews 1:1-4, where Christ is the agent of God in creation and also "sustains all things by his powerful word" (Heb 1:3). This sustaining work of Christ also casts a quasi-philosophical tone to this passage since it was the Logos in Stoic and Middle Platonic thought that carried this role.

Wisdom traditions. Given the polyvalence of each of the few terms noted above, the Jewish wisdom tradition appears to be a primary lens through which many of the claims of the Colossian hymn can be read. Ben Witherington III's assessment is that the hymn is "profoundly indebted to Jewish wisdom literature."[60] Dunn likewise identifies a "wisdom Christology" as underlying the Colossian hymn.[61] This tradition, rooted in the Hebrew Bible, continued to develop in the Jewish writings of the Second Temple period.[62] It was thus a tradition that provided a connection to foundational texts and shared norms of Judaism while also providing a vehicle for innovation based on the needs of a given community. We saw an example of this in chapter two in the brief look at the praise of Sophia in Wisdom of Solomon 10. This tradition depicts

---

[57]Gregory E. Sterling, "Prepositional Metaphysics in Jewish Wisdom Speculation and Early Christological Hymns," in *Wisdom and Logos: Studies in Jewish Thought in Honor of David Winston*, ed. D. T. Runia and Gregory E. Sterling, SPhiloA 9 (Atlanta: Scholars Press, 1997), 219-38.

[58]Ibid., 233.

[59]Ibid., 238.

[60]Witherington, *Letters to Philemon, the Colossians, and the Ephesians*, 130.

[61]James D. G. Dunn, *Christology in the Making: A New Testament Inquiry into the Origins of the Doctrine of the Incarnation* (Grand Rapids: Eerdmans, 1996), 187-97.

[62]See ibid., 168-75.

personified Wisdom as present with God before creation (Prov 8), as the agent of God in the act of creation (Wis 7–9), and as an agent of God actively at work among God's people (Wis 10). Witherington has shown that many of the claims of the Colossian hymn have very close parallels within Second Temple–period Jewish wisdom texts (see table 4.1[63]). Though Witherington identifies "remote echoes" from Proverbs 3, 8, and 9, he rightly notes that "the more evident and close parallels are from the later Jewish wisdom literature."[64]

Table 4.1. The Colossian hymn and Wisdom of Solomon

Colossians	Wisdom of Solomon
Col 1:15a	"For she is . . . a spotless mirror of the working of God and an image of his goodness" (7.26); cf. Philo, *Leg All* 1.43
Col 1:15b	"I tell you what Wisdom is and how she came to be . . . I will trace her *course from the beginning of creation*" (6.22); cf. Prov 8:22, 25
Col 1:16a	"For he created all things so that they might exist" (1.14); "Wisdom that effects all things" (8.5); cf. Wis 8.4-6
Col 1:16d	On thrones and scepters (5.23d; 6.21; 7.8)
Col 1:16-17, 19	"For Wisdom . . . because of her purity pervades and penetrates all things" (7.24b)
Col 1:17b	"that which holds all things together knows what is said" (1.7); "she reaches mightily from one end of the earth to the other, and she orders all things well" (8.1b); cf. Sir 43:26
Col 1:17a, 18d	On priority and superiority (7.29c)
Col 1:19	Wisdom dwelling; fullness, God's filling (1.4, 6-7)

With these connections in view, we can see that there are very close associations between Jesus in the Colossian hymn and the figure of Wisdom in early Judaism. Dunn explains,

> What pre-Christian Judaism said of Wisdom and Philo of the Logos, Paul and the others say of Jesus. The role that Proverbs, ben Sira, etc. ascribe to Wisdom, these earliest Christians ascribe to Jesus. That is to say, for those who were familiar with this obviously widespread cosmological speculation, the implication was presumably clear: *Jesus was being identified as Wisdom.*[65]

While a majority of scholars speak confidently of ways in which Jesus came to be understood as embodying the actions that had been attributed to

---

[63]Adapted from Witherington, *Letters to Philemon, the Colossians, and the Ephesians*, 130.

[64]Witherington, *Letters to Philemon, the Colossians, and the Ephesians*, 131. See also the parallels in Dunn, *Christology in the Making*, 165-66.

[65]Dunn, *Christology in the Making*, 167 (emphasis original).

personified Wisdom in the Old Testament and other early Jewish texts, this view is not without its critics. Gordon Fee, for example, dismisses what he calls "Wisdom Christology" as nothing more than a scholarly invention.[66] With regard to Colossians 1:15-20 in particular, Fee argues that the alleged linguistic parallels are either nonexistent or not true parallels, and the thematic and conceptual parallels are only "in the mind of the beholder" and not in Paul's own writing.[67] According to Fee, "There is a rather complete lack of linguistic and conceptual ties to this tradition."[68] A similar argument is made by Sean McDonough, who follows Fee in seeking to place some distance between Paul's claims and Wisdom.[69] Though arguing against what has now become a fairly well-accepted scholarly perspective (according to Fee this view has become "the unquestioned coin of the realm"), it is important to note that their argument is not simply a negative one.[70] Both Fee and McDonough seek to give a more prominent place to what they see as Paul's own claims about Jesus as seen throughout his writings. Thus Fee claims of the Colossian hymn that "the whole passage fits presuppositionally within Paul's standard Son of God christology."[71] McDonough points to echoes of Genesis 1 and an Adam Christology, in which Jesus is revealed as the true Lord over all creation.[72]

---

[66]See his extensive analysis in Fee, *Pauline Christology*, 595-629.

[67]Ibid., 325.

[68]Ibid., 320. In order to make this claims Fee reviews all of the key passages in the wisdom tradition that are regularly cited (609-18). He dismisses all of the texts from Wisdom of Solomon as irrelevant for Paul and claims that even if they were known by Paul they do not indicate that personified wisdom was understood as the agent of God in creation. Relevance for Paul can be addressed by noting that even if Paul was not familiar with Wisdom of Solomon, he was very familiar with the wisdom tradition (as Fee allows). I also disagree with Fee's assessment of what is said about Wisdom in these texts, especially Wis 7:22 (7:21 LXX); 8:4-6; 9:1-2, 9 (616-17). Though the vocabulary may not be the precise vocabulary of the Old Testament creation accounts or of Paul in the Colossian hymn, the notion of Wisdom's role as "an associate in his works" (Wis 8:4) who "works all things" (Wis 8:5) and who is the "fashioner of all things" (Wis 7:22) seems hard to ignore. The emphasis in these passages on "all things," which is an emphasis in the Colossian hymn, is clear as well and should not be dismissed (e.g., Wis 7:22; 8:5; 9:1). Even if Paul did not know Wisdom of Solomon, that text shows us how the thinking about Wisdom developed from the earlier biblical texts (e.g., Prov 8:22-31) to later Hellenistic Jewish ones. And even further along this trajectory we can also consider Philo, who made the connection between the Logos and the Wisdom of God.

[69]Sean M. McDonough, *Christ as Creator: Origins of a New Testament Doctrine* (Oxford: Oxford University Press, 2009), 175-79.

[70]Fee, *Pauline Christology*, 597.

[71]Ibid., 317.

[72]McDonough's connections with Gen 1 are intriguing and should be considered, particularly his claims about the connections between Col 1:6 and Gen 1:28 related to the "be fruitful and multiply" tradition, which may also have come to be associated with David's kingship. See McDonough, *Christ as Creator*, 180-82. However, the same criteria by which he dismisses the

My judgment is that the claims made about Jesus in Colossians 1, particularly those relating to his role as agent of God in creation, actually do resonate with features of the wisdom tradition. That is not to say that Jesus was simply slotted into a preexisting role as Wisdom of God or that a preexisting hymn to Wisdom was adapted to include Jesus. Rather, through his role as agent of God in redemption, it came to be understood that Jesus was also necessarily the agent of God in creation.[73] And it is hard to deny the significance of Paul's claims elsewhere that Christ embodies the Wisdom of God (1 Cor 1:24) such that Paul does indicate the importance of this tradition in his thinking. Engagement with this tradition is also evident in Hebrews 1 and John 1, suggesting it was a widespread view and not an isolated one. Fee and McDonough have overstated their case against the Wisdom connections, it seems to me, in the interest of pointing out other important streams of thought. However, this is not a case where one must choose one set of conceptual echoes or another. Instead, the allusive language of poetry allows for multiple strands of earlier tradition that Paul has reflected on and used in his portrayal of the exalted Jesus.

As we saw in the examination of the Philippian hymn, Thomas Tobin has put forward another intriguing possibility through his discussion of the heavenly man tradition and its engagement with the two creation accounts in Genesis 1 and Genesis 2.[74] In this view the three states of Jesus' existence (preexistence, earthly life, exaltation) represent a view shared in common among the authors of the Philippian hymn, the Colossian hymn, John 1, and Hebrews 1.[75] But as is evident, the explicit mention of the role of Christ as agent of creation occurs only in Colossians, John, and Hebrews. Tobin writes, "None of them can be explained simply on the basis of Jewish wisdom literature. All three texts move well beyond the Jewish wisdom tradition and are part of a broader tradition of Hellenistic Jewish speculation represented by a writer such as Philo of Alexandria."[76] Tobin points to a merging or assimilation of

---

Wisdom connections would also undermine his own position: precise verbal parallels cannot be produced, and the thematic connections between Jesus and Adam are very limited, particularly when it comes to Christ's having a role in the process of creation.

[73]In this respect, one can agree with McDonough (ibid., 89) about the development of this doctrine even if one cannot agree with him on the conceptual background for it.

[74]Thomas Tobin, "The World of Thought in the Philippians Hymn (Philippians 2:6-11)," in *The New Testament and Early Christian Literature in Greco-Roman Context: Studies in Honor of David E. Aune*, ed. John Fotopoulos (Leiden: Brill, 2006), 91-104.

[75]Ibid., 93.

[76]Ibid., 94.

the two distinct concepts of the Logos and the heavenly man that is evident in Philo. Tobin also explains that "the function given to the Logos in Stoicism is quite similar to that given to Wisdom in Jewish wisdom literature."[77] As Philo illustrates, then, "the Logos figure offered educated Jews a way of speaking of Wisdom that was comprehensible to educated members of the larger Greco-Roman world, Jews and non-Jews alike."[78] Tobin's proposed amalgamation of Logos/Wisdom and heavenly man traditions "would have offered an interpretive bridge by means of which the pre-existing reality of Christ found in Phil 2:6-11 could have taken on the much more cosmological role found in John 1:1-18; Col 1:15-20; and Heb 1:3-4."[79] This is an intriguing hypothesis that takes seriously both the likely biblical background as well as first-century developments in Hellenistic Jewish cosmological speculation. What is important to note here is the availability of a number of Jewish interpretive traditions related to the Genesis creation accounts as well as to the role of Wisdom in creation, but that also go beyond the wisdom tradition.

Further, it is clear that the Wisdom connections do not explain everything about the Colossian hymn. While the Wisdom material is important for the Colossian hymn, its value appears to be predominantly with regard to background for the first strophe. An additional set of connections to biblical literature and Second Temple writings may be seen in strophe two. The references to the resurrection, the dwelling of the fullness of God, as well as to reconciliation and making peace point to a different set of ideas, namely, the prophetic promises of the new age to be initiated by God in the eschaton. We saw allusions to the prophetic promises of renewal in the Philippian hymn with its echoes of Isaiah 42. In the Colossian hymn this complex of ideas drawn from the prophets can be seen in several ways.

First, in the notion that Jesus is hailed as firstborn from among the dead (Col 1:18b) we can note the prophetic expectation that the resurrection would be a part of the new age. Prophetic passages like Isaiah 26:19 and Ezekiel 37:1-14 make this clear, although without the notion that only one person might rise first.[80] N. T. Wright explains that, for Paul, "*that which Jewish eschatology looked for in the future*, the overthrow of the enslaving evil powers and the

---

[77]Ibid., 95.
[78]Ibid., 95-96.
[79]Ibid., 104.
[80]See N. T. Wright, *The Resurrection of the Son of God* (Minneapolis: Fortress, 2003), chaps. 3–4.

establishment of YHWH's reign instead, *had truly been inaugurated in and through the messianic events of Jesus' death and resurrection.*[81] Though the nature of Jewish expectations of resurrection in the first century CE remain debated, it is at least clear that the Colossian hymn has this tradition in view.

A second connection between the Colossian hymn and the prophetic promises of renewal can be seen in the notion of "all the fullness" dwelling in him (Col 1:19). Though we may note that the concept of *plērōma* (fullness) is also used of God's wisdom in Hellenistic Judaism, the notion in Colossians 1:19 that all of the fullness of God was pleased to dwell in Christ seems to draw more directly on the biblical idea of the dwelling of God within the temple.[82] This is seen most explicitly in Psalm 68:16 (67:17 LXX), a psalm that celebrates God's victory for his people, including mention of the idea that God was pleased to dwell on his holy mount until the end of time.[83] The broader perspective of Psalm 68 is quite significant. Not only does this psalm celebrate God's victory (Ps 68:17-20) but it also celebrates the destruction of God's enemies (Ps 68:21-23) and the return of God's people from exile (Ps 68:18). Praise of God is a prominent theme of this psalm as well (Ps 68:24-27, 32-35). The idea that the dwelling of God on God's mountain is now understood as the dwelling of the fullness of God in Jesus thus carries with it some important implications both in terms of God's restoration of all things and in terms of the location of true worship.[84]

The return of the glory of God to God's temple was not just a theme of the Psalms; it was also a major theme of the prophetic promises of renewal.[85]

---

[81]N. T. Wright, *Paul and the Faithfulness of God* (Minneapolis: Fortress, 2013), 1068 (emphasis original).

[82]For connections with Wisdom and Hellenistic Judaism see Dunn, *Epistles to the Colossians and to Philemon*, 99-100.

[83]O'Brien adds the following references to round out the picture: LXX Ps 131:13; Is 8:18; 49:20. He also points to the importance in Deuteronomic theology of God's choosing a place for his name to dwell (see Deut 12:5, 11; 14:23; 16:2, 6, 11; 26:2). O'Brien, *Colossians, Philemon*, 52-53.

[84]Sumney finds in this deployment of the temple theme from Ps 68 evidence that it was the early community's experience of worship that shaped its understanding of the Jewish Scriptures. He explains, "The liturgy in Colossians transfers the psalm's declaration about a place to a person. Beyond this psalm, there are a number of passages that speak of God dwelling in Jerusalem or the temple, enough that we may see it as a recognizable theme. The combination of the presence of εὐδοκέω with κατοικέω makes Ps 68 the more likely immediate source of the theme." Sumney adds, "The liturgy adds 'all the fullness' to the psalm's declaration about Jerusalem as it shifts its reference to Christ. This is the earliest extant instance of the church using this language to claim that all of God's fullness was present in Christ." Sumney, "Writing 'In the Image' of Scripture," 200.

[85]Wright, *Paul and the Faithfulness of God*, 1051-53. Wright cites Ezek 40–48 and in particular Ezek 43:1-9; 48:35. See also N. T. Wright, *Jesus and the Victory of God* (Minneapolis: Fortress, 1996), 615-24.

Through its engagement with this theme of the dwelling place of God, now centered on Christ, the Colossian hymn points to the idea that the return of YHWH has now been accomplished. This has been done through Christ in a surprising twist unforeseen by the prophets. Along these lines, Wright explains,

> The long awaited return of YHWH to Zion is, I suggest, the hidden clue to the origin of Christology. . . . The most important thing was that in his life, death and resurrection Jesus had accomplished the new Exodus, had done in person what Israel's God had said he would do in person. He had inaugurated God's kingdom on earth as in heaven.[86]

We will see that another similar deployment of this theme develops in the Johannine prologue. For now, it is important to note the diversity of Old Testament biblical motifs that are brought together around the person of Jesus in elaborating the significance of his life, death, resurrection, and redemptive work for humanity.

Of course, these concepts are now irreversibly modified by the necessity of understanding them in light of Jesus. As Wilson explains, "In any case, if our author has adopted any concepts, from whatever source, he has also adapted them to give expression to his faith in the supremacy and sufficiency of Christ."[87] Further, while these biblical motifs and ideas reflected in Second Temple Jewish writings are clearly of importance for the author of this hymn, they are not the only cultural context that needs to be considered. The Roman context of Colossae and the Roman context of Paul potentially writing from prison in Rome call for consideration of the extent to which the Colossian hymn engages themes that derive from the situation of Roman imperial occupation.

ROMAN IMPERIAL THEMES IN THE COLOSSIAN HYMN

In the first part of this chapter we noted that engagement of themes related to the pervasive Roman imperial ideology is a feature of Colossians as a whole. With close attention to the realities of life in first-century Colossae, Maier summarizes this feature well when he writes, "Colossians has achieved a social construction of Paul's Gospel by drawing from elements of imperial ideology in a way that must have found particular resonance amongst the inhabitants of an Asia Minor city in

---

[86]Wright, *Paul and the Faithfulness of God*, 654-55. See the development of this argument on 649-56.

[87]Wilson, *Colossians and Philemon*, 144.

the heartland of an enthusiastic cult of the emperor."[88] When we examine the hymn in light of this overall understanding we can see that it also employs concepts that were important within the Roman imperial construction of reality.[89]

In particular, titles and claims of supremacy such as those used of Christ in Colossians 1:15-20 were a feature of ancient Greco-Roman discourse about rulers. More importantly, the Roman provinces were not shy about ascribing divine greatness to the emperor in their inscriptions, public decrees, and other works. The imperial cult institutionalized the honoring of the emperor in these ways. This institution also helped popularize the idea that the emperor was closely associated with the gods, if not divine himself. As we saw in chapter two, the provinces had their hymn-singers, hymn-instructors, and professional choirs whose task it was to compose and sing hymns in honor of Augustus.[90] The promotion of such a close association with the divine is also a feature of the Colossian hymn as Jesus is presented as the visible manifestation—*eikōn*— of God. Further, the Roman emperors, and particularly Caesar Augustus in his *Res Gestae*, made high claims about their benefactions to humanity including the bringing about of peace and the reconciliation of warring tribes.[91] Such claims are echoed in the praise poetry of Roman poets like Horace who likened the emperor's benefactions to the gifts of a god.[92]

The following chart shows where claims about Christ in Colossians 1:15-20 have a similarity with claims made for the emperor or other rulers in antiquity. As table 4.2 makes clear,[93] many of the claims about Christ are represented in the wider Roman culture. If not word-for-word parallels, the concepts resonate with one another as they paint a portrait of reality in which a particular human being manifests the will and benefactions of the gods to humanity in tangible ways.

---

[88]Maier, "Reading Colossians in the Ruins," 213. See also S. R. F. Price, *Rituals and Power: The Roman Imperial Cult in Asia Minor* (Cambridge: Cambridge University Press, 1986).

[89]Cognizant of the critique of imperial readings offered by Bevere (noted above), I am not reading Colossians as an "anti-imperial tract" but rather paying attention to concepts in the hymn which seem to be at home in the Roman imperial context.

[90]See above, chap. 2. Cf. Philip A. Harland, *Greco-Roman Associations: Texts, Translations, and Commentary*, vol. 2, *North Coast of the Black Sea, Asia Minor*, BZNW 204 (Berlin: de Gruyter, 2011), 128-40.

[91]See esp. Caesar Augustus, *Res Gestae* 1.34, 2.42-43, 5.9-13. Cited in Frederick W. Danker, *Benefactor: Epigraphic Study of a Graeco-Roman and New Testament Semantic Field* (St. Louis: Clayton, 1982), 259-70.

[92]For example, Horace, *Odes* 4.5 and 4.15.

[93]Matthew E. Gordley, *Teaching Through Song in Antiquity: Didactic Hymnody Among Greeks, Romans, Jews and Christians*, WUNT 2/331 (Tübingen: Mohr Siebeck, 2011), 298.

Table 4.2. The Colossian hymn and select ancient witnesses to Roman imperial ideology

He is the image of the invisible God,	Plutarch, *Themistocles* 27.4.4-5; Ecphantes, *On Kingship* 80.3-7; 81.9-13; various inscriptions
the firstborn over all creation.	Letter of the Proconsul of Asia in Praise of Caesar 1-12 (*OGIS* 2:458)
For by him all things were created: things in heaven and on earth, visible and invisible, whether thrones or powers or rulers or authorities; all things were created by him and for him. He is before all things,	
and in him all things hold together.	Aristides, *Or.* 23.76–78; Seneca, *Clem.* 1.1.2; 1.3.4
And he is the head of the body, the church.	Lucian, *Apology* 13; Seneca, *Clem.* 1.3.4; 1.5.1; 1.13.4; 2.2.1-2
He is the beginning	Letter of the Proconsul of Asia 1-12 (*OGIS* 2:458)
and the firstborn from among the dead,	
so that in all things he might have the supremacy.	Lucian, *Apology* 13
For God was pleased to have all his fullness dwell in him, and through him to reconcile all things to himself making peace	Ecphantes, *On Kingship* 80.3-7; 81.9-13; Calpurnius Siculus, *Ecl.* 4.142-46 Pliny, *Panegyricus*, 80.1-2 *Res Gestae* 13.42-43; 26.11-12; Cassius Dio 44.49.2
through the blood of his cross—	
through him, whether things on earth or things in heaven.	Plutarch, *Fort. Rom.* 2.316e–317c; *Princ. iner.* 5.781f-82a; Suetonius, *Augustus* 98.2-3

From this brief comparison we may draw out several important points. First, the claims about Christ in the Colossian hymn were not merely religious ideas but would have resonated with wider claims about the emperor in first-century culture. These claims thus had a political aspect to them. Second, the widespread availability of such claims in the broader culture would mean that the author's use of these concepts in the Colossian hymn would not have been missed by Colossian readers. Along these lines, Maier explains,

> The Colossian representation in 1:15-20 of a Jesus above all rule and authority, through whom and for whom all things exist, who brings all into reconciliation is at home in the contact zone of imperial ideology, and one can understand how persuasive and recognizeable such ideas would have been once related to

the repertoire of Roman imperial imagery carefully and self-consciously deployed everywhere in the Roman Empire.[94]

If such ideas were as recognizable as Maier claims, then their inclusion in the Colossian hymn and their application to Jesus would have been striking.

But in spite of recognizable similarities we can also note some very sharp differences between the Colossian hymn and what is claimed about the emperors. As table 4.2 makes clear through blank spaces in the right column, there are several unparalleled aspects of the Colossian hymn. These unparalleled areas include the claims about the role of Christ in the creation of all things, reference to his crucifixion, and allusion to his resurrection. Apart from these vital claims, other aspects of the hymn have some kind of parallel in the discourse about rulers in antiquity. These unique claims about Jesus suggest that something unprecedented is going on in this hymn. It is not simply an echoing of imperial themes, but rather a matter of supplementing those themes with new and other guiding ideas. Walsh and Keesmaat suggest that the claims of Rome are undermined and destabilized in the hymn:

> In the space of a short, well-crafted, three-stanza poem, Paul subverts every major claim of the empire, turning them on their heads, and proclaims Christ to be the Creator, Redeemer and Lord of all creation, including the empire.[95]

These claims about the passage's use and reworking of Roman imperial themes provide the starting point for a consideration of the extent to which the hymn may be seen to be participating in the wider Jewish practices of resistance literature that we have already seen elsewhere.

READING THE COLOSSIAN HYMN AS RESISTANCE POETRY

While scholars like Maier, Walsh, and Keesmaat are now reading the hymn as countering the claims of Roman imperial ideology, the extent to which Colossians 1:15-20 may be viewed as participating in the wider Jewish practices of resistance literature has not yet been fully explored. By resistance literature I refer to scribal literary practices that articulated opposition to the narratives of empire emanating from the ruling authorities of the places in which the Jews

---

[94]Maier, "Reading Colossians in the Ruins," 215.
[95]Walsh and Keesmaat, *Colossians Remixed*, 84.

found themselves.[96] While apocalypses and narratives of the Second Temple period are the most obvious vehicles of this tradition of scribal resistance, as we have seen psalms can also be read for the ways in which they resist ideologies of empire and promote Jewish ways of thinking, being, and responding to crisis.[97] In addition to the examples we reviewed in chapter two, we have likewise now seen that the Philippian hymn shares features with this material.

While recognizing the differences between a New Testament hymnic passage like Colossians 1:15-20 and any other examples of resistance poetry, it is still possible to consider the ways in which the Colossians passage does indeed reflect the features of Jewish resistance poetry. Recall that the resistance poetry of early Judaism has several features. First, it often recounts horrors of the past as it facilitates remembering for the sake of the oppressed. Second, through its imagery, language, descriptions, and metaphors resistance poetry articulates and provides resources for shaping the identity of the community in contrast to the identity of the oppressors. Third, poetry of resistance promotes hope through the articulation of a desirable future that serves to motivate the kind of resistance the poem advocates.[98] Bringing the Colossian hymn into conversation with this larger feature of early Judaism provides helpful context and added nuance for appreciating other features of the Colossian hymn that have long been recognized and puzzled over. Features such as its resonance with scriptural motifs, its use of quasi-philosophical ideas, its engagement with themes of Roman imperial ideology, and its apparently disruptive mention of "the blood of the cross" and "the church" can be understood more adequately when viewed in light of traditions of Jewish resistance poetry.[99]

---

[96]See the discussion in chap. 2. See also the discussion of these ideas in Richard A. Horsley, *Revolt of the Scribes: Resistance and Apocalyptic Origins* (Minneapolis: Fortress, 2010); Anathea Portier-Young, "Jewish Apocalyptic Literature as Resistance Literature," in *The Oxford Handbook of Apocalyptic Literature*, ed. John Joseph Collins (Oxford: Oxford University Press, 2014), 135-62.

[97]For particular attention to Old Testament psalms and poems as resistance, see Hugh R. Page Jr., *Israel's Poetry of Resistance: Africana Perspectives on Early Hebrew Verse* (Minneapolis: Fortress, 2013).

[98]See my forthcoming article, Matthew E. Gordley, "Psalms of Solomon as Resistance Poetry," *JAJ* (forthcoming 2018).

[99]Bevere's critique of finding an anti-imperial message in Colossians is that the Jewish background is thereby minimized; Bevere, "Colossians and the Rhetoric of Empire," 192-93. He claims that in identifying the Colossian heresy as closely related to Judaism (which we must note is a contested claim in itself) he thereby gives proper recognition of the importance of the Jewish traditions that Paul draws on and adapts. The anti-imperial reading of Walsh and Keesmaat, he claims, cannot account for the prominent role of Jewish traditions. While their analysis may not, my analysis suggests that the Jewish tradition provided the materials necessary to construct a view of Jesus in which he is supreme over all other powers.

Remembering history and past traumas. An important characteristic of resistance poetry is that it provides a kind of communal memory of history both in terms of what is remembered and the way in which it is remembered. While it is evident that Jesus is remembered in the Colossian hymn, it is significant to note what is remembered about Jesus as well as the significance given to those past events. Rather than a narrative such as is found in the Philippian hymn, in which the "death of the cross" is the central turning point of the hymn, Colossians makes more direct claims about its subject through its repeated use of the verb *eimi* ("he is," four times). Nevertheless, in Colossians these direct claims are then supported by additional descriptors, which have the effect of articulating some of the actions of the redeemer. Taken together, the direct statements and the additional descriptors, though not creating an overarching narrative to the hymn, do provide ways of remembering Jesus, both who he is and what he has accomplished.

With regard to the memory of traumatic events, Jesus is remembered for his death on the cross. It is noteworthy here, as in Philippians, that the cross (here, "the blood of his cross," Col 1:20) brings with it a whole narrative in and of itself, as it remembers in a central way the gruesome death of Jesus at the hands of the Romans. Being directly mentioned at the climactic point of the second strophe, the trauma of the crucifixion is not downplayed but rather celebrated in the hymn. In this way, the hymn functions as a "countermemory."[100] It does not deny that the crucifixion occurred, but reinvests it with new meaning.

Further, Jesus is remembered as having risen from the dead. He is celebrated as the "firstborn from among the dead so that in all things he might have the supremacy" (Col 1:18). Just as the mention of the cross brings to mind the historical reality of the crucifixion, so the accolade "firstborn from among the dead" brings into focus the historical claims for the resurrection of Jesus. With the resurrection in view, crucifixion is no longer a symbol of Rome's defeat of Jesus but rather the means by which Jesus attains a new level of supremacy as he rises from the dead. As we have seen, the notion of the resurrection also has implications for the future as it taps into a Jewish narrative about the coming eschatological renewal of all things.

---

[100]The term *countermemory* is used in reference to John's Gospel by Tom Thatcher, *Greater Than Caesar: Christology and Empire in the Fourth Gospel* (Minneapolis: Fortress, 2009), 16. On Jn 1:1-18 as countermemory, see below, chap. 5.

Jesus is also remembered in other ways that go far beyond the trauma of the cross. He is remembered as the image of God and thus a revelation of the divine in visible form—in contrast to Roman claims that the emperor was in some way the visible manifestation of the divine. Jesus is remembered as God's agent in the creation of all things, a claim that calls to mind the Jewish creation narratives and poems. He is remembered as the one in whom the fullness of God was pleased to dwell, calling into focus the national history of the Jewish people and the dwelling of God in the temple. Such a memory sharply contrasts with Jewish claims about the temple as well as claims of other temples and those who were memorialized within them. Jesus is also remembered as God's agent in the redemption of all things, drawing on Jewish prophetic promises associated with God's renewal of all things. Such a claim would stand in contrast to the claim that the Roman emperor had himself brought about the reconciliation and renewal of all things. As Maier explains,

> That it is from Jesus' crucifixion and resurrection that a universal peace and renewal comes presumes that the old Augustan order is no real peace (its *pax deum* is an illusion), and that the violence on which it rests offers no genuine reconciliation.[101]

The claims about Jesus noted above thus call on a variety of rich narrative traditions that call into question prevailing Roman claims about the nature of reality within the Roman Empire.

In addition, Jesus is remembered in light of a very specific relationship of authority to the church: "He is the head of the body, the church" (Col 1:18a). These aspects of the memory of Jesus connect deeply with wisdom traditions of the Old Testament and Hebrew Bible, even as they, through their praise of Jesus, break new ground in their claims about Christ. For example, while preexistence may plausibly be inferred from the Philippian hymn, here the role of agent of God in the creation of all things makes such a belief explicit. Taken together, these hymnic acclamations of Christ craft a memory of Jesus, his divine nature, and his accomplishments that facilitates a particular kind of response for the community to its present circumstances. As with resistance poetry, which facilitates a community's memory of the past in a certain way, the Colossian hymn remembers Jesus using some very specific and loaded imagery.[102]

---

[101]Maier, "Colossians and Empire," 348.

[102]Maier explains, "If it echoes imperial-sounding ideals, it does not replicate them. Colossians twists Empire and makes it slip. This hybrid vision from the cross disavows Empire even at it mimics it." Ibid., 349.

Identity of the community and its oppressors. As we have seen, in resistance poetry, concerns of identity are paramount. The identity of the oppressors is part of the mental picture that is created and reinforced through the composition. Likewise, the identity of the community is often a prominent theme. We have just seen that the identity of Jesus is a major focus of the Colossian hymn through its memory of him in terms of his identity, his accomplishments, and his death on the cross. Does the Colossian hymn also address the identity of the community or the identity of the oppressors?

The identity of the community is seen in the first strophe. The first strophe suggests that the community consists of those who are part of "the church" and, as such, are under the headship of Christ, in contrast to those who fall under the headship of Caesar. The second strophe suggests that the community consists of those who are already reconciled to Christ, and who experience the peace that came about through the cross. Taken as a whole the hymn implies that the community members are those who recognize and acknowledge the supremacy of Christ in all things. They already embrace the vision of Christ that the hymn promotes.[103]

Regarding the identity of the oppressors to whom the Colossians are subject, we receive a mixed message. On the one hand, Christ is the one through whom all things were created (Col 1:16) and in whom all things hold together (Col 1:17). The exact nature of "all things" is clarified in Colossians 1:16 to include "things in heaven and on earth, visible and invisible, whether thrones or powers or rulers or authorities." The fact that Christ is the agent of creation of these entities and is "before all things" (Col 1:17) suggests his supremacy over all of these entities and that they would be subject to him.

On the other hand, the second strophe of the hymn presents a more complex picture. In the second strophe we learn that all things were in need of reconciliation, and that, while Christ makes peace, there was apparently a very real lack of peace prior to his making peace.[104] This warring has led, in fact, to death (Col 1:18) and to the cross (Col 1:20). While Christ is hymned as the "firstborn from among the dead" as an honorific title, this is surely also because he was subjected to death at the hands of the Romans. How the

---

[103]If the hymn implies these ways of thinking about the identity of the Colossian believers, the surrounding verses that introduce and explain the hymn tell us more directly about this community. The community consists of those who were "rescued," were formerly part of the kingdom of darkness, and are now part of the kingdom of the beloved son (Col 1:12-14).

[104]Wilson, *Colossians and Philemon*, 155-56.

forces that were created by him have run amok to the point that they are no longer at peace and need to be reconciled is not addressed, but rather assumed. In this way it is similar to Cleanthes's *Hymn to Zeus*, in which Zeus (the universal reason) directs all things. And yet, even in the imaginal world in which Zeus controls all, there are those who defy reason and go against Zeus. The reason for this is their own folly. It is in the list in Colossians 1:16 that we may gain a glimpse of the kinds of oppressors that the Colossian hymn has in mind.

According to Colossians 1:16 the oppressors are those forces that currently are not pacified but are at war with the Creator and his agent. The description of such forces is noteworthy, but the identity of these thrones, powers, rulers, and authorities is debated.[105] These may be cosmic forces; they may also be local ruling authorities. Ulrich Huttner explains how these terms might have been heard by those living in the Lycus valley: "If the addressees of Colossians associated the 'powers' listed by the sender with their own high-ranking local official and municipal functionaries, they could not have avoided the idea of a political and perhaps also religious revolution."[106] It may be that the lines are blurred between the cosmic kinds of powers that are certainly included here and the human institutions that are under the direct influence or perhaps are even the manifestation of those powers. In this way the hymn can be read as an "attack on 'legitimation of imperial power.'"[107]

In the context of this imagery, the hymn puts forward a picture of Jesus as the agent of God in both creation and redemption of all things. The opponents, those who are being actively resisted, are those who are yet neither pacified nor reconciled. Yet the promise of reconciliation and pacification is held out in our hymn, providing a vision of the future that is different from the past or present.

Promoting a hopeful vision of the future. In spite of the realities of the Roman cross and the opposing powers, the Colossian hymn offers its readers an optimistic portrait of a world in which Christ is supreme as God's agent and in which there is peace since all things are reconciled through Christ. Such a portrait draws on a wealth of ideas current in both Jewish and Greco-Roman thought. The language of universal peace and reconciliation takes up a major theme of the imperial ideology that pervaded the Roman Empire in

---

[105]Dunn, *Epistles to the Colossians and to Philemon*, 92-93.
[106]Huttner, *Early Christianity in the Lycus Valley*, 121.
[107]Ibid.

this era.[108] By utilizing these concepts the Colossian hymn also engages with deeply rooted Jewish motifs.[109] As we saw above, several indicators in the hymn suggest that the author understood that the long-awaited prophecies of renewal and restoration have come to pass in Jesus. First, the resurrection was a signal that the new age had begun. Second, all the fullness dwelling "in him" may point to the return of the glory of God to his temple, another major theme of the prophetic promises of renewal.[110] Third, that God was pleased to reconcile all things to himself taps into this narrative as well, suggesting that even those nations hostile to God would turn to him and be reconciled.[111] And fourth, that it was done through the blood of the cross, while not anticipated by the prophetic texts, is key. The point of the Colossian hymn is that through the blood of Jesus this long-awaited new era has now begun. The comprehensive picture of Christ through the hymn is thus eschatological in the sense that what God does in and through Christ is a revelation to the world of the renewing actions of God.[112]

In the context of Roman claims to have initiated a new era of peace and prosperity—what Maier has called a kind of "realized eschatology"—the Colossian hymn paints a vivid portrait of reality in which the new age has arrived through Christ. The new age has been inaugurated through the most unlikely of means: the cross. The Roman tool of fear and control has become the means of the triumph of Christ (cf. Col 2:15).

The hymn's eschatological focus on the revelation of God through Jesus aligns to a large extent with the eschatological stance of the letter as a whole. Sumney explains, "In a way found in no earlier letter, Colossians focuses steadfastly on believers' present possession of eschatological blessings."[113] But Sumney also points out that Colossians has a view of a future act of God that has direct importance for the Colossians as well (see Col 1:22; 3:4, 25). What the hymn claims about the present and implies about the future is thus clarified through the remainder of the letter as the Colossians are urged to live their lives in the present in light of the reality of the resurrection (Col 3:1-11).

[108]Maier, "Reading Colossians in the Ruins."
[109]On this see Wright, *Paul and the Faithfulness of God*, 1067-68.
[110]Ibid., 1051-53. As pointed out above, Wright cites Ezek 40–48 and in particular Ezek 43:1-9; 48:35. See also, Wright, *Jesus and the Victory of God*, 615-24.
[111]On the theme of the pilgrimage of the nations to Zion as part of the age of renewal, see Wright, *Paul and the Faithfulness of God*, 1056-58.
[112]Lohmeyer, *Die Briefe*, 47.
[113]Sumney, *Colossians*, 5.

CONCLUSIONS

We have now seen that Colossians 1:15-20 has many features that associate it with the hymnody of the ancient world. Specifically, it has as its subject a divine being, his deeds in history, and his benefits to humanity. Further, there is much in Colossians 1:15-20 that draws on Jewish trajectories of Wisdom hymns and poetry that resist human empire by co-opting its language and themes for a different vision of reality. In addition, it contains some language and concepts that are broadly philosophical in nature. It is also found in a letter that can be considered a kind of philosophical paraenesis. This combination of features justifies our considering this passage hymnic in a broad sense and, more specifically, a prose hymn with philosophical and anti-imperial content.

We are unable to draw a firm conclusion as to whether this was a hymn that Paul was quoting, or if it was a composition of his own. If the passage is a hymn he was quoting, then it can be considered likely that he was quoting traditional material that allowed him to make his points throughout the epistle and connect with his audience over shared tradition.[114] If not a pre-existing hymn but a composition of Paul's own creation, the passage still shows many markers of hymnic style, content, form, and function. Though the passage itself would not then be a piece of shared tradition, its hymnic content and claims about Jesus were apparently part of the tradition since Paul did not need to argue for their validity.[115] Further, its hymnic style would likely be reflective of early Christian practice, enabling us to derive from the passage some further conclusions about early Christian worship.

First, as early Christian worship developed it continued to associate Jesus more closely with the divine. The associations with the divine in Philippians 2:5-11 are supplemented by the claims made in the Colossian hymn. Second, while associating Jesus more closely with the divine, early Christian worship maintained a distinction between God and Jesus. It is clear in the Colossian hymn that Jesus was the agent of God in creation and redemption, and also distinct from God. Third, at the same time, early Christian worship declared that what had come about in Jesus was the work and actions of God. Fourth, current traditions of Jewish thought provided rich material for understanding

---

[114]This is the view of Wilson, *Colossians and Philemon*, 127. Cf. Sumney, *Colossians*, 61.

[115]Wilson takes this seriously, noting that though it is perhaps a hymn, "It is also possible that our author was himself responsible for the composition, drawing together elements from earlier tradition into an almost creedal statement of the status and supremacy of Christ." Wilson, *Colossians and Philemon*, 156.

Christ. The Colossian hymn adds to the Jewish traditions that were part of the Philippian hymn, especially drawing more explicitly on Wisdom and creation themes. Finally, language of imperial praise and concepts of imperial ideology also provided an important backdrop for the language used in praise of Jesus. It is in its echoing, mimicking, and refuting of contemporary praise of the Roman emperor that the early Christian praise of Jesus can be seen as a practice of resistance. Seen as resistance poetry, this poem does not advocate any kind of physical uprising against the Roman Empire. Instead the hymn promotes a spirituality of resistance through its portrait of reality that is centered on the cross. Further, by infusing deep revelatory and theological meaning to the cross—Rome's tool of domination—early Christian praise of Jesus embodies the idea of countermemory. The fact of the crucifixion is remembered, but its significance is altered dramatically as the crucified one is also praised as the firstborn from among the dead and as the one who brought about peace through the blood of his cross.

In contrast to those who live their lives under the control of rulers and authorities and with a sense of being enslaved in the kingdom of darkness, early Christians who worship the Christ of the Colossian hymn could embrace a new way of living "through him":

> Let the peace of Christ rule in your hearts, since as members of one body you were called to peace. And be thankful. Let the message of Christ dwell among you richly as you teach and admonish one another with all wisdom through psalms, hymns, and songs from the Spirit, singing to God with gratitude in your hearts. And whatever you do, whether in word or deed, do it all in the name of the Lord Jesus, giving thanks to God the Father through him. (Col 3:15-17 NIV)

Rather than deliberative discourse about Jesus or rational argument, these claims about Christ are presented in the allusive and effusive language of praise poetry. The surplus of meaning contained in this praise language would make the Colossian hymn a rich text for the early church fathers as they sought to clarify the divine nature of Jesus.[116] It likewise provides a rich resource for contemporary reflection about the significance of Jesus, a topic I will examine in my concluding chapter.

---

[116]For its extensive use in the early Church see Edsall and Strawbridge, "Songs We Used to Sing," 301-3.

Five

THE PROLOGUE OF
THE GOSPEL OF JOHN

The mysteries of the Johannine prologue are many. As one recent volume devoted to the prologue puts it: "The prologue is an inexhaustible, literally unfathomable, text."[1] Without much exaggeration the same claim could be made about scholarship on the prologue.[2] In light of how much has been written about the prologue, Martinus de Boer recently noted, "It is most unlikely that anyone can in fact say anything really new about it."[3] But as we will see, there are new things that can be said about the prologue. On the one hand, new tools and interpretive approaches continue to emerge, and these allow contemporary readers to discern shades of meaning that may previously have been undetected. On the other hand, each new generation of readers brings its own questions and perspectives that benefit from an integration of the findings of the past even as they add to them.

Among scholars who have attempted to probe the depths of the prologue, there is, not surprisingly, a general consensus on some issues but still wide

---

[1]Jan G. Van der Watt, Richard Alan Culpepper, and Udo Schnelle, eds., *The Prologue of the Gospel of John: Its Literary, Theological, and Philosophical Contexts: Papers Read at the Colloquium Ioanneum 2013*, WUNT 359 (Tübingen: Mohr Siebeck, 2016), xviii.

[2]Over fifty years ago Robinson already expressed a similar sentiment: "The effect of reading too much on the Fourth Gospel is to make one feel either that everything has been said about it that conceivably could be said or that it really does not matter what one says, for one is just as likely to be right as anyone else." J. A. T. Robinson, "The Relation of the Prologue to the Gospel of St. John," *NTS* 9 (1962): 120-29.

[3]Martinus C. de Boer, "The Original Prologue to the Gospel of John," *NTS* 61 (2015): 448-67.

disagreement on others. To judge from the commentaries themselves, one area of widespread agreement is on how to approach an analysis of the prologue. In general, scholars approach the prologue by addressing a constellation of related issues in which answers to one issue lead to answers on other issues. In the end, each interpreter ends up with a perspective on the prologue that can be located somewhere on the map with all the others.

Readers of the prologue owe a great debt to several commentators within the last decade who have done a fine job of both introducing and summarizing the issues and the main lines of debate.[4] With gratitude for their work, my aim is neither to point out all the disputed topics nor to review all the previous proposals. Rather, given the approach of this volume as a whole—considering early Christian hymns in their broadest cultural context—I take the opportunity to expand on and make connections between several aspects of earlier research on the prologue. The result will be, if not a new perspective on the prologue, at least a more fully informed one.

Of the many thorny issues in the prologue, discerning the poetic structure of the passage remains a particularly difficult challenge. J. A. T. Robinson captures the difficulty well: "The very variety of the solutions suggests that this may be a hopeless task."[5] And as we have seen, this is one argument that opponents of "hymn-hunting" in the New Testament have continued to make. However, Robinson goes on: "That there is something in it is however confirmed by the persistence of the attempts."[6] John McHugh makes a similar remark when he suggests that varying interpretations are not a symptom of scholarly hubris or bad interpretive instinct but rather a result of the genius of the work: "The fact that the plans differ from one another is not significant. It is always so with great literature, and the variety of interpretation which is legitimately possible with Virgil, Dante or Shakespeare only bears witness to the richness of the thought."[7] These lines of thought offer encouragement to

---

[4]Among the most thorough treatments of the prologue in recent years, see John F. McHugh, *A Critical and Exegetical Commentary on John 1–4*, ed. Graham Stanton, ICC (London: T&T Clark, 2009); Craig S. Keener, *The Gospel of John: A Commentary* (Peabody, MA: Hendrickson, 2003), vol. 1; J. Ramsey Michaels, *The Gospel of John*, NICNT (Grand Rapids: Eerdmans, 2010). An extensive review and summary of earlier scholarship on the prologue from the nineteenth and twentieth centuries can be found in Michael Theobald, *Die Fleischwerdung des Logos: Studien zum Verhältnis des Johannesprologs zum Corpus des Evangeliums und zu 1 Joh*, NTAbh 20 (Münster: Aschendorff, 1988).

[5]Robinson, "Relation of the Prologue," 126.

[6]Ibid.

[7]McHugh, *John 1–4*, 90.

us to continue probing the riches of the prologue and to seek new vantage points from which the treasures of the prologue can be perceived. In order to discover these vantage points, we begin in this chapter by tackling the issue of the structure of the prologue. As a foundation for all that follows, I will outline an arrangement of the prologue that accounts for what many scholars believe to be its organizing principle: the historical development of the role of the Logos in history from creation to the present day of the community. With such an arrangement in place, we can then move to examine the prologue in several ways that relate to the larger focus of this volume.

First, cognizance of the features of Jewish hymnody from the Second Temple period can aid in identification of important features of the prologue that connect with Jewish traditions in ways that have not always been fully articulated. Certainly the value of wisdom traditions for the prologue have been thoroughly explored. However, we will see that there is more that can be said as a result of a comparison with early Jewish didactic hymns, Wisdom hymns, and hymns that review history.

Second, in a similar vein we will examine the extent to which the prologue can be said to be engaging with the realities of the Roman Empire. While most commentators have not imagined the Fourth Gospel as engaging directly with issues relating to Roman imperial ideology, our awareness of hymnic praise of gods and men can help us to read the prologue in its widest first-century context.

Third, our understanding of the ways in which hymns at times functioned as part of a strategy of resistance for Jewish and Greco-Roman communities during this era allows us to consider how a hymn with this kind of language might have functioned similarly for the Johannine community. We will see that, like other kinds of resistance literature, the prologue exhibits a concern for remembering key events of the past in a way that challenges the prevailing narrative of the dominant group. It also promotes a very clear sense of identity both for the community itself and for its opponents. While not seemingly as future-oriented in its provision of hope for the community as other resistance poems, the realized eschatology of the prologue can also be understood as an important aspect of the prologue's strategy of resistance.

Finally, with the larger goal of gaining an understanding of early Christian worship, we will consider the importance of worship for the Fourth Gospel as a whole, and then note how the prologue contributes to and supports this leitmotif. Based on the understanding that the prologue does not predate the Fourth Gospel but is the fruit of reflection on its contents,[8] we will ask the question, where does the Gospel's concern for worship find a place in the prologue? With regard to worship, this passage can be understood to represent the kind of worshipful response to the news about Jesus that the Fourth Gospel as a whole advocates. The prologue is the community's declaration about Jesus and confession of praise to Jesus that mirrors the worship and confession of those in the Fourth Gospel who come to recognize and acknowledge the glory of God in the person of Jesus.

In short, I will put forward the claim that the prologue is a Christian hymnic composition that was written in light of deep reflection on an earlier edition of the Gospel of John, in light of Jewish traditions (i.e., Wisdom, historical psalms, Moses, Sinai, memra), edited by a final redactor who may have been the author himself, and added to the beginning of the Gospel. The hymn presents Jesus as the revelation of God and the culmination of God's work in history; Jewish history is to be understood, and valued, within the framework of Jesus as the Word made flesh. Further, all of history, including Roman history, is to be understood within this larger framework. In addition, the prologue points to the reality that true worship centers on Jesus as the locus of divine revelation. Such a portrayal of Jesus provides a worldview framework that can allow believers to navigate the challenges of life under Rome as they recognize that forces of darkness in the world are unable to overcome the revelation of light and life through the Logos.

THE STRUCTURE OF THE PROLOGUE

In order to advance these points of discussion it is important to sketch briefly my understanding of the nature, form, and function of the prologue. I begin by laying out an arrangement of the prologue that helps to bring out the ways in which the passage resonates with hymnic reviews of history in the tradition of Jewish didactic hymns. Where possible the rationale for each decision will be spelled out with reference to some of the history of scholarship on this rich passage.[9]

---

[8]Robinson, "Relation of the Prologue," 128.

[9]For the case for this arrangement see Matthew E. Gordley, "The Johannine Prologue and Jewish Didactic Hymn Traditions: A New Case for Reading the Prologue as a Hymn," *JBL* 128 (2009): 781-802.

Although I view the prologue as a Christian hymnic composition, my claim in presenting this arrangement is not that it represents an original, preexisting hymn that predated the Gospel of John. The origins of the prologue cannot be determined with any degree of certainty, but it seems most likely to me that the prologue was written in a hymnic register for the purpose of introducing the Gospel and is itself the result of deep and extended reflection on the contents of this Gospel. Though admittedly a scholarly construction, an arrangement like the one I provide here helps to make visible some of the logic that is present in the final version of the text. It seems most likely that the author of the Gospel of John, or the final editor, wrote the prologue in a hymnic style that, if not based on one specific preexisting hymn, reflects the style of Jewish didactic hymns that review history. This was the author's sense of the best way to begin the Gospel, rather than beginning with a narrative, a genealogy, or some other opening.

First Strophe (Jn 1:1-2): *The Word with God*
In the beginning was the Word,
and the Word was with God,
and the Word was God.
He was in the beginning with God.

Second Strophe (Jn 1:3-4): *The Word and Creation*
All things came into being through him,
and without him nothing came into being.
What came to be in him was life,
and the life was the light of men;

Third Strophe (Jn 1:5, 9): *The Word in the World*
The light shines in the darkness,
and the darkness has not overcome it.
The true light,
which enlightens every person,
was coming into the world.

Fourth Strophe (Jn 1:10-11): *The Rejection of the Word in the World*
He was in the world,
and the world came into being through him,
but the world did not know him.
He came to his own,
but his own did not receive him.

Fifth Strophe (Jn 1:12-13): *The Word and Those Who Receive Him*
But to as many as received him,
he gave them authority
to become children of God—
to those who believed in his name.
Those not of blood
neither of the will of flesh
nor of the will of man
but born of God.

Sixth Strophe (Jn 1:14): *The Community's Experience of the Word*
And the Word became flesh
and tented among us,
and we have beheld his glory,
glory as an only begotten from the father,
full of grace and truth.

Seventh Strophe (Jn 1:16-17): *The Community's Reception of Grace Through*
Jesus Christ
For out of his fullness
we all received,
even grace upon grace.
For the law was given through Moses,
grace and truth came through Jesus Christ.

It will immediately be clear that this arrangement assumes that the material about John the Baptist and his testimony is a kind of commentary by the author or editor that interrupts the hymnic flow.

John the Baptist Interlude Number One (Jn 1:6-8)

There came a man sent from God, his name was John. He came as a witness, that he might testify concerning the light, that all people might believe through him. He was not the light, but he came that he might testify concerning the light.

John the Baptist Interlude Number Two (Jn 1:15)

John testifies concerning him and cried out saying, "This is he of whom I said, 'The one coming after me was before me, for he is prior to me.'"

Whether these verses were included originally as the author composed the prologue or represent even later additions based on the editor's perception of a need for clarification is difficult to say. These lines are now integral to the final text, but I remove them to showcase the otherwise clear temporal and strophic development of the non-Baptist materials. I also consider that the hymn formally ends with the naming of Jesus Christ and that John 1:18 represents a transition to the narrative that follows.

Editorial Explanation and Summary (Jn 1:18)

No one has ever seen God; God the only begotten who is at the bosom of the father, has made him known.

This line provides an editorial explanation of what has preceded. It also summarizes the point of the prologue as a means of transitioning to the body of the Gospel proper.

This particular arrangement has a number of points in its favor. To begin with, it is aligned with several of the consensus views about the prologue. It is inclusive of the portions of the prologue on which there is general agreement. In his day Robinson noted a "wide measure of agreement that the following verses *at least* . . . form some kind of ode or rhythmic meditation" and went on to list John 1:1, 3-5, 10-11, and 1:14a.[10] Over fifty years later, McHugh states confidently, "It is now almost universally accepted that there was a pre-Gospel hymn containing at least vv. 1, 3-5, and 10-11."[11] Though my arrangement also contains some additional verses (i.e., Jn 1:2, 9, 12-13, 14, 16-17), the initial point here is that it contains all the verses on which there is somewhat of a consensus. I will argue for the centrality of the additional verses below.

In the same vein, this arrangement brackets out the material that is generally agreed to be secondary or inserted as explanatory comments, namely, the verses related to the testimony of John the Baptist (Jn 1:6-8, 15).[12] My arrangement also brackets out John 1:18 as an explanatory comment, which I will support below. Even so, on these first two points my arrangement aligns well with two aspects of general consensus: what should definitely be included, and what should definitely be excluded.

One further aspect of this arrangement also aligns with the most supported (though not a consensus) view, namely, the interpretation of this passage as developing in historical periods. McHugh explains and notes his own approval:

---

[10]Robinson, "Relation of the Prologue," 126 (emphasis original).

[11]McHugh, *John 1–4*, 89.

[12]McHugh notes the "equally firm consensus that the verses about the Baptist (6-8 and 15) should be excluded." Ibid.

"By far the most popular description (and in the present writer's view, rightly so) is that which sees vv. 1-5 as speaking of the primordial existence of the Logos, and of its role in creation and history, of vv. 6-13 as outlining the historical advent of the Logos into the world, and of vv. 14-18 as celebrating the Incarnation of the Logos."[13] Certainly not all agree on this, and there are those who see the incarnation in view as early as John 1:6 or even John 1:3. But this review of history in periodic fashion from creation to incarnation represents the most common view among scholars, and is the view that my arrangement helps bring out more clearly.

Beyond the general consensus points, my specific arrangement has several additional points in its favor.

First, one can readily observe clear verbal, thematic, and conceptual connections from strophe to strophe (see table 5.1). This kind of staircase parallelism has been cited by other scholars in favor of the view that this passage as a whole is a carefully composed poetic passage.[14] It has also been cited in smaller sections of the prologue to argue that only the smaller section should be considered hymnic.[15] However, table 5.1[16] shows the extent to which this device is carried through throughout John 1:1-17.

Table 5.1. Thematic connections between strophes' ending and opening lines

Transition from	Key phrase in last line of previous strophe	Key phrase in first line of following strophe	Connection
First to Second Strophe	in the beginning (Jn 1:2)	All things were made . . . (Jn 1:3)	Genesis 1 creation account
Second to Third Strophe	light of men (Jn 1:4)	The light shines . . . (Jn 1:5)	Light imagery
Third to Fourth Strophe	coming into the world (Jn 1:9)	He was in the world . . . (Jn 1:10)	The world
Fourth to Fifth Strophe	did not receive him (Jn 1:11)	But to as many as received him . . . (Jn 1:12)	Receiving the Word
Fifth to Sixth Strophe	born of God (Jn 1:13)	The Word became flesh . . . (Jn 1:14)	Contrasting images relating to birth
Sixth to Seventh Strophe	full of grace and truth (Jn 1:14)	For out of his fullness . . . (Jn 1:16)	Fullness imagery and grace and truth

---

[13]Ibid., 79.

[14]Raymond E. Brown, *The Gospel According to John I–XII*, AB 29 (Garden City, NY: Doubleday, 1986), 6.

[15]Boer, "Original Prologue," 449-50.

[16]Gordley, "Johannine Prologue," 792.

Second, the notion that this hymn ends at John 1:17 and not John 1:18 is supported, at least in part, by the most recent research into the ancient manuscript evidence for how the prologue was read by its earliest interpreters. For example, P. J. Williams has shown that no early Greek manuscript and no early lectionary includes a break in the text after John 1:18, but some do have a break after John 1:17.[17]

Third, sweeping hymnic reviews of history were part of Jewish literary culture. While each example strikes its own unique stamp on that history, the prevalence of this device—both prior to and subsequent to John's Gospel (e.g., see the later psalms and prayers within the Odes of Solomon and the Hellenistic Synagogal Prayers)—suggests its importance to Jewish and early Christian communities seeking to articulate their place within the history of God's work in the world.

Fourth, it is widely agreed that the Fourth Gospel is a Gospel that shows other clear evidence of editing over time.[18] Accordingly, it is not surprising that the opening would have been edited and supplemented just as other aspects of the Gospel were (including the ending). Seeing the prologue as a hymn grafted on later (following Robinson's notion that the prologue is the fruit of meditation on the Gospel) can accommodate insights about the origins and development of ideas.

Finally, the hymnic arrangement as a hymnic review of history can give a good reason for why the John the Baptist material would be inserted where it is. Explanatory glosses link the hymn to the narrative and clarify the relationship of the Logos in history to the recent events of the advent of Jesus.

While each of the above points are important, there is however one potentially significant problem with this arrangement. This problem centers on our understanding that the incarnation of Jesus is directly in view only in John 1:14 and not prior.[19] Such a view makes sense if the hymn takes a chronological development since this is the place where the incarnation is first clearly and explicitly described. However, the problem with this view is that other

---

[17]P. J. Williams, "Not the Prologue of John," *JSNT* 33 (2011): 375-86. This piece of information is not the whole story, however, since ancient mss have breaks in other places as well, including after Jn 1:5. This information has led de Boer to prefer Jn 1:1-5 as the prologue, a view that creates additional problems, which I discuss below.

[18]See Brown, *John*, xxxiv-xxxix.

[19]This has been an ongoing issue in the study of the prologue. See the recent overview in Richard Alan Culpepper, "The Prologue as Theological Prolegomenon to the Gospel of John," in Van der Watt, Culpepper, and Schnelle, *Prologue of the Gospel of John*, 3-26, esp. 17-20.

language earlier in the prologue can easily (some might even say more naturally) be read as referring to the earthly ministry of Jesus, presupposing the incarnation. Specifically, the fourth strophe is at issue (Jn 1:10-11):

He was in the world,
and the world came into being through him,
but the world did not know him.
He came to his own,
but his own did not receive him.

The phrase "He was in the world" could be read as a reference to the incarnate Jesus. To support my view that the incarnation does not occur until John 1:14, these verses can be read as referring to the *Logos asarkos*, the Logos revealed in history prior to the incarnation. In this way what follows (Jn 1:12-13) would need also to refer to those in history who received or did not receive the Logos, again prior to the incarnation:

But to as many as received him,
he gave them authority
to become children of God—
to those who believed in his name.
Those not of blood
neither of the will of flesh
nor of the will of man
but born of God.

Many have indeed taken this view that these verses refer to the reception of the Logos in history prior to the incarnation. Martin Hengel, for example, writes:

Even when most of his own children "received him not" and became faithless, some of them remained faithful and proved themselves as true "sons of God" and even witnesses of the Logos, beginning with Abraham via Moses and all the prophets up to John the Baptist the last witness in Israel and the first disciple of the Logos incarnate.[20]

Still, it is hard to overlook the thought that the people mentioned in John 1:12-13 also sound very much like the members of the Johannine community

---

[20]Martin Hengel, "The Prologue of the Gospel of John as the Gateway to Christological Truth," in *The Gospel of John and Christian Theology*, ed. Richard Bauckham and Carl Mosser (Grand Rapids: Eerdmans, 2008), 282.

who have received Jesus and thus become children of God. Ernst Käsemann, in fact, argued that there is no mention of the *Logos asarkos* after John 1:5, and that the only way this could be argued was if one were to claim that John 1:12 was not original, a view he would not accept.[21] Ernst Haenchen, however, was quite happy to accept John 1:12-13 as editorial insertion, claiming that once those verses are removed, the logic of the hymn's historical scope and development becomes clear.[22] In a different kind of attempt to explain the apparent disconnect, Bultmann famously claimed that the final editor of the prologue misunderstood the original hymn that he had adapted.[23] Unfortunately, the problem with removing John 1:12-13 on these grounds alone is that these verses seem very much wedded to the overall hymn by means of the staircase parallelism that is a feature of the rest of the hymn, but not a feature of the commonly accepted interpolations. Must we then accept that the third, fourth, and fifth strophes refer to the incarnation and thus refer to the earthly ministry of Jesus? If so, my chronological-historical reading is undermined.

Fortunately, it is possible to accept the view that John 1:5-11 reflects the actions of the Word in history prior to the incarnation, while also maintaining that John 1:12-13 should not be considered an editorial insertion. The solution is provided by C. H. Dodd, who explains the matter as being not a case of either/or but of both/and. In Dodd's view John 1:5-13 speaks primarily of the Logos in history, but only in light of the author's understanding that the Logos made flesh is the ultimate revelation of the Logos in history in John 1:14.[24] Dodd explains,

> The life of Jesus *is* the history of the Logos, as incarnate, and this must be, upon the stage of limited time, the same thing as the history of the Logos in perpetual relations with man and the world. Thus not only vv. 11-13 but the whole passage from verse 4, is *at once* an account of the relations of the Logos with the world, *and* an account of the ministry of Jesus Christ, which in every essential particular reproduces those relations.[25]

---

[21]Ernst Käsemann, "The Structure and Purpose of the Prologue to John's Gospel," in *New Testament Questions of Today* (Philadelphia: Fortress, 1969), 138-67, here 166.

[22]Ernst Haenchen, *A Commentary on the Gospel of John*, trans. Robert W. Funk, Hermeneia (Philadelphia: Fortress, 1984). He explains, "Once one treats this passage as an insertion, the structure of the hymn emerges and the work of the redactor becomes evident" (119). And further, "If verse 14 is connected with v. 11, these difficulties disappear" (119).

[23]But that is another issue.

[24]C. H. Dodd, *The Interpretation of the Fourth Gospel* (Cambridge: Cambridge University Press, 1968), 282-85.

[25]Ibid., 284 (emphasis original).

He claims that this "double significance is thoroughly characteristic of the method of this evangelist."[26] From the conceptual starting point of the incarnation of Jesus, the Evangelist can look backward at history and see the history of the Logos in the world through the lens of the reality that he perceives in the incarnation of the Logos in Jesus.

Hengel takes the same view. He explains, "In reality it is the case that this concise sketch of creation history, which in four strophes moves to the decisive point, the incarnation, anticipates as a type the activity and fate of the incarnate Word with this movement. John loves such ambivalences."[27] In light of this explanation it remains reasonable to view the prologue as reflecting historical periods in the strophic outline that I have provided here.

Furthermore, in light of Dodd's interpretation it is possible to note now that the inclusion of the John the Baptist materials in John 1:6-8 actually supports this view. Through the parenthetical inclusion of this recent testimony, the author is already connecting the themes of the Logos in history with the themes of the incarnation and ministry of Jesus even though the incarnation is not explicitly stated until John 1:14.

Thus we can see that the author of the prologue is looking back at history from the perspective of the time after the Gospel was written. The prologue, especially John 1:5-13, contains clear Johannine themes read backward into the mythic past. In other words, the era before Jesus is now interpreted by the author in light of the perspective of the Johannine community. What is now fully revealed by the Word made flesh is understood to have been available to people of earlier generations. By taking this approach the author of the prologue affirms the wisdom of the Jews and their entire tradition. He also then uses that tradition in an effort to legitimize the community's understanding that Jesus is the ultimate culmination of this history.

In light of this discussion that some see the incarnation in view as early as John 1:10, it is noteworthy that de Boer has recently proposed that the incarnation and ministry of the earthly Jesus occurs even earlier in the hymn. He sees the incarnation already in John 1:4 beginning with the phrase "What came to be in him was life." He writes that this expression is "not about the role of the Word in creation but about the salvation that has been effected through him."[28]

---

[26]Ibid.

[27]Hengel, "Prologue of the Gospel of John," 282.

[28]Boer, "Original Prologue," 465.

In this view we would therefore have a reference to the ministry of the incarnate Jesus as early as John 1:4.

De Boer provides a detailed analysis of John 1:1-5 and concludes that this discrete unit is a hymn of the Johannine community that serves alone as the prologue to the Fourth Gospel. He bases his argument on a three-strophe rendering of these verses, a move that is supported by the recognition of staircase parallelism, and the following of the alternative punctuation in John 1:4. He then argues that the first strophe is about Christology and the divine identity of the Word, while his strophes two and three are about soteriology using the language of life and light to show that the saving work of the Word is the work of new creation.

While de Boer's thesis is well-informed and makes a good effort to untangle a knotty problem, it is ultimately not compelling. First, his claim is based largely on the strophic structure that he creates based on recognition of staircase parallelism. While he is right to observe the staircase parallelism that occurs here on a micro-level, he fails to take into account the same kind of staircase parallelism that occurs on a larger, macro-level throughout John 1:1-17. In fact, the staircase parallelism that is present in these verses does not necessarily lead to the arrangement that de Boer has outlined, but points to a different arrangement, namely, the one presented here. The extent of the staircase parallelism beyond John 1:1-5 is problematic for his claim that the hymn ends at John 1:5.

A second problem with de Boer's reading is that it cuts against the grain of the trajectory that the passage seems to be setting up. Creation language reflective of Genesis 1 is clearly in view in John 1:1-2. The most natural reading would be that it remains in view in John 1:3 as the Genesis 1 imagery continues to be in view, particularly with the concepts of light and life.

A third problem is that de Boer has created an unnatural division between his second and third strophes. This is what allows him to read strophe two as new creation and not original creation.[29] De Boer's understanding is at least as challenging, if not more so, than viewing the fourth and fifth strophes as the reception and rejection of the Word in history.

Given these problems, de Boer's argument that the hymn shifts immediately to soteriology is not compelling. Nevertheless, de Boer's insight is not

---

[29]Ibid.

without merit. It can in fact be seen to bear some fruit by taking it in line with Dodd's remarks above. Surely this initial work of the Logos in creation (in Jn 1:1-3) can now be more fully understood in light of the incarnation of the Logos in John 1:14. Looking back at this history from the perspective of the incarnation, one can see that the work of the Logos even in creation was a work of enlightening humanity and ultimately *is* closely connected with the saving work of the incarnate Logos. The polyvalence of John's imagery relating to life and light is present here as well.

To echo some of the quotations that began this chapter, given the complexity of these issues, it is unlikely that a simple and satisfying solution to the structure of the prologue can be found. In part, this is due to the genius of the author, who is able to use images and themes with rich pedigrees and to infuse them with new meaning related to his understanding of Jesus.[30] However, when viewed as a review of history the overall emphasis of the prologue seems to be this: all of the actions of the Logos in history should now be seen through the lens of the incarnation of the Logos in the person of Jesus Christ.

JEWISH THEMES IN THE PROLOGUE

With this arrangement into strophes in place, we can briefly consider some of the elements of the prologue that reflect a Jewish background. These have been discussed extensively, and what follows here is only a summary of the main connections between the prologue and Jewish traditions. The one aspect of the Jewish context that has been noted but, to my knowledge, not fully explored is the connection of the prologue with Jewish hymns that review history. This is a dimension that I will examine in more detail.

To begin with, there is no doubt that the creation account of Genesis 1 is part of the conceptual framework of the author. The opening words "In the beginning" (Jn 1:1) make this clear. One dimension of the much-studied term *Logos*, which I will discuss further below, is its connection with God's act of creation through God's spoken word: "and God said" (Gen 1:3). The entire second strophe has its focus on the creation of all things with a particular emphasis on life and light, two themes of Genesis 1:1-31. The first two strophes thus tap into some very foundational aspects of Jewish tradition by alluding

---

[30]Culpepper, "Prologue as Theological Prolegomena," 25.

to an ancient poem about creation.[31] These creation themes are also prominent in the hymnic oracles of Isaiah 40–55, which highlight God's sovereignty by pointing to God as the sole creator of all things.[32]

However, already in the first two strophes the prologue indicates that it will move in other directions as well. With the term *Logos* the prologue strikes out in a conceptual direction that has captured the imagination of readers for centuries. I have already noted that the term has a connection with Genesis 1. It also connects with Jewish psalm traditions through the same motif: creation by God's word (e.g., Ps 33:6). While it is possible to claim that this term is colored by connections with Genesis 1, it seems more likely that the concept of the Logos has its origin in other dimensions of Jewish thought. This becomes particularly clear as the prologue continues and the reader learns more about the Logos in history. The Logos appears to embody the functions ascribed in the Bible to God's Wisdom.[33]

According to Proverbs and other early Jewish writings, Wisdom was a mediating agent of God in the act of creation and is closely associated with life (Prov 3:19; 8:30, 35; Sir 24:8; Wis 7:22; 8:5; 9:1-2; Bar 4:1). Wisdom enlightened humanity (Sir 24:1-33; Wis 7:29-30; Bar 4:2; 1 En. 42.2). Wisdom was available to humanity though rejected by many (Bar 3:37; Wis 8:1; Sir 24). Those who love Wisdom are loved by God (Sir 4:14), and Wisdom enables people to become friends of God (Wis 7:27). Wisdom is even equated with the Torah (Sir 24:23; Bar 4:1). The author of Wisdom of Solomon notes that God made all things by his word and by his Wisdom (Wis 9:1-2). With these clear connections to the figure of Wisdom, John's Logos figure seems to be taking on the qualities of divine Wisdom.[34] As Marianne Meye Thompson explains, "These are categories of agency that allow for the closest possible unity of the means of God's revelation and the God who reveals."[35]

---

[31]As de Boer explains, "That Gen 1.1-5 served as a source of inspiration for John 1.1-5 can scarcely be denied" ("Original Prologue," 462).

[32]For example, Is 40:28; 44:24; 45:7; 45:18; 48:12-13. See Marianne Meye Thompson, *John: A Commentary*, NTL (Louisville, KY: Westminster John Knox, 2015), 28-29.

[33]See the summary of the connections in Brown, *John*, cxxii-cxxv, and 519-24. He concludes, "In the OT presentation of Wisdom there are good parallels for almost every detail of the Prologue's description of the Word" (523). See also James D. G. Dunn, *Christology in the Making: A New Testament Inquiry into the Origins of the Doctrine of the Incarnation* (Grand Rapids: Eerdmans, 1996), 164-65; Thompson, *John*, 37-39.

[34]For an extended discussion of Christ as the Wisdom of God in the New Testament, see Dunn, *Christology in the Making*, 167-212.

[35]Thompson, *John*, 39.

Thus far it is at least clear that the mediating role of God's Wisdom in creation is clearly in view. However, whether this concept is derived through Hellenistic Jewish speculation or through some other development of this kind of discourse is difficult to say. A variety of views have been proposed. Thom Tobin finds that the concept of the Logos in the prologue is indebted to the kinds of ideas found in Philo and Hellenistic Jewish speculation on Genesis 1-2.[36] Martin Scott argues that it is not from Philo at all but rather from wisdom traditions describing personified Sophia.[37] Jarl Fossum argues that the concepts in the prologue do not derive from discourse about Sophia but rather from an understanding of the divine name.[38] Daniel Boyarin has made a compelling case for seeing targumic reflections on the memra (the Aramaic term for "word") as the primary background for the prologue's claims.[39] McHugh likewise finds the concept of the Logos derived from Aramaic conceptions of the memra along with Old Testament traditions.[40] The variety of views that have been articulated and supported by appeals to relevant primary texts from antiquity suggest that the Logos concept in the prologue engages with several important streams of Jewish thought in the Second Temple period rather than just one.[41]

However, lending support to the Wisdom background, Second Temple-period Jewish understandings of Wisdom can be seen elsewhere in the prologue, particularly in John 1:4-6, 10-13. These sections seem to echo the notion of divine Wisdom's sojourn and ultimate rejection by humanity as seen in places like Sirach 15:7 and 1 Enoch 42.2.[42] One other important aspect of

---

[36]Thomas Tobin, "The Prologue of John and Hellenistic Jewish Speculation," *CBQ* 52 (1990): 252-69.

[37]Martin Scott, *Sophia and the Johannine Jesus*, LNTS 71 (Sheffield: JSOT Press, 1992).

[38]Jarl E. Fossum, "In the Beginning Was the Name: Onomanology as the Key to Johannine Christology," in *The Image of the Invisible God: Essays on the Influence of Jewish Mysticism on Early Christology*, ed. Jarl E. Fossum, NTOA 30 (Göttingen: Vandenhoeck & Ruprecht, 1995), 109-34.

[39]Daniel Boyarin, "The Gospel of the *Memra*: Jewish Binitarianism and the Prologue to John," *HTR* 94 (2001): 243-84.

[40]McHugh, *John 1-4*.

[41]For an opposing view see McDonough, who dismisses these connections with traditions represented in early Jewish writings as being of little value compared to the biblical background and the community's experience of Jesus. Sean M. McDonough, *Christ as Creator: Origins of a New Testament Doctrine* (Oxford: Oxford University Press, 2009), 212-17. Though his arguments cannot be addressed fully here, my assessment is that McDonough too hastily dismisses the relevance of the early Jewish literature for understanding concepts in the early Christian hymns.

[42]See Peder Borgen, "The Gospel of John and Hellenism," in *The Gospel of John: More Light from Philo, Paul and Archaeology; The Scriptures, Tradition, Exposition, Settings, Meaning*, ed. Peder Borgen, NovTSup 154 (Leiden: Brill, 2014), 79-99, 107-9.

Second Temple Jewish writings about Wisdom was the equation of Wisdom with God's law, as I noted above.

Law allusions are noteworthy particularly as the prologue continues on to describe the incarnation using language and imagery that echoes the revelation to Moses at Sinai. Several elements of the final two strophes of the prologue (Jn 1:14-15, 16-17) help to link the incarnation of Jesus with the revelation of the law to Moses on Mt. Sinai. First, the verb used to describe the dwelling of the Logos among humanity, *skenoō* (which I have translated above as "tented"), is a fascinating choice in that its root meaning is linked to the tabernacle. Second, the whole idea of seeing his glory (Jn 1:14) likewise calls to mind the glory of God that was present in the tabernacle. These phrases thus call to mind a whole set of events that are foundational to Jewish self-understanding. Third, the giving of the law through Moses is explicitly mentioned in the final strophe. Moses is shown to be a mediator through whom the law was given. By comparison, Jesus is portrayed as the one through whom grace and truth came. Both Moses and Jesus are mediators of God's gifts. These allusions suggest the value of these past events for the community even as they invest the life and ministry of Jesus with deep significance.

With the imagery related to Moses and the tabernacle in the final two strophes, we can see that the focus of the prologue has shifted. From Wisdom's role in creation and history in general the prologue moves to describe the revelation of Jesus in ways that draw on foundational historical narratives related to God's covenant with Israel through Moses. Along these lines, Charles Giblin sees the prologue developing in two parts: the first part uses cosmological imagery related to creation, light, and life; the second uses theophanic imagery associated with Moses and the covenant.[43] The shift occurs, notably, with the notion of becoming children of God (Jn 1:12-13). Thus we find here the interface of two grand stories of the Jewish tradition: Wisdom and covenant.

Finally, we can see glimpses in the Johannine prologue of prophetic promises of renewal such as those outlined in Isaiah 40–66. This is of particular significance with the term *glory*, seen twice in the prologue (both

---

[43]Giblin explains, "The 'cosmological' imagery of X [part 1] has been supplanted in Y [part 2] by what may be labeled 'covenantal, historical' imagery." Charles Homer Giblin, "Two Complementary Literary Structures in John 1:1-18," *JBL* 104 (1985): 91.

times in Jn 1:14) and a major theme of John's Gospel.[44] On its connections with Isaiah, Larry Hurtado explains that in Isaiah 40–66, "'glory' is frequently used in statements about a future manifestation of God that will involve redemption for Israel and even the illumination of Gentile nations."[45] He points especially to the connection of themes of light and glory in Isaiah 60:1-3. Hurtado concludes, "The Johannine treatment of Jesus amounts to him being the one in whom God's glory is manifested, the unique human embodiment of God's glory on earth."[46] Though we did not see the emphasis on the term in Philippians or Colossians (though note the "glory of God the Father" in Phil 2:11), we did see clear evidence that both hymns likewise viewed Jesus in light of the fulfillment of the promises of the return of YHWH to dwell among his people. The Johannine prologue thus reflects this same understanding through some more explicit terminology that associated Jesus with the glory of God.[47]

At this point in the analysis of Jewish themes in the prologue, we may readily agree with Hartmut Gese, who writes: "The relationship of the prologue to the Old Testament is extensive and intimate. . . . The prologue is not dependent on various details of the Old Testament. It is related to the Old Testament tradition itself, and the total conception of the prologue grew out of this tradition."[48] The vision of reality portrayed in the prologue grows not out of any one aspect of Jewish tradition alone, but is rooted deeply in many aspects of it.

Taken as a whole, the connections between the prologue and the Old Testament do indeed show that the prologue grew out of this broad background. And yet, there are some aspects which show that it is not the Old Testament as an ancient document but rather as a living tradition that the prologue engages with. The issues that the prologue raises are issues that other Jewish communities were raising as well. And they were raising these kinds of issues in their hymnic praise of God.

---

[44]See Larry W. Hurtado, *Lord Jesus Christ: Devotion to Jesus in Earliest Christianity* (Grand Rapids: Eerdmans, 2003), 374-89.

[45]Ibid., 378.

[46]Ibid., 380.

[47]Ibid., 389. Hurtado pictures "fervent mining of material from Isaiah, especially 40–66, in the service of a radical Christological interpretation of these chapters that was underway with explosive rapidity in circles of Jewish Christians, and within the first few years (at most) of the Christian movement" (389).

[48]Hartmut Gese, *Essays on Biblical Theology* (Minneapolis: Augsburg, 1981), 222.

And so, finally, it should be noted that the kinds of themes outlined above—creation, Wisdom, Sinai, the covenant, the law, Moses as a mediator of God's benefactions, and the glory of God—find their place in Jewish psalms and hymns that review history.[49] As we have seen, hymnic reviews of history were well-suited to enable an author or community to utilize its tradition and history in ways that help it to navigate its current context. Accordingly, it is not a stretch to consider that the deployment of these kinds of images and ideas in a hymnic reflection about the incarnation of Jesus is a carefully considered response to the challenges facing the early Christian community in which the Gospel of John was written and treasured.

A full consideration of the context of the Johannine community would take us far afield from the current task. Here I note simply that it is widely held that a conflict with Jewish synagogue leaders is indicated by the contents of the Fourth Gospel (see Jn 16:1-3).[50] Not surprisingly, the Johannine prologue takes up several aspects of Jewish tradition to support its view of the working of God in history and in the life and ministry of Jesus, presumably in contrast to other conflicting views. But beyond the Jewish context it is also the case that the Fourth Gospel comes out of a context in which the Roman Empire was in full power. It is to the Roman context that we now turn.

THE PROLOGUE IN ROMAN IMPERIAL CONTEXT

As with many New Testament writings, in recent years the Fourth Gospel has received increasing attention for the ways in which it engages with the realities of empire.[51] There are some notable aspects of the Fourth Gospel that have invited such consideration. For example, Rome is explicitly

---

[49]Matthew E. Gordley, *Teaching Through Song in Antiquity: Didactic Hymnody Among Greeks, Romans, Jews and Christians*, WUNT 2/331 (Tübingen: Mohr Siebeck, 2011), 213-14, 230.

[50]See Raymond E. Brown, *The Community of the Beloved Disciple* (New York: Paulist, 1979).

[51]See N. T. Wright and J. P. Davies, "John, Jesus, and 'The Ruler of This World': Demonic Politics in the Fourth Gospel?," in *Conception, Reception, and the Spirit: Essays in Honor of Andrew T. Lincoln*, ed. J. G. McConville and Lloyd Pietersen (Eugene, OR: Cascade, 2015), 71-89. See also the recent full-length studies by Warren Carter, *John and Empire: Initial Explorations* (New York: T&T Clark, 2008); Lance Byron Richey, *Roman Imperial Ideology and the Gospel of John*, CBQMS (Washington, DC: Catholic Biblical Association of America, 2007); Tom Thatcher, *Greater Than Caesar: Christology and Empire in the Fourth Gospel* (Minneapolis: Fortress, 2009). For a critical review see Christopher W. Skinner, "John's Gospel and the Roman Imperial Context: An Evaluation of Recent Proposals," in *Jesus Is Lord, Caesar Is Not: Evaluating Empire in New Testament Studies*, ed. Scot McKnight and Joseph B. Modica (Downers Grove, IL: IVP Academic, 2013), 116-29. Also note Stephen D. Moore, *Empire and Apocalypse: Postcolonialism and the New Testament*, Bible in the Modern World (Sheffield: Sheffield Phoenix, 2006), esp. chap. 3.

brought into view in John 11 and in John 18–19. In fact, the Gospel of John is the only Gospel to specifically mention "the Romans" (Jn 11:48). This Gospel also creates a stark and explicit contrast between being a friend of the emperor and affirming the kingship of Jesus (Jn 19:12). Finally, it is only in this Gospel that Pilate asks, "Shall I crucify your king?" to which the chief priests answer, "We have no king but the emperor" (Jn 19:15). Although scholars debate the significance of the inclusion of such details, the presence of this material suggests that issues relating to how to negotiate Roman imperial realities were important to the author of the Fourth Gospel and are not simply a recent scholarly invention. In light of this understanding, the prologue can be read with attention to the ways in which it participates in this engagement not only with Jewish themes but also Roman imperial ones. When we read the prologue with this larger context in view, we will see that the prologue engages its Roman context subtly and indirectly in at least three ways: (1) it uses a strategy of resembling but contesting; (2) it employs a strategy of going beyond what was said about the emperor to make unique and startling claims about Jesus; (3) it incorporates a rejection motif that highlights the contrast between the Roman rejection of Jesus and the reception of Jesus by those who have become children of God.

Before considering the prologue's engagement with imperial realities, we should acknowledge that, at first glance, such an approach may seem unwarranted. A surface reading of the prologue shows no explicit mention of the Roman Empire and does not appear to call out the Roman emperor as an object of comparison. Recent scholarship on the prologue generally ignores Roman imperial themes altogether, strengthening the impression that it is only the Jewish context that matters.[52] And even among those who have considered the Fourth Gospel's Roman context, the Gospel's absence of more explicit and more extended engagement with political themes has caused some to conclude that connections to the Roman context are of secondary importance, at best, and therefore not as significant as Jewish concerns. For example, in a review of recent scholarship that reads John in the context of the

---

[52]The recently published proceedings of the Colloquium Ioannaeum 2013, for example, while engaging profitably with Jewish and Greek philosophical perspectives, are silent on matters relating to Roman imperial themes. Van der Watt, Culpepper, and Schnelle, *Prologue of the Gospel of John.*

Roman Empire, Christopher Skinner concludes that Roman characters and issues "do not constitute a major emphasis for the Fourth Gospel."[53] Thus, while Skinner can claim to see the value in attending to the Roman cultural context, he is not convinced that the Roman Empire is a major concern for the Fourth Gospel. He argues instead that the Fourth Gospel more explicitly and pointedly addresses Jewish concerns, and that a focus on Rome gives too much attention to a very minor theme. Further, he contends that efforts to see Roman imperial engagement in the prologue are not convincing since the presumed imperial-themed concepts are not prominent in the rest of the Gospel.[54] Jewish themes, however, are carried on throughout.

This issue is complicated even further when one considers Stephen Moore's claim that "John is at once the most—and least—political of the canonical gospels."[55] Those who view John as the least political of the Gospels note that John does not provide the reader with the same kind of clear teaching about how to engage with political realities in the world around them. In this perspective, John is viewed more as a spiritual gospel advocating universal truths. If there is any sustained critique in John, it is with Jewish leaders who reject Jesus.

Fortunately, readers do not need to choose between these options. Instead, it seems clear that the Fourth Gospel is explicit in some places about issues concerning Jewish tradition and in other places about issues concerning Rome. Furthermore, N. T. Wright's contribution to this discussion shows that John's engagement with Rome is reflective of a very Jewish set of themes including creation, new creation, and even "a Daniel-based apocalyptic . . . message."[56] Even so, Skinner also observes, as have others, that certain themes of the prologue are dropped and do not reappear elsewhere, suggesting that they are not really that important to the author of the Gospel. However, I contend that is not an indication that they are not important for the author of the prologue or the final editor of the Gospel. That observation is better explained by the consensus view that the prologue was added later. Thus it could more readily be claimed that if imperial themes are found in the prologue,

---

[53]Skinner, "John's Gospel," 128. Thatcher reviews a number of features of John's Gospel that have led interpreters to believe that the Roman Empire is not a significant concern for the author or the community. However, he provides much additional material to argue the opposite position.
[54]Ibid., 127.
[55]Moore, *Empire and Apocalypse*, 50.
[56]Wright and Davies, "John, Jesus, and 'The Ruler of This World,'" 88-89.

they were important at the time period of the latest stage of development of the Fourth Gospel. The prologue thus brings those issues into focus that otherwise might have more readily been overlooked in the rest of the Gospel.

With regard to these observations, it is fair to say that at most the Roman themes touched on in the prologue are implied rather than explicit. But this should not be surprising. Warren Carter and Tom Thatcher both draw on the work of James C. Scott to better appreciate the subtle ways in which resistance can occur.[57] The forms of resistance are often very subtle, for good reason. Carter summarizes,

> An expectation of explicit naming is unlikely in a text that originates with those subjected to imperial power and yet are concerned, in part, to contest it. The powerless rarely engage in direct and open confrontation but employ self-protective, calculated, disguised arts of resistance along with continual acts of accommodation.[58]

Just because the allusions and engagement are subtle does not mean they are not significant.

Finally, these observations about the prologue take on even greater significance when one considers the ways in which the Fourth Gospel engages with its imperial context elsewhere. While he does not analyze the prologue directly, Thatcher takes a holistic approach in considering the ways in which the Gospel as a whole engages with the realities of its Roman context. In summary Thatcher explains,

> The Gospel of John may be seen as a response to Rome at two levels: the very fact of writing a Jesus book may be viewed as a subversive act, and the specific contents of John's Gospel may be viewed as a specific counter to the claims of imperial power.[59]

A key to Thatcher's approach is the notion of countermemory, an idea we noted while looking at the Colossian hymn.[60] This strategy accepts the reality

---

[57]Thatcher, *Greater Than Caesar*, esp. 26-29 and 33-39; Carter, *John and Empire*, 149-50. Cf. James C. Scott, *Domination and the Arts of Resistance: Hidden Transcripts* (New Haven, CT: Yale University Press, 1990).

[58]Carter, *John and Empire*, 150.

[59]Thatcher, *Greater Than Caesar*, 4.

[60]Tom Thatcher, "'I Have Conquered the World': The Death of Jesus and the End of Empire in the Gospel of John," in *Empire in the New Testament*, ed. Stanley E. Porter and Cynthia Long Westfall, McMaster New Testament Studies Series 10 (Eugene, OR: Pickwick, 2011), 140-63; Thatcher, *Greater Than Caesar*.

that certain events have occurred, but by remembering them in a certain way an author shapes the significance of those events in ways that are quite different than the prevailing narrative of the dominant group. Adapting Thatcher's two-level observation above, I suggest that the prologue itself embodies a similar strategy of resistance on two levels. The first is the very act of composing and preserving a hymn in honor of Jesus. As we have noted, only gods, heroes, and semi-divine rulers such as the emperor received such hymnic acclamation. The second level of response to Rome is that of the specific contents of the prologue, and the ways in which these claims stand in tension with claims made about the emperor. It is to these claims that we now turn.

There are several ways in which the prologue engages its Roman context. Overall, the prologue evokes a strategy of "resembling but contesting" in which claims of the prologue, read in their cultural context, imitate aspects of Roman claims about the emperor and the nature of Rome's rule, and make competing claims about those realities. For example, as we have seen Roman claims about the emperor include notions that the emperor is creator of the new world, that his rule is divinely sanctioned, that he reveals the will of the gods, and that he is a gracious benefactor.[61] The prologue shows instead that Jesus takes precedence over the emperor in each of these domains. The prologue demonstrates Jesus' priority over the emperor by starting its hymnic acclamation not with his birth but rather much, much earlier: "in the beginning" (Jn 1:1). This appeal to antiquity prior to Rome follows a strategy used by other subjects of Rome's rule who sought to show that their way of life preceded the rise of Rome.[62] The prologue presents Jesus as God's agent of creation in all that exists, including benefactions to humanity such as life, light, grace, and truth. As such his actions and benefactions are unmatched by the emperor. Finally, Jesus is depicted in the final version of the prologue as one who is legitimated through the prophetic witness of John the Baptist.[63] Through these kinds of claims the prologue counters "imperial claims of divine sanction, sovereignty, agency, and revelation."[64] Carter explains,

> [The prologue] contests Rome by mimicking and disqualifying its claims to ultimate sovereignty and agency, by summoning prophetic legitimation for

---

[61]See chap. 2.
[62]Carter, *John and Empire*, 93-122.
[63]Cf. Richey, *Roman Imperial Ideology*, 133.
[64]Carter, *John and Empire*, 152.

Jesus, and by asserting divine sanction for Jesus "in the beginning . . . with God."[65]

Without denying that such claims participate in Jewish disputes about their own tradition, I agree with Carter, who rightly claims that they also "contest Roman claims even as they imitate them."[66]

Rather than just resembling and contesting, Lance Byron Richey goes further, claiming that the function of the prologue is primarily contrastive, using language of contrast and difference: "John upsets and inverts the language of power and divinity used by the Roman world."[67] This dimension of the prologue's strategy of resistance is developed through the use of concepts that go well beyond Roman imperial claims about the emperor. Richey sees this in the choice of language used about Jesus as compared to the opening sections of the other Gospels. By beginning with a hymnic prologue rather than a birth narrative, and by avoiding "son of God" language and using instead the concept of the Logos, the prologue avoids the risk that Jesus would be understood as simply on par with the emperor, who also had birth narratives and was identified as a son of God.[68] Rather than seeing the work of the Logos in creation as resembling and contesting claims of the emperor's role in the creation of a new world, Richey sees it as adding a unique dimension to claims about Jesus that are never made about the Roman emperor. We observed a similar dynamic in the Colossian hymn, in which some of the claims about Jesus reflect claims made about the emperor in wider Greco-Roman discourse, while some of the claims about Jesus are unique and clearly set him apart from the emperor. Such a strategy is arguably at work here as well.

Finally, in addition to its language of implied contrast, the prologue sets up an explicit tension between the rejection of Jesus by the world (see Jn 12:31, with Pilate as "the ruler of this world"), and the reception of Jesus by the community of children of God.[69] The prologue thus "divides the world into two groups on the basis of relation to Jesus."[70] Rome's system and allies are "the world," which rejected Jesus and crucified him. The alternate community are

[65]Ibid., 156.
[66]Ibid., 152.
[67]Richey, *Roman Imperial Ideology*, 152.
[68]Ibid., 124-27.
[69]On the polyvalence of the expression "ruler of this world" as it relates to this discussion, see Wright and Davies, "John, Jesus, and 'The Ruler of This World,'" 76-77, 83, and 87.
[70]Carter, *John and Empire*, 156.

the children of God—those who receive him.[71] These twin themes of rejection and acceptance are developed and illustrated throughout the remainder of the Gospel.[72]

Analysis of the prologue with regard to its engagement with Roman imperial themes leads to the conclusion that in its first-century Roman context the claims about God's activities in the world through Jesus paint a portrait of reality that differs considerably from the picture painted by Roman imperial propaganda. The means of painting this verbal portrait—through hymnic reflection on the work of the Logos in history and now incarnate in Jesus—is not insignificant. Given the important role of hymnody in the Greco-Roman world and among Jewish groups, the use of a hymnic composition in this way carries significant implications about the community that utilized it and about the one being praised. With this clearer understanding of the prologue's engagement with imperial themes, we turn now to consider the ways in which this passage may be seen to reflect some of the dynamics of resistance poetry that we have observed in other hymnic compositions.

DYNAMICS OF RESISTANCE POETRY IN THE PROLOGUE

As we have seen in previous chapters, resistance poetry commonly demonstrates a concern for remembering history for the marginalized community, constructing the identity of the community and its oppressors, and articulating a sense of hope for a new day. The prologue provides indications of each of these features in some very interesting ways.

Remembering the past; concern for history. For starters, with its references to creation, the Logos in history, allusions to Sinai, and the incarnation, the prologue certainly is concerned with the past. And even though likely secondary, the references to the testimony of John the Baptist only serve to enhance this feature of remembering the past in a certain way. It is of particular importance that Jesus is remembered as having glory, the glory of the father (Jn 1:14). The incarnation is remembered as a revelation of God's glory using imagery that is foundational to Jewish self-understanding.

---

[71]Cf. Richey, *Roman Imperial Ideology*, 141-42, on becoming clients of Caesar.
[72]Brown (*John*, 19) observes that the hymn in Jn 1:11 and Jn 1:12 mirrors the two halves of the Gospel of John, with its narrative of the rejection and the acceptance of Jesus in the Book of Signs (Jn 1–12) and the Book of Glory (Jn 13–20). Thus the hymn anticipates the structure of the Gospel as a whole.

As noted briefly above, a turn to the past was one strategy used by many communities, both Greek and Jewish, to respond to and adapt to the reality of the Roman conquest.[73] In some cases, these works did not directly or explicitly counter Rome, but instead they simply placed Rome within a larger and more ancient context, which had the effect of showing that Rome, despite its present dominance, was not ultimate.[74] In other cases, ancient myths and figures were presented in new ways that allowed the community to maintain its ancient traditions but in a way that enabled fruitful engagement with the new realities. Carter shows that the figures of Abraham, Moses, and Wisdom were utilized in this way by Jewish authors during the Roman era.[75] The identities of these figures also play an important role in John's Gospel. Specifically in the prologue we have already seen that Jesus is associated closely with divine Wisdom, and also that his connection with (and superiority over) Moses is explicit. As we have also seen, the idea of showing that Jesus was "in the beginning with God" (Jn 1:2) denotes his primacy over any Roman claims to antiquity and surely participates in this subtle dynamic of resistance. In whatever way Jesus was remembered by Romans and Jews at the end of the first century, for this community he was remembered as revealing divine glory—a glory that goes back to his being with God in the beginning.

Resistance poetry is generally concerned not with history in a general sense but often shows a propensity to remember specific traumatic events of the past, as a form of witness to what has occurred. Though this hymn does not explicitly mention the crucifixion as other hymns do (Phil 2:8 and Col 1:20; cf. Eph 2:16), the whole concept of the rejection of the Logos by the world (Jn 1:10-11) provides a reminder of painful events of the distant and not-so-distant past, as well as the community's present. In this way the trauma of the rejection of Jesus is inscribed in the hymn. Though not spelled out in detail, the rejection of Jesus is alluded to through the broader notion of the rejection of the Logos in history.[76] As we have noted, the effect of this review of periods of

---

[73]Carter, *John and Empire*, 93-122.

[74]This is particularly the case with the three examples Carter cites in ibid., 97-101.

[75]Ibid., 101-17.

[76]It may be that the phrase "we have seen his glory" (Jn 1:14) refers broadly to all that Jesus said and did, with the understanding that even the crucifixion was a revelation of God's glory. Even so, the crucifixion is not explicitly mentioned in the prologue. Given the lateness of this Gospel and especially the prologue, it may be that by the time of its writing, the trauma of the crucifixion of Jesus was less in focus while the trauma of the rejection of the message about Jesus was the real and present experience of the community.

history is to show that the recent rejection of Jesus by the Jews and Romans—
a traumatic and defining event for the community—is to be understood as the
latest instance of the rejection of the Logos by the world that was created
through him. This way of remembering the rejection of Jesus aligns well with
Thatcher's explanation of a countermemory: "Countermemories do not challenge normative views of the past by insisting that certain things never really
happened, but rather by reinterpreting the significance of events that are
widely accepted as historical."[77] By placing the rejection of Jesus in the broader
context of the rejection of the Logos in history, the significance of the event is
reinterpreted. Thatcher explains, "Countermemories *reconfigure the value of
accepted facts* by forcing those facts into a new social vision that is radically at
odds with the values of a great tradition."[78] The prologue affirms the rejection
of Jesus by the world as a historical reality but invests it with deep significance
by tying it to the rejection of the Logos throughout history. In addition, by
including this theme in the hymn, the community cannot forget that the possibility of rejection continues for them in the present.

On the other hand, the community's acceptance of the message about Jesus
is also invested with value that is counter to what the prevailing social vision
suggests. Their acceptance of Jesus is remembered and now experienced as in
line with the acceptance of God's Logos by God's people throughout history.
This leads us to consider the prologue's concern with identity.

Concern with identity. The community is referenced in the hymn in very
clear ways, as are those outside the community. As with resistance poetry in
general, there is a clear sense of who "we" are versus who "they" are. For the
author of the prologue "we" are those who receive him (Jn 1:12), believe in his
name (Jn 1:12), see his glory (Jn 1:14), receive power to become children of God
(Jn 1:12), are born of God (Jn 1:13), and experience grace on grace (Jn 1:16).
Richard Alan Culpepper, in his chiastic arrangement of the prologue, argues
that the phrase about becoming children of God is the pivot of the prologue,
and thus the focus around which all else turns.[79] The meaning of this phrase
gains clarification throughout the remainder of the Fourth Gospel, but this
central theme is introduced here in the center of the prologue.[80] Even apart

---

[77]Thatcher, *Greater Than Caesar*, 16.
[78]Ibid., 38 (emphasis original).
[79]Richard Alan Culpepper, "The Pivot of John's Prologue," *NTS* 27 (1980): 1-31.
[80]Culpepper, "Prologue as Theological Prolegomena," 20-24.

from accepting Culpepper's chiastic arrangement of the prologue, it is clear that this idea is vital to the prologue.

By contrast, the opponents are those who did not know him (Jn 1:10) and did not receive him (Jn 1:11), thereby rejecting God's *charis*, rejecting the Logos, and ultimately participating in a futile attempt to quench the life-giving light of the Logos (Jn 1:5). Such opponents will come into clearer view throughout the Gospel, with the Roman governor Pilate being the explicit locus of the rejection of Jesus that leads to his death. In addition to the Romans as represented by Pilate, the opponents may also be those who may place primacy on any other revealer, whether John the Baptist or Moses. Both of those individuals are explicitly shown to be less than Jesus, signaling to contemporary readers that there was a need within the community to clarify their roles.[81] Even so, both John and Moses are not accorded the negative place given to the Romans but are fully affirmed as participants in God's ongoing plan of revelation. The "we" of the community thus accepts Jesus as the Logos, and accepts and honors John the Baptist and Moses as participants in God's revealing of his life-giving purposes throughout history.

The identity of Jesus himself is also important to the prologue. However, the concern is not so much to explain the identity of Jesus as to focus on the great extent to which the incarnation is a revelation of God's glory. And this notion points back to the identity of the community, since the community are those who recognize the divine glory in the earthly life and ministry of Jesus.

Vision of the future? Resistance poetry often includes reference to a particular vision of an imagined, desirable future that incorporates the idea of a reversal or a renewal of some kind. In Christian and Jewish texts this tends to look like eschatological judgment on the oppressors of God's people and the renewal of the people of God through God's agent.[82] When looked for in those terms, the prologue's focus seems to be almost entirely on the latter notion (renewal) rather than on the former (judgment). Its focus also concerns more the past (remembering history) and the present (shaping identity) than the future. This is not to say that prologue does not suggest a particular vison of the future. It does. However, it is a future that is based on the present reality that the community is already experiencing. In theological terms, it is

---

[81]We can note here an aspect of Thatcher's notion of "greater than" Christology. Thatcher, *Greater Than Caesar*, 41.

[82]E.g., Pss. Sol. 17.

a realized eschatology.[83] The community does not need to wait to see the glory of the exalted Jesus before whom every knee will bow and every tongue acknowledge his lordship (Phil 2:10). That glory has already been revealed in the recent past and the present: "we have seen his glory" (Jn 1:14). As Raymond Brown puts it, "The Gospel very clearly regards the coming of Jesus as an eschatological event which marked the change of the aeons."[84]

If the Fourth Gospel as a whole demonstrates a realized eschatology, the prologue does so even more consistently. W. Robert Cook notes six themes throughout the Gospel of John that bear on its eschatological teaching and suggest that the author's eschatology included additional expectations for the future: death, eternal life, resurrection, heaven, judgment, and Christ's return.[85] Interestingly, none of these future-oriented eschatological touch points are present in the prologue. In this light we can see that the prologue is indeed concerned largely with history, and identity, but less so with a vision of hope for the future. Indeed, the vision for the future seems to be implied but not stated: that the community would live as children of God in light of the grace on grace, and the grace and truth that has come to them through Jesus Christ. Cook cites Bultmann in this regard: "Jesus is the eschatological salvation bringer . . . [and] his coming *is* the eschatological event."[86]

A window into the eschatological perspective of the prologue can be seen in the notion of the community's becoming children of God by being born of God (Jn 1:12-13).[87] Culpepper agrees with Bultmann that becoming children of God "is intended in an eschatological sense" and suggests that this is confirmed elsewhere in John (see Jn 11:52).[88] What this means is that the concept of becoming children of God points to the prophetic expectation for the restoration of Israel in the last days that would then signal the gathering of the nations.[89] Culpepper explains, "What the prophet Isaiah looked forward to in the future had already begun in the ministry of the Revealer and was being

[83]For a concise overview of the complicated picture of eschatology in the Gospel of John, see Brown, *John*, cxv-cxxi.
[84]Ibid., cxxi.
[85]W. Robert Cook, "Eschatology in John's Gospel," *CTR* 3 (1988): 79-99.
[86]Bultmann, cited in ibid., 82 (emphasis added).
[87]Culpepper, "Prologue as Theological Prolegomena," 20-24.
[88]Ibid., 22.
[89]Culpepper notes Is 56:7-8; 66:18; Mic 4:1-2; Pss. Sol. 17:30-31, all of which provide indications that the restoration of Israel would be a signal of the gathering of the nations. For this understanding in John, see Jn 10:16; 11:52; 12:32.

accomplished in the mission of the church. It was no longer a future expectation therefore but a reality already in process."[90] We can agree with this view but also then ask whether Rome is in view in this eschatological understanding.

Thatcher is helpful here as he expands on this eschatological idea with specific reference to Rome. In particular he notes the absence of motifs of judgment, noting especially the absence of any judgment against the Romans. He explains, "For John, in other words, there is little need for a future act of divine vengeance against Rome, simply because *Rome has already been conquered and judged in the ministry of Jesus and the faith of his disciples.*"[91] The Gospel of John as a whole thus differs from the Gospel of Mark and from Revelation in not projecting this power reversal onto an eschatological future of judgment. Thatcher goes on, "Instead, John seeks to demonstrate that Jesus has already conquered the world, and that he did so at the very moments when he seemed the weakest."[92] Other scholars have drawn similar conclusions. For example, George R. Beasley-Murray explains that "expectation of future glory is not a theme of the prologue; rather the emphasis lies on the revelation of the glory awaited from the future made in the present."[93] And for Käsemann the prologue "bears witness to the presence of Christ . . . as the Creator of eschatological sonship to God and of the new world."[94]

Each of these scholars, approaching the prologue from different angles, helps explain the extent to which a particular vision of the future (namely, the prophetic promises of the restoration of Israel and the gathering of the nations through the work of God's agent) is already underway through the ministry of Jesus. It may also be that what I am identifying in John 1:18 as the editorial explanation and summary gives us a hint at the future dimension of eschatology as it points to the presence of Christ "at the bosom of the father" (Jn 1:18). This idea thus opens up the possibility of a return that is explicitly addressed later in the Gospel (Jn 14:3).

We can conclude that, with regard to its concern for a particular view of history that includes the remembrance of traumatic events, its emphasis on the identity of the community in contrast to its opponents, and its implications

---

[90]Ibid., 23. He adds, "In these various ways the Gospel of John recognizes the eschatological role of Jesus as the Messiah who would gather the children of God from all nations."
[91]Thatcher, *Greater Than Caesar*, 15 (emphasis original).
[92]Ibid., 40.
[93]George R. Beasley-Murray, *John*, WBC 36 (Waco, TX: Word, 1987), 17.
[94]Käsemann, "Structure and Purpose," 165.

of a positive vision of the future coming out of a belief that the eschatological revelation has already occurred, the prologue participates in many of the conventions of resistance poetry. As with other early Christian and early Jewish examples, it seemingly does not advocate any kind of physical resistance to imperial powers, but rather a conceptual resistance centered on the person of Jesus. As we will see in the following section, the prologue's connections with notions of worship strengthen this case.

WORSHIP IN THE FOURTH GOSPEL
AND THE PROLOGUE

Worship is a recurring theme in the Gospel of John, both as a point of discussion between Jesus and other characters and through narratives that involve places of worship or acts of worship.[95] Given this Gospel's explicit concern with worship, it is not surprising that the prologue to the volume touches directly on matters related to worship. To explore those touch points, we first examine briefly the primary places where worship is discussed in the Gospel of John.

The notions of worship fostered by the Gospel of John are complex and multifaceted. To begin with, the location where worship occurs is a point of obvious concern. Early on in the narrative Jesus' cleansing of the temple at the beginning of his ministry problematizes the locus of worship (Jn 2:13-22). In this scene Jesus himself is identified as the temple (Jn 2:21), picking up already on hints within the prologue, where Jesus is described in language suggestive of the tabernacle and the abiding glory of God in the temple.[96] Next, Jesus' encounter with the Samaritan woman at the well brings this issue fully into view and adds the question of the nature of true worship (Jn 4:14-42; esp. Jn 4:20-24).[97] In addition, the question of who is the appropriate object of worship is problematized as Jesus is shown to be an appropriate recipient of worship. When he is healed and later encounters Jesus, the man born blind literally

---

[95]For scholarly treatment of this theme, see Dorothy Lee, "In the Spirit of Truth: Worship and Prayer in the Gospel of John and the Early Fathers," *VC* 58 (2004): 277-97; Jerome Neyrey, "Worship in the Fourth Gospel: A Cultural Interpretation of John 14–17," *BTB* 36 (2006): 107-17.

[96]Brown, *John*, 124-25.

[97]"Jesus is speaking of the eschatological replacement of the Temple, resuming the theme of ii 13-22. In ii 21 it was Jesus himself who was to take the place of the Temple, and here it is the Spirit given by Jesus that is to animate the worship that replaces the Temple" (Brown, *John*, 180).

worships Jesus (Jn 9:1-41; esp. Jn 9:38).[98] Finally, Jesus himself is portrayed in the Gospel as a worshiper of God who also claims a unique place in the relationship between the Father and humanity. In Jesus' prayer in John 17, for example, Jesus models prayer for the community but also articulates the nature of his presence among them. As agent of God, he is the mediator of God's gifts to humanity, and he enables humans to become children of God.

The prologue itself touches on each of these aspects of worship, at least to a certain degree. First, the tabernacle imagery, related to the tent and to the glory of God, raises the issue of the location and focus of worship. Connections between the Greek verb *skenoō* and biblical passages such as Exodus 27:21, Leviticus 1:1, and Numbers 1:1 have been long noted. D. Moody Smith captures the connection with the verb *skenoō* and explains, "The very word suggests a subtle but important theme of the prologue and of the gospel, namely, that Jesus will become the place where the people will meet God, displacing the tent and its successor, the Jerusalem temple (cf. 2:19-21; 4:20-24)."[99] The glory of God is to be seen in Jesus (Jn 1:14), and Jesus is revealed to be the location and focal point of worship. This perspective is not unlike what we saw in Colossians regarding the dwelling of the fullness of God in Christ as a reference to the temple.

As we have already seen, Jesus is also the unique agent of God, the mediator of God's gifts to humanity. Along these lines there are a surprising number of connections between the prologue itself and Jesus' own prayer in John 17.[100] The prologue introduces this mediator while John 17 shows the mediator in action. Taken together both John 1 and John 17 reflect the realities of a worshiping community centered on Jesus as mediator of God's gifts.

Finally, does the prologue suggest that Jesus is the appropriate object of worship? In key places in the Gospel, a growing understanding of the identity of Jesus leads to belief in him, or in his name, and also to worship (e.g., the man born blind). Thomas's confession is the climactic expression of a clarified understanding of Jesus' identity: "My Lord and my God!" (Jn 20:28). This

---

[98]Note, however, that the explicit worshiping of Jesus in Jn 9:38 is not present in some mss traditions. Brown, *John*, 375-76. Even if not original, this verse is but one of many references to worship so that the overall argument is not undermined.

[99]D. Moody Smith, *John*, ANTC (Nashville: Abingdon, 1999), 59.

[100]John F. O'Grady, "The Prologue and Chapter 17 of the Gospel of John," in *What We Have Heard from the Beginning: The Past, Present, and Future of Johannine Studies*, ed. Tom Thatcher (Waco, TX: Baylor University Press, 2007), 215-28.

belief in Jesus is what is already espoused in the prologue. The prologue con-
stitutes a confession of Jesus as uniquely participating in the divine (Jn 1:1-2),
the source of light and life (Jn 1:3-5), revealing God's glory in his flesh (Jn 1:14),
and the source of grace and truth (Jn 1:16-17). Recognizing that other Second
Temple–period psalms embody the worshipful result that their authors
promote (e.g., Sir 39:12-35; 4Q437; Pss. Sol.), it is not a stretch to imagine that
the prologue itself reflects this same dynamic.[101] The prologue embodies the
confession of an appropriate response by one who has seen God's glory in
Jesus and become a child of God. As a hymnic confession it models for the
reader an appropriate response of worship. Even if not a preformed hymn
itself, it nevertheless reflects the kinds of acclamations of praise that were the
appropriate response of the community to the presence of the risen Jesus
among them. The prologue does not *tell* us about early Christian worship;
rather, it *invites* us into the narrative about Jesus and *models* a confessional
response to the revelation of the glory of God in Jesus.

CONCLUSION

Considering what we have seen of how hymns and hymnic texts played a role
for communities in the ancient world, we conclude with several observations.
First, for the Romans, from the kinds of examples scholars like Thatcher,
Richey, and Carter cite, and from others we have looked at in this volume,
hymns played a role in promoting a particular view of the emperor. What was
said about the emperor was significant, as was the fact that hymns were composed in his honor. From the Roman side we thus have the example of an
individual who was accorded hymnic praise that included such topics as his
divine origins, divine legitimation of his reign, and his blessings to humanity.

Second, within Judaism, we have noted the multifaceted role of psalms and
hymns for Jewish communities seeking to come to grips with their time and
place in the divine story. We have seen that psalms could function for them as
a kind of scribal resistance to claims and ideas that were in competition with the
beliefs and self-understanding of a particular community. This was true in
Qumran as well as in texts like the Wisdom of Solomon and Psalms of Solomon,

---

[101]Gordley, *Teaching Through Song in Antiquity*, 212, 214, 266. Cf. Rodney A. Werline's view of Pss.
Sol. 3 in his "The Experience of God's *Paideia* in the Psalms of Solomon," in *Experientia*, vol. 2,
Linking Text and Experience, ed. Colleen Shantz and Rodney A. Werline (Atlanta: Society of
Biblical Literature, 2012), 17-44.

where personified Wisdom or a divinely appointed messiah could be extolled for divine origins as well as for blessings given to or forthcoming for humanity.

Third, for the early Christians the situation does not seem to have been fundamentally different. We have already detected a degree of poetic resistance in both the Philippian and Colossian hymns as they portray Jesus as the one who, in unique and unmatched fashion, embodied the divine among humanity. Utilizing aspects of the rich Jewish psalm tradition, the early Christian hymns came into use in a context in which Roman imperial propaganda invited the inhabitants of the Roman Empire to see themselves as recipients of divine blessings through the emperor.

Taking these realities into account from the Roman side, the Jewish side, and the Christian side, it is not difficult to see that the Johannine prologue, whatever its origins, is also participating in these same dynamics and staking a claim in this cultural context. Accordingly, the prologue presents praise of Jesus, in exalted terms, that invites an understanding of Jesus that puts him in a position in which his role is greater than that of any other claimant on the loyalties and worship of the community. Moses and John the Baptist are named in the prologue and assume their places as witnesses to the Logos in history. The emperor is not named in the prologue, but it is clear that the author of John's Gospel numbered him as a chief member of the world that did not recognize Jesus and as part of the darkness that attempted to extinguish the light of the Logos. For all of the empire's grand claims for the emperor, he is not worthy even to be named but only to take his place in the shadow of the exalted Jesus of the Johannine prologue. Readers of John's Gospel are invited to embrace this exalted view of Jesus. As they encounter the words and works of Jesus in the Gospel narrative they are prepared by the prologue to understand that the work of Jesus as agent of God had its origins in the mythic past, before Rome, before Moses, before Abraham—"in the beginning."

– Six –

A WIDER LOOK

Philippians, Colossians, and the Gospel of John each offered us
an example of a lengthy and elaborate hymn of Christ. The scope,
content, and style of these passages allowed the conclusion that they are early
christological hymns. Whether composed by the author of the epistle or
Gospel, or a citation of an earlier composition, these passages give us a glimpse
of aspects of early Christian worship of Jesus. But these are not the only places
in the New Testament where such hymnic praise is found. In addition to the
long christological hymns of John 1:1-17, Philippians 2:6-11, and Colossians
1:15-20 there are numerous other passages that reflect some of the features of
early Christian hymnody. Taken together, these shorter passages from
throughout the New Testament help to round out the picture of the earliest
Christian hymns and show us just how important hymnic praise of Christ was
for the early Christians.

In this chapter I cast a broad net and look at a selection of other New Testament passages that reflect the features we have seen in the major hymns.
These hymns or hymn fragments come from Ephesians, 1 Timothy, Hebrews,
1 Peter, the Gospel of Luke, and Revelation. The passages in Ephesians,
1 Timothy, Hebrews, and 1 Peter are generally quite short, the explicitly hymnic
portions being as short as two lines. We will see that it is likely that they represent earlier traditions and may, in some cases, be excerpted lines from longer
hymns. The passages in Luke and Revelation are longer and appear to be
complete compositions in and of themselves. However, their incorporation
into a larger narrative framework makes it more likely that they are the

product of the authors of these larger literary works. Even so, as with the major hymns for which certainty regarding their authorship was not an option, we are on more solid ground to recognize that these hymns reflect aspects of early Christian worship even though they themselves may not be word-for-word transcriptions of actual hymns.

The functions of these texts vary, and we will explore each of them individually below. However, it is safe to say that in each case the use of a hymn, a hymn fragment, or a hymnic couplet served multiple purposes. In all cases they helped to ground the teaching of the letter or the message of the larger composition in already accepted affirmations about the person and work of Christ. By appealing to tradition or to material presented in a way that coheres with traditional formulations about Christ, the authors were able to lend weight to their own message. Further, by portraying Christ in a verbal portrait by means of hymnic language, these authors were able to engage not only the minds of their readers but also their imaginations. These hymnic passages seem to have been useful in tapping into the power of the affective dimensions of poetic discourse. Finally, in almost every case, the hymnic acclamations of Christ were not radically unique or made up from scratch. Rather each one appears to have drawn on important Jewish traditions, again lending weight to the ultimate point being made by each author by linking to wider traditions of discourse.

We begin this chapter by looking at the hymnic expressions found in the following passages: Ephesians 2:14-16; 1 Timothy 3:16; 1 Peter 3:18-22; and Hebrews 1:1-4. We turn next to the psalms that are included in the Lukan infancy narrative: the Magnificat (Lk 1:46-55), the Benedictus (Lk 1:68-79), the Gloria in excelsis (Lk 2:14), and the Nunc Dimittis (Lk 2:29-32). We then conclude with a look at the hymnic acclamation of Christ around the heavenly throne in Revelation 4–5. Without minimizing the differences between these passages, we will see that the employment of hymnic resources in these very diverse texts and contexts attests to the widespread use of hymnic praise of Christ among many early Christian groups.

EPHESIANS 2:14-16

It will come as no surprise that a letter by Paul, or at least in the Pauline tradition, would include a hymn or a hymnic section. In Ephesians 2:14-16 we find a hymnically styled passage that reflects a number of features of the kinds of hymnody we have already encountered. It has been called a hymn, part of a hymn, a "hymn of peace," a "liturgical piece,"[1] and a "christological excursus."[2] However, for a number of reasons it is not likely that this was a preexisting composition. Reinhard Deichgräber points to matters of style and the important observation that the passage requires the broader context of Ephesians 2, with its explicit identification of the two groups, in order to be fully understood.[3] In English translation, the passage reads:

> For he is our peace:
> Who has made both groups one
> and the dividing wall has broken down,
> the hostility between us, in his flesh.
> The law with its commandments and ordinances, he has abolished
> that the two he might create in himself
> into one new humanity, making peace,
> and might reconcile both groups
> in one body to God through the cross,
> putting to death that hostility through it. (Eph 2:14-16)

As for what might be considered hymnic features, we can note that, in addition to its content, which focuses on Christ and his actions including mention of the cross, there is a clear change of style from first-person plural ("he is *our* peace" in Eph 2:14a) to third-person discourse (Eph 2:14b-16). After this passage, the author returns to direct address in Ephesians 2:17 and first-person address in Ephesians 2:18. This change of address is one feature commonly used as evidence in support of the claim that a passage is a preexisting hymn. However, Deichgräber points out that this change of style (*stilwechsel*) is a feature that the author uses throughout Ephesians so that here it cannot be utilized as a definitive criterion that this is a citation of an earlier hymn.[4] Further, as already noted, apart from its context in Ephesians, the hymn does

---

[1] William Harry Rader, *The Church and Racial Hostility: A History of Interpretation of Ephesians 2, 11-22*, BGBE (Tübingen: Mohr, 1978), 196-200.

[2] Reinhard Deichgräber, *Gotteshymnus und Christushymnus in der frühen Christenheit*, SUNT 5 (Göttingen: Vandenhoeck & Ruprecht, 1967), 167. Deichgräber approves of Conzelman, who calls it a "christologischen Exkurs" that explicates Is 57:19.

[3] Ibid., 165-66.

[4] Ibid., 165-67. As we have seen, Brucker has argued that *stilwechsel* is a common feature of ancient writing, and cannot be used by itself to argue that a passage may be a preexisting unit of tradition. Ralph Brucker, *"Christushymnen" oder "epideiktische Passagen"? Studien zum Stilwechsel im Neuen Testament und seiner Umwelt*, FRLANT 176 (Göttingen: Vandenhoeck & Ruprecht, 1997).

not make sense on its own. The reference point of "the two" is not contained within the hymn but is only found within the context in Ephesians 2:11-13. These preceding verses make it clear that the two groups are Jews and Gentiles. We can safely conclude then that this is a passage with many hymnic features and hymnic style, but not necessarily a preexisting hymn.[5]

A number of phrases and concepts in this passage echo what we have already seen in other hymns. The concepts of reconciliation (Eph 2:16a) and making peace (Eph 2:15c; Eph 2:14a) have clear parallels with the Colossian hymn both on a conceptual level and on a verbal level. The use of prepositional phrases to describe the work of Christ is also noteworthy: in his flesh (Eph 2:14c), in him (Eph 2:15b; Eph 2:16b), and through the cross (Eph 2:16b). We may also note the explicit reference to the crucifixion (Eph 2:16b) in language that sounds similar to both the Colossian and Philippian hymn. The explicit mention of his flesh (Eph 2:14c) calls to mind the important phrase of the Johannine prologue: "and the Word became flesh" (Jn 1:14). We will also see the mention of "flesh" in 1 Timothy 3:16 and 1 Peter 3:18b. "One body" is reminiscent of the Colossian idea that he is the "head of the body" (Col 1:18a). That the reconciling work of Christ is done "to God" (Eph 2:16b) is reminiscent of the idea in the Philippian hymn that all that had occurred through Christ was "to the glory of God the Father" (Phil 2:12). Stylistically, the use of multiple participles (Eph 2:14b, 14c, 15a, 16c) is a hymnic feature and the fact that they are aorist participles creates an audible rhyming pattern.[6] The same verb for create (*ktizō*) was also used in Colossians (twice in Col 1:16) and is also used of God in Revelation 4:11. Other hymns that mention the idea of creation use *poieō* (Heb 1:2) or *ginomai* (Jn 1:3).

A major theme of this passage is the idea that there was enmity that needed to be overcome. A similar assumption underlies the Philippian hymn and the Johannine prologue. The Colossian hymn also refers to related ideas using similar language of peacemaking and reconciliation. While Ephesians speaks of "making peace" and the idea that he would "reconcile both groups" (*poiōn eirēnēn kai apokatallaxē tous amphoterous*), Colossians 1:20 uses a verbal form for "making peace" (*eirēnopoiēsas*) and speaks not of reconciling the two but of reconciling all things (*apokatallaxai ta panta*). Such close connections between the Colossian hymn and Ephesians 2:14-16 have led one interpreter to propose that this passage

---

[5]Deichgräber, *Gotteshymnus und Christushymnus*, 166.
[6]An even clearer example of this occurs in 1 Tim 3:16 with its series of six aorist passive verbs.

represents the missing third strophe of the two-strophe Colossian hymn.[7] In this view the first strophe focused on creation (Col 1:15-18a), the second on redemption (Col 1:18b-20), and this third one (Eph 2:14-16) on the reconciliation and unification of Jews and Gentiles in Christ in the church. Such a claim, while possible, is unprovable. Instead, it is much more likely that the tradition found in the Colossian hymn is known by this author (however one decides the two letters are related), and that the author of Ephesians is spelling out the implications of Christ's reconciling work as they apply to Jewish and Gentile believers.

There are also some ideas in Ephesians 2:14-16 that are not present in other hymns. While some assumption of conflict is not unique, the explicit mention of two hostile groups is new. Two groups may be an exegetical reflection of Exodus 21:8 and Exodus 22:20, and the entire passage has been viewed as a midrash on the synagogue lectionary readings of Exodus 21:1–22:21.[8] The notion of Christ's bringing peace might also be an indication of early Christian reflection on a passage like Isaiah 57:19.[9] New creation themes are not unknown in early Christian hymns (see Col 1:18b), but the idea of creating one new humanity out of the two groups is unique. Reference to "the law with its commandments and ordinances" (Eph 2:15) is noteworthy as an indicator of Jewish traditions being in view. However, explicit mention of the law in a hymnic context is seen only in the Johannine prologue (Jn 1:17).

The extension of the focus of hymnic acclamation to include the present experience of the church is also noteworthy. This is implied in other hymns but not explicit. For example, in Colossians Christ "is the head of the body, the church" (Col 1:18a), suggesting the present experience of the believers in Colossae. In Philippians every tongue confessing "that Jesus Christ is Lord to the glory of God the Father" (Phil 2:11) likewise points to the present experience of the community in confessing that lordship. Here the present experience of the community is in view and explicitly identified as one in which a former state of hostility has now been replaced by a state of peace and unity through the reconciling work of Christ. As we saw in the examination of Colossians, this peacemaking and reconciling was an accomplishment for which the Roman emperor was praised. Interestingly, here the Roman tool for subjugation of its enemies and the enforcement of peace among its conquered peoples, the cross, is the same tool

---

[7]Rader, *The Church and Racial Hostility*, 198, citing E. Testa's 1969 study (in Italian).
[8]Ibid., 200.
[9]Deichgräber, *Gotteshymnus und Christushymnus*, 167.

through which Christ accomplishes his peacemaking work. As with the explicit mention of the cross in the Philippian and Colossian hymns, there may be a reference to Rome's power here as well. The extent to which the Ephesians were presently experiencing the peace and unity that Christ's death had made possible, or whether this was part of the author's case for pursuing such unity, is an open question. But it is clear that the hymnic passage with its emphasis on unity has immediate application for the community (see Eph 4:3-16).

In addition to this hymnic passage, elsewhere in the letter the author of Ephesians makes use of a significant number of what might be called "traditional materials." Deichgräber, for example, considers Ephesians 1:20-23 to be reflective of an early Christian hymn as well.[10] Clinton Arnold notes the inclusion of blessings, prayer reports and thanksgivings, and confessional and liturgical materials, all of which may reflect a worship setting.[11] While I am hesitant to conclude that Ephesians 2:14-16 is a preexisting hymn in its own right, it is safe to posit a close connection between this passage and the worship activities of the early church. It is likely then reflective of the kinds of confessions and acclamations made about Christ in the church's communal gatherings. It also provides evidence of the fruits of the early Christians' reflections on the promises of the Jewish Scriptures fulfilled in Christ.

Accordingly, the following conclusions can be drawn about Ephesians 2:14-16 and early Christian worship. Early Christian worship and its hymnody centered on Christ, placed an emphasis on his incarnation and crucifixion, and maintained a clear distinction between God and Christ. In addition, early Christian worship extolled Christ as uniquely suited to be the mediator of God's blessing to all of humanity. This worship of Christ also had a focus on the very practical implications of it claims for those who gathered in his name. Finally, it included explicit engagement with Jewish motifs and traditions.

1 TIMOTHY 3:16

We turn next to another letter in the Pauline tradition, this time one of the Pastoral Epistles, to examine 1 Timothy 3:16.[12] In addition to being called a

---

[10]Ibid., 161-65.

[11]Clinton E. Arnold, *Ephesians*, Zondervan Exegetical Commentary on the New Testament (Grand Rapids: Zondervan, 2010), 55-56.

[12]On creedal expressions about Jesus in the Pastoral Epistles and their relation to earlier Pauline writings, see Larry W. Hurtado, *Lord Jesus Christ: Devotion to Jesus in Earliest Christianity* (Grand Rapids: Eerdmans, 2003), 512-18.

hymn, this short passage of eighteen words has also been called a "liturgical confessional formula,"[13] a preformed tradition,[14] a "doxological confession,"[15] and "a believer's confessional, hymnic prayer about Christ."[16] For such a short hymn, 1 Timothy 3:16 contains a surprising number of interpretive challenges. These relate to the extent of the hymn (is this a complete hymn or just a fragment of a larger hymn?), its structure (two strophes? three strophes? no strophes?), its logical development (is it chronological or does it follow some other pattern of development?), its background, and the meaning of each individual line. Here I provide a brief sketch of answers to these questions in the context of the concerns of our larger study.

In 1 Timothy 3:16 an introductory phrase precedes the hymn: "Without any doubt, the mystery of our religion is great." The hymn proper reads,

He was revealed in flesh,	(line 1)
vindicated in spirit,	(line 2)
seen by angels,	(line 3)
proclaimed among Gentiles,	(line 4)
believed in throughout the world,	(line 5)
taken up in glory.	(line 6)

In an extensive study of the use earlier traditions in 1 Timothy, Mark Yarbrough utilizes eight criteria relating to structure, content, and style to determine if a particular passage can be considered a "preformed tradition." His eight criteria (formulaic introduction or conclusion, texts that are self-contained or contextually dislocated, emphasis on central theological concepts, emphasis on parametric content, identifiable external parallels, poetic nuances, abnormal vocabulary, unusual syntactical structure) are reflective of those that have been used by scholars to make their case for preexisting hymnic materials.[17] While we noted the limitations of such criteria in chapter one, the presence of some of these features in 1 Timothy 3:16 is an observation that requires assessment. Yarbrough determines that 1 Timothy 3:16 meets

---

[13]Deborah Krause, *1 Timothy*, Readings, a New Biblical Commentary (London: T&T Clark, 2004), 79.

[14]Mark M. Yarbrough, *Paul's Utilization of Preformed Traditions in 1 Timothy: An Evaluation of the Apostle's Literary, Rhetorical, and Theological Tactics*, LNTS 417 (London: T&T Clark, 2009), 102.

[15]Krause, *1 Timothy*, 80.

[16]Jerome D. Quinn and William C. Wacker, *The First and Second Letters to Timothy: A New Translation with Notes and Commentary*, ECC (Grand Rapids: Eerdmans, 2000), 322.

[17]Yarbrough, *Paul's Utilization*, 200.

seven of the eight criteria and should therefore be considered a preformed tradition.[18] Agreeing with earlier scholars who referred to it as a hymn, Yarbrough determines that this is one of twelve citations of preformed traditions in 1 Timothy, and thus was part of a larger rhetorical and organizational strategy of the author.[19]

While some have seen this verse as a complete hymn in and of itself, others see it as just a fragment of a larger hymn. Along these lines, Jerome Quinn and William Wacker consider it "a fragment, a headless torso, and one can only surmise what a preceding (and/or following) strophe contained."[20] However, given that the focus of the hymn includes the incarnation and exaltation of Christ, and that the passage makes no reference to concepts that need to be explained by the wider epistolary context, it is possible to consider this as a complete unit. This observation will be the starting point for the present analysis.

As for its contents, this very carefully constructed hymnic composition focuses on Christ. There is a clear use of the pattern of incarnation and exaltation such as we saw in the Philippian hymn. Incarnation is clearly seen in the first line with his being manifest in the flesh. The term *flesh* is noteworthy, as the same term is used in John 1:14. Several lines suggest the theme of the exaltation of Jesus, especially "seen by angels" and "taken up in glory." In the Hebrews hymn we will see that Jesus is superior to the angels as well as the exact representation of God's glory (Heb 1:2). In John's prologue the term *glory* is also used but in a different sense: the believers were the ones who "saw his glory" (Jn 1:14). *Glory* also occurs in the Philippian hymn but is used in yet another way: all that occurred in Christ was "to the glory of God the Father" (Phil 2:11). We will also see that the exaltation of Jesus is explicit in 1 Peter 3:22 but without the use of the term *glory*. The exalted status of Jesus is also dramatically portrayed in Revelation 4–5, where he is acclaimed as worthy to receive glory (Rev 5:12, 13b).[21] First Timothy 3:16, with its emphases on incarnation and exaltation, is in good company with the other hymns we have seen and with those we will examine.

---

[18]Ibid., 95-102.

[19]The other preformed traditions are 1 Tim 1:8-10; 1:15a-b; 1:17; 2:5-6a; 3:1; 4:8; 4:9, 10b; 5:24-25; 6:7; 6:10a; 6:11-16. Ibid., 201.

[20]Quinn and Wacker, *First and Second Letters to Timothy*, 323.

[21]On the significance of giving glory to Christ and to God, see Richard Bauckham, *Jesus and the God of Israel: God Crucified and Other Studies on the New Testament's Christology of Divine Identity* (Grand Rapids: Eerdmans, 2009), 132-35.

As for other facets of the praise of Jesus in other early hymns, the resurrection may be in view with the phrase "vindicated in spirit," although this phrase is notoriously difficult to interpret. In very similar language and style (a passive verb with the dative of *pneumati*), a more explicit reference to the resurrection is found in 1 Peter 3:18, "made alive in spirit." It may be that this phrase in line two of 1 Timothy 3:16 is synonymous. That he was "believed in throughout the world" (line 5) is loosely connected with the Johannine prologue, where believing is explicitly called forth: "To as many as received him, to those who *believed* in his name, he gave the right to become children of God" (Jn 1:12). The use of aorist passive verbs is noteworthy, as is the lack of articles, both of which are indicators of poetic material.

Interestingly, Robert Gundry interprets line two to refer not to the resurrection proper but to "that vindication in spirit *prior to* the resurrection."[22] Further, he interprets line three, "seen by angels," not to refer to the exaltation of Christ but to refer to the descent of Christ to the "spirits in prison" described in 1 Peter 3:19. Gundry claims that 1 Timothy 3:16 thus follows the pattern that is present in 1 Peter 3:18-20. In his view the angels are not "the good angels around the throne" but "fallen angels" since line three describes "the sight of the vivified Christ in spirit-form by the 'spirits in prison.'"[23] His interpretation is possible because of the uniqueness of the phrasing in these lines in 1 Timothy 3:16. However, although it is supported by the presence of this tradition in 1 Peter 3:18-22, the broader scope of early Christian hymnic expressions that we have seen suggests a more natural reading as referring to the resurrection (in line 2) and the exaltation (in line 3).[24] Either way, the passage is closely connected with hymnic praise of Christ throughout the New Testament.

Structurally, there are many connections and interrelationships between the six short lines. In the first two lines we can observe an antithetical relationship between flesh and spirit. There may also be such a relationship between angels and Gentiles (lines 3 and 4) and the world and glory (lines 5 and 6). It can also be noted that three terms relate to a heavenly exalted state

---

[22]Robert H. Gundry, "The Form, Meaning and Background of the Hymn Quoted in 1 Timothy 3:16," in *Apostolic History and the Gospel: Biblical and Historical Essays Presented to F. F. Bruce on His 60th Birthday*, ed. W. Ward Gasque and Ralph P. Martin (Exeter: Paternoster, 1970), 203-22, here 214 (emphasis added).

[23]Ibid., 213-15.

[24]This is the view taken by Hurtado, *Lord Jesus Christ*, 514-15.

("spirit," "angels," "glory" in lines 2, 3, and 6) while three terms have a much more earthly focus ("flesh," "Gentiles," "world" in lines 1, 4, and 5). On a verbal level each of the six lines begins with a passive verb. The first three have a long *o* sound, the next two have a *u* sound, while the final one has an eta. The very obvious patterning here has led scholars as early as 1870 to suggest a chiastic pattern along the lines of ABBAAB.[25]

In terms of its logical development, given that the first line is a clear reference to the incarnation and that the last line suggests the ascension, it is tempting to see a chronological development in this short passage as we have seen in others (e.g., Phil 2:6-11; Jn 1:1-17). This could be plausible if the third line were to refer to Jesus' being seen by the angels during his earthly ministry.[26] Likewise, in a chronological reading the fourth and fifth lines would need to refer to belief in Jesus during his lifetime. However, this kind of chronological view is difficult to maintain since it appears that the fourth and fifth lines refer much more naturally to the proclamation of the message about Jesus by the early believers (as in Acts) rather than anything from the lifetime of Jesus. A different kind of chronological reading can be defended, however, if one sees two strophes, or two parts, to the hymn. The first strophe (lines 1-3) refers to the events of the life of Jesus, and the second strophe (lines 4-6) refers to the early church. The phrase "taken up in glory" (line 6) would then refer not to Jesus but to the raising up of the church into the realm of the divine. Ralph Martin suggests this when he explains that the hymn "shows how Christ has brought together the two spheres by His coming from the glory of the Father's presence into the world . . . and by his lifting up of humanity back again into the divine realm."[27] In this way line six could be seen as an eschatological ascent by the church, the body of which Christ is the head (cf. Eph 1:22-23; 2:16; Col 1:18a) at the parousia.

Interestingly, more so than others we have looked at, this passage includes the actions of the early Christians as part of the hymn itself: proclamation of the message about Jesus and belief in him are both included in the hymn (lines 4 and 5). The mystery (*mysterion*) referenced in the introductory phrase of 1 Timothy 3:16 thus extends beyond the essentials of Jesus' life,

---

[25]Yarbrough, *Paul's Utilization*, 100. Yarbrough cites Jamieson, Fausset, and Brown's 1870 commentary.

[26]During the temptation in the wilderness, for example. Krause, *1 Timothy*, 80.

[27]Ralph P. Martin, *Worship in the Early Church* (Grand Rapids: Eerdmans, 1974), 48-49.

death, resurrection, and exaltation to include the coming to faith of the Gentiles and the whole world. The fulfillment of the prophetic promises of the inclusion of the Gentiles in the people of God is thus part of the complex of ideas promoted in the hymn (cf. Is 19:18-25; Amos 9:11-12; Zech 14:16; Ps 45:17). In a way, this broader focus that includes the activities of the church as part of the story of Jesus can be seen to be reflective of Luke's emphasis in Luke-Acts. Deborah Krause explains, "Both the hymn and Luke's two-volume work claim that the church's activities of proclaiming the gospel and promoting belief in the whole world are a part of the redeeming work of God in Jesus Christ."[28] While the writer of 1 Timothy surely embraces those dimensions of the hymn, the focus of 1 Timothy as a whole seems to show an even further development, as it is less focused on proclaiming this gospel throughout the world and more intent on "guarding and protecting the belief of the church in the world."[29] This observation leads us briefly to consider the function of the hymn in the letter as a whole.

As for the function of the hymn in its context, it plays an important role in the author's concern to protect right belief and encourage right behavior in the church (1 Tim 3:15). This concern, evident from the beginning of the letter (see 1 Tim 1:3), is present throughout. The author desires to protect "sound teaching that conforms to the glorious gospel of the blessed God, which he entrusted to me" (1 Tim 1:10b-11). Krause explains that the hymn provided the author with "a pedagogical tool for imparting the essential elements of the faith and a means of counterbalancing and challenging those 'other teachings' that would focus simply on elements of spirit, angels, and glory."[30] In the hymn the explicit mention of flesh, the nations, and the world supports the author's efforts to challenge "elements of Gnostic belief that may be operative in the 'other' teachings he seeks to refute."[31] It is to refuting those other teachings that the letter then turns in 1 Timothy 4:1-5.

Regarding the hymn's cultural and conceptual background, some scholars have seen the background of the hymn in the schema of an enthronement ritual.[32] As seen in other texts, both biblical and extrabiblical, such a ritual includes three phases: elevation, presentation, and enthronement. Each of

---

[28]Krause, *1 Timothy*, 81.
[29]Ibid., 82.
[30]Ibid.
[31]Ibid.
[32]Deichgräber, *Gotteshymnus und Christushymnus*, 133-37.

these phases is present in this passage, to a degree. The final line remains a challenge to this approach since it would seem to be out of sequence.[33] However, line six can be seen as the resounding climax and conclusion to the hymn, recognizing the exaltation and enthronement of Christ above all. Such a view might enable us to imagine that such a claim resonates with the more political messages we have seen in other early hymns. Christ, in this view, would be portrayed in the garb of a divinely appointed world ruler and thus a challenge to those who presently hold power in the Roman world.

Not all scholars see such a framework as relevant for 1 Timothy 3:16. Gundry dismisses the enthronement ritual as the background for this passage. Instead, he notes that the couplets "successively indicate the revelation, proclamation, and reception of Christ; the pairs of antithetical nouns indicate contrasting spheres in which each of the three basic actions take place."[34] For Gundry, such a portrayal comes out of a Palestinian Jewish matrix for the original composition.[35] He shows convincingly that each line of the hymn can be read in light of Jewish traditions more readily than Hellenistic conceptions. In particular, he notes a number of biblical texts related to theophanies and to vindication, as well as to "the Enochian world of thought" including the ascensions of Enoch and Elijah.[36] Given the very different ideas that scholars see in the background of this passage, it appears that the polyvalent and allusive nature of the poetic language allows for readers to hear echoes of a number of earlier traditions.

Since part of our concern in this volume is to consider the place of these hymns within early Christian worship, we can pause briefly to consider how this hymn fits into the picture of worship put forward in 1 Timothy. Unlike Colossians or Ephesians, which mention hymn singing (Eph 3:16; Col 3:16), 1 Timothy does not. However, the author does mention "supplications, prayers, intercessions, and thanksgivings" (1 Tim 2:1) and refers to lifting up holy hands in prayer (1 Tim 2:8). He mentions food being received with thanksgiving and sanctified with prayer (1 Tim 4:4-5), as well as reading of Scripture (1 Tim 4:13). These are all features suggestive of early Christian worship. The

---

[33]Ibid., 136.

[34]Gundry, "Form, Meaning and Background," 208.

[35]Ibid., 216-22.

[36]Ibid., 221. While he does not go so far as to posit an Aramaic or Hebrew original, he believes that its being composed originally in Greek does not mean that it must be considered Hellenistic in its origins.

author also uses a worship-related term in *theosebeian*, reverence for God (1 Tim 2:10). However, the overriding concern for the author seems to be less with worship and more with preaching and teaching (1 Tim 4:13; 5:17), which accords with the letter's overall concern for right doctrine and behavior. Notoriously, 1 Timothy includes the injunction for women to dress modestly and learn "in silence and full submission" (1 Tim 2:11). It may be that such a reference in this context suggests that in some places women actually did have a voice in early Christian worship gatherings, and that the question of who had a voice remained a contested one at this time.[37] Unfortunately, the issue of the extent to which women, in particular, participated in the recitation of psalms, hymns, and spiritual songs is not addressed.[38]

Aside from the above indications, the letter is peppered throughout with liturgical-sounding materials. In addition to the hymn we are examining, there are doxologies in 1 Timothy 1:17; 6:15-16 and a confession in 1 Timothy 2:5-6.[39] Broadening the context to include the Pastoral Epistles as a whole, we see other clear indicators of liturgically shaped passages throughout these letters.[40] These features in 1 Timothy and in the Pastoral Epistles more broadly support the idea that in 1 Timothy 3:16 the author is drawing from a tradition in which the worldview of Christians is shaped by their worship.

Quinn and Wacker discuss possibilities for what might have been the liturgical setting of the use of such a creedal hymn. They conclude rightly that there is a "lack of convincing evidence for an ecclesial setting."[41] Deichgräber likewise urges caution, noting that precise settings are mere guesses rather than anything that can be proved.[42] Regardless of its possible original setting, in a letter in which correct belief and proper behavior are in view, it is not surprising that such a hymn would play an important role.

---

[37]Krause, *1 Timothy*, 8-17. Krause embraces this as showing that the issue of who had a voice in the early church was still contested at this time.

[38]Although along those lines it is noteworthy that the first song of praise in the Gospel of Luke is recited by a woman (Lk 1:46-55). On the roles of women in the early Christian movement see the important study by Ross Shepard Kraemer, *Her Share of the Blessings: Women's Religions Among Pagans, Jews and Christians in the Greco-Roman World* (New York: Oxford University Press, 1992), esp. 128-56.

[39]For analysis of all the preformed traditions in 1 Timothy, not just hymnic or confessional, see Yarbrough, *Paul's Utilization*, chap. 3.

[40]Quinn and Wacker, *First and Second Letters to Timothy*, 11.

[41]Ibid., 323.

[42]Deichgräber, *Gotteshymnus und Christushymnus*, 137.

HEBREWS 1:1-4

Hebrews 1:1-4 provides an elaborate expression of Christ's agency in creation and in redemption, a familiar pattern in early Christian hymns. This passage echoes many of the ideas and some of the features we have already seen elsewhere. Along these lines Harold Attridge notes an "implicit Christological pattern of pre-existence, incarnation, death, and exaltation."[43] However, in spite of thematic connections to other early Christian hymns it is unlikely that these four verses constitute an actual hymn that the author is quoting. Instead, much like Ephesians 2:14-16 this passage shows the marks of being carefully composed for its present context, in this case serving as an exordium for the composition as a whole.[44] Even so, we are on firm ground to notice the hymnic features of this passage and to identify its multiple connections with early Christian hymnody. The passage reads,

> Long ago God spoke to our ancestors in many and various ways by the prophets,
> but in these last days he has spoken to us by a Son, whom he appointed heir of
> all things, through whom he also created the worlds. He is the reflection of God's
> glory and the exact imprint of God's very being, and he sustains all things by his
> powerful word. When he had made purification for sins, he sat down at the right
> hand of the Majesty on high, having become as much superior to angels as the
> name he has inherited is more excellent than theirs. (Heb 1:1-4 NRSV)

Differences from and similarities with the other verses are readily apparent. Phrases like "whom he appointed heir of all things [*hon ethēken klēronomon pantōn*]" and "through whom he made the worlds [*di' hou kai epoiēsen tous aiōnas*]" illustrate this. Some familiar expressions greet the reader here. As in several other hymns we learn through the use of the preposition *dia* with a genitive pronoun what God has accomplished through him. We also learn that Christ is the agent of God in creation of all things (see Col 1:16 and Jn 1:3). In this case, however, it is the term *tous aiōnas* instead of *ta panta* to denote the worlds God created.[45] Interestingly, though, in a second reference to "all things" the author does use the term *ta panta* (Heb 1:3), and

---

[43]Harold W. Attridge, *A Commentary on the Epistle to the Hebrews*, Hermeneia (Philadelphia: Fortress, 1989), 36.

[44]Attridge notes the way these verses function as an exordium: "the exordium also prepares for the reflection on Christ's incarnation in 2:5-18" (ibid., 36).

[45]McDonough draws out the eschatological impact of this term as being particularly significant. Sean M. McDonough, *Christ as Creator: Origins of a New Testament Doctrine* (Oxford: Oxford University Press, 2009), 200-204.

Christ is also the heir of all things (*ta panta*, Heb 1:2). Hebrews also uses a verb for the act of creation that we have not seen in the earlier hymns. While we have seen *ktizein* and *ginomai* elsewhere, Hebrews uses *poiein*. The identity of the agent here is "a Son" who is both an exalted Son and heir. Both John and Colossians speak of Christ using Son terminology, though they do so using either a different noun (in John's case), or with different descriptors (in the case of Colossians). First Corinthians 8:6 indicates through parallelism that Christ is the Son, though it is not spelled out in precise terms. While there is a clear degree of resonance with this conception of the agent being God's Son in each of these passages, it must also be recognized that the forms of expression of the identity of the agent are not identical. The similarities and differences noted here suggest that these verses in Hebrews draw on a developing common framework for understanding the person and work of Jesus as God's unique agent.

Hebrews has a unique point of connection with Colossians in further indicating that the Son not only was the agent of creation, but is also God's agent in sustaining all things. The expression used in Hebrews 1:3 is *pherōn te ta panta tō rhēmati tēs dunameōs autou* (bearing all things by the word of his power). Colossians reflects on this same concept but uses a different form of expression in Colossians 1:17: *ta panta en autō synestēken* (all things hold together in him). The notions of creating and sustaining all things, and of the agency of Christ expressed in these ways, call to mind ancient philosophical discussions of divine agency. While it seems unlikely that the early Christians possessed a deep understanding of these philosophical discussions, as we saw in Colossians it does appear that some of the language they employed came not from the Old Testament but through Hellenistic Jewish speculation.[46]

As we have seen elsewhere, for early Christian authors these concepts certainly have their roots in wisdom traditions. Hebrews 1:1-4 thus appears to be connected to other early Christian hymns that espouse a wisdom Christology.[47]

---

[46]See Gregory E. Sterling, "Prepositional Metaphysics in Jewish Wisdom Speculation and Early Christological Hymns," in *Wisdom and Logos: Studies in Jewish Thought in Honor of David Winston*, ed. D. T. Runia and Gregory E. Sterling, SPhiloA 9 (Atlanta: Scholars Press, 1997), 219-38; Ronald R. Cox, *By the Same Word: Creation and Salvation in Hellenistic Judaism and Early Christianity*, BZNW 145 (Berlin: de Gruyter, 2007). Even McDonough acknowledges the Jewish Hellenistic language although he dismisses its significance in favor of Old Testament and messianic Son of God themes as being primary; see McDonough, *Christ as Creator*, 192-96.

[47]James D. G. Dunn, *Christology in the Making: A New Testament Inquiry into the Origins of the Doctrine of the Incarnation* (Grand Rapids: Eerdmans, 1996), 163-212.

The explicit mentioning of the "word" (Heb 1:3) may have several connections. Of course, God creates by God's word (Gen 1:3, 6, 9, 11, 14; Wis 9:1; Sir 42:15; Ps 32:6; 2 Pet 3:5; Heb 11:3). In addition, this idea connects with the word of the Lord as addressed to and through the prophets of old (see Heb 1:1).[48] Thus in Hebrews 1:1-4 the agent of creation is also the agent of revelation of eschatological salvation.

Overall, like other hymns, Hebrews makes a strong case that the agent of God in creation is also the agent of God in redemption. Here redemption is expressed in two ways: making purification for sins (Heb 1:3), and representing God to humanity both audibly (Heb 1:2) and visibly (Heb 1:3). According to Hebrews the Son is the one who both reveals God to humanity and cleanses people of their impurity. Attridge explains, "Here the decisive nature of God's eschatological salvific action in and through Christ is affirmed. That decisiveness is based upon the two elements which determine the whole Christology of Hebrews, the status of Christ as the exalted Son and the sacrificial, priestly act by which he effected the atonement for sin."[49] This sacrificial, priestly dimension in Hebrews goes beyond what we have seen in other hymns so far. However, this theme will become a focal point of heavenly praise in Revelation 5:9-12.

As for the revelatory dimension of the Son in Hebrews 1:1-4, we have seen that the Johannine agent of God is largely a revealer of God as well (Jn 1:18). John Meier explains, "If we grasp that the whole purpose of chapter 1 is to ground the claim that the Son is the supreme revealer-and-revelation, even the quasi-metaphysical designation in 1,3a takes on a salvation-historical function. He who is eternally the effulgence of God's glory and the image of his substance is alone the adequate revealer and content of revelation."[50] Similarly, the Colossian agent is one who reconciles God and humanity (Col 1:20), in part through the forgiveness of sins (but not in the hymn proper; see Col 1:13), but also through representing the invisible God in visible form (Col 1:15). Thus in similar though not identical ways

---

[48]Craig R. Koester, *Hebrews: A New Translation with Introduction and Commentary*, AB (New York: Doubleday, 2001), 71.

[49]Attridge, *Epistle to the Hebrews*, 36.

[50]John P. Meier, "Symmetry and Theology in the Old Testament Citations of Heb 1,5-14," *Bib* 66 (1985): 504-33. Meier cites Mary Rose D'Angelo, who makes the same connection that I have: "Such a revelation-Christology brings us very close to the position of the fourth gospel, especially John 1,18" (522 n. 57). See also John P. Meier, "Structure and Theology in Heb 1,1-14," *Bib* 66 (1985): 168-89.

the opening passage of Hebrews presents the Son as agent in God's work of creation and redemption.

While we would not want to make too much of each individual term, the choice of the term "glory" (Heb 1:3) may draw on themes associated with the visible manifestation of God in the tabernacle. The term itself is certainly common in early Christian hymnic material including John 1, Philippians 2, and 1 Timothy 3:16. Tabernacle and temple themes are clearly present in early Christian hymns as well, particularly in the Johannine prologue. The network of connected ideas within these multiple texts is perhaps what is most significant.

Hebrews 1:1-4 also strongly emphasizes the notion of superiority and supremacy, including an exaltation at the right hand of God. The superiority of Christ was a prominent feature of the Colossian hymn and of the Johannine prologue. Likewise, Philippians describes the exaltation of Christ to the highest place and the investiture of the divine name. We have seen the same emphasis in 1 Timothy 3:16 and we will see it next in 1 Peter 3:22. Here in Hebrews 1, Craig Koester has shown that the theme of Jesus' exaltation alludes to Psalm 109:1 (LXX), a classic resurrection prooftext of the earliest Christian movement.[51] This reference shows that resurrection is not mere resuscitation but "an exaltation or enthronement by which he entered fully into the life and rule of God as 'Lord.'"[52] As Koester explains, "No other early Christian writing makes such creative use of this psalm in order to make the powerful christological argument that Jesus is at once king and priest."[53]

In terms of the background of this material, Deichgräber notes some Semiticisms that could be suggestive of a Semitic background. However, he also notes that some of the language and expression has no easy background in Hebrew or Aramaic. His conclusion is that it is unlikely then that the background is to be found in a Hebrew hymn but rather the background should be sought in a Hellenistic context.[54] Such a conclusion aligns with what we have seen as indicated by the philosophical terminology used in this passage.

---

[51]Koester, *Hebrews*, 72. For allusions to this psalm in the New Testament, see Mt 22:44; 26:24; Mk 12:36; 14:62; 16:19; Luke 20:42; 22:69; Acts 2:34; Rom 8:34; 1 Cor 15:25; Eph 1:20; Col 3:1. On its use in 1 Pet 3:22 see Paul J. Achtemeier, *A Commentary on First Peter*, Hermeneia (Minneapolis: Fortress, 1996), 273. See also Donald Juel, *Messianic Exegesis: Christological Interpretation of the Old Testament in Early Christianity* (Philadelphia: Fortress, 1988), 135-50.

[52]Koester, *Hebrews*, 72.

[53]Ibid.

[54]Deichgräber, *Gotteshymnus und Christushymnus*, 137-40.

Finally, we observed initially that Hebrews 1:1-4 is better seen as an exordium in hymnic style rather than a hymn in and of itself. Some scholars have sought to view phrases or parts of the passage as fragments of an early hymn. However, the view that sees Hebrews 1:2 or Hebrews 1:3 as a hymn fragment is rendered improbable by the careful stylistic construction of the entire long passage that begins in Hebrews 1:1 and runs through Hebrews 1:4. The whole unit is a carefully constructed sentence that then connects closely with the series of Scripture quotations in the remainder of the chapter.[55] In fact, Meier has shown that the seven claims about Christ in this exordium are then supported by the seven Old Testament citations in the remainder of the chapter. The close organic connection of each phrase with its context makes it difficult to see this as a hymn or part of a hymn. More likely the elevated language and style of the opening verses of Hebrews are reflective of the author's familiarity with the hymnic language of praise and confession in the Christian community.[56] Accordingly, while reflecting to some extent a hymnic style, Hebrews 1:1-4 stands apart from the larger hymns we have explored. This passage also stands apart from a verse like 1 Corinthians 8:6, which is an acclamation that can stand on its own.

In terms of its function as an exordium, Hebrews 1:1-4 prepares the reader for what is to come. Koester summarizes this function well and is worth quoting at length:

> The opening sentence of Hebrews is a prologue to the composition that establishes the basic premises of the argument to follow. Above all, it sketches the basic mythic pattern out of which the discourse of Hebrews grows: God's Son has entered the plane of human existence (and sin) and has again been exalted. This pattern of descent and ascent (from God to humans and back to God) also defines the path of pilgrimage for the readers: they are to follow the one who has come to them back to the place that is properly his and, by gift, theirs.[57]

This pattern of descent and ascent is one we have seen already in Philippians 2 and 1 Timothy 3:16, and will also see in 1 Peter 3:18-22. Its widespread presence in hymnic praise of Christ suggests its importance as a theme in early Christian worship.

---

[55]Meier, "Structure and Theology in Heb 1:1-14."
[56]While Deichgräber refers to the text as a hymn, the hymnic features he cites should, in this particular instance, be seen as being part of the elevated style of the author who is influenced by early Christian liturgical practice. Deichgräber, *Gotteshymnus und Christushymnus*, 137-40.
[57]Koester, *Hebrews*, 74.

1 PETER 3:18-22

The possibility that there are early Christian hymn fragments embedded in 1 Peter has long been discussed. Hymnic or, more broadly, liturgical-confessional backgrounds have been proposed for 1 Peter 1:18-21; 2:21-25; 3:18-22; 5:5-9.[58] Whether they are earlier hymns or not, these statements about Christ relate closely to the main themes of the letter and support the author's discourse around suffering and hope. Paul Achtemeier explains, "His passion, death, and subsequent resurrection show the way present suffering is related to future glory, and thus provide Christians with a model for the way they are to live a faithful life in the midst of a hostile society."[59] The suffering, death, resurrection, ascension, exaltation, and subjugation of all powers to Christ all are found within 1 Peter 3:18-22 and thus make it a good place to examine the author's use of hymnic materials. At the same time, this passage has been referred to as "the most difficult passage in the entire letter."[60] This is due to its language, style, and possible use of earlier traditional material, as well as how the passage relates to the larger context. While we cannot hope to untangle all of these knots here, we can at least explore the extent to which this passage reflects what we have seen in the other New Testament christological hymns.

The scholarly reception of 1 Peter 3:18-22 as being reflective of early Christian hymnody has been mixed. Several of the phrases and expressions in the passage show a poetic style and have the kind of content that is the focus of the early christological hymns.[61] In addition, the passage seems to be a digression on the theme of suffering from 1 Peter 3:17, which the author then resumes in 1 Peter 4:1. However, the passage as a whole does not give the impression of being a unified hymn. Prose and poetic styles are intermingled as finite verbs (e.g., "Christ suffered" and "that he might bring," 1 Pet 3:18a) are combined with passive participles (e.g., "put to death" and "made manifest," 1 Pet 3:18b). Some lines address the community directly in a second-person style (e.g., "that he might bring you to God," 1 Pet 3:18a), while others describe cosmic events in a

---

[58] Achtemeier, *1 Peter*, 22. While Achtemeier allows for the possibility that 1 Pet 1:18-19 and 1 Pet 1:20-21 reflect the language of early hymns, he argues that it is not possible to extricate them from the use made of them by the author in the present context (126, 130-31). He discounts the likelihood of a preformed hymn for 1 Pet 2:21-25 (192-93).

[59] Ibid., 65. Further, "The theological logic of 1 Peter is grounded in the events of the passion of Jesus Christ: his suffering (2:21) and death (1:19) and his subsequent resurrection (1:21) and glorification (3:21)" (66). On Israel as the controlling metaphor for the Christian community, see 69-73.

[60] Ibid., 240.

[61] Ibid., 240-43.

third-person style (1 Pet 3:22).[62] Efforts to reconstruct an original hymn with the author's redactions and editorial comments have not been convincing.[63]

Given the challenges inherent in this passage, rather than examine the whole passage as a hymn, I will instead examine those lines that demonstrate a clear poetic style and that connect closely with the hymnic material we have already encountered. Those lines are 1 Peter 3:18b and 1 Peter 3:22, which I set apart below as quotations within the larger passage for emphasis:

> For Christ also suffered for sins once for all, the righteous for the unrighteous, in order to bring you to God: (1 Pet 3:18a)

> "He was put to death in the flesh, but made alive in the spirit," (1 Pet 3:18b)

> In which also he went and made a proclamation to the spirits in prison, who in former times did not obey, when God waited patiently in the days of Noah, during the building of the ark, in which a few, that is, eight persons, were saved through water. And baptism, which this prefigured, now saves you—not as a removal of dirt from the body, but as an appeal to God for a good conscience, through the resurrection of Jesus Christ, (1 Pet 3:19-21)

> "who is at the right hand of God, having gone into heaven,
> with angels, authorities, and powers made subject to him." (1 Pet 3:22)[64]

In between these hymnic lines of 1 Peter 3:18b and 1 Peter 3:22, 1 Peter 3:19-21 can be viewed as more of an instructional excursus in which the author elaborates on the phrase "made alive in the spirit" (1 Pet 3:18b) and then returns to the same theme with the phrase "through the resurrection of Jesus Christ, who" (1 Pet 3:21). Like the hymnic lines, 1 Peter 3:19-21 also certainly draws on earlier traditions; however, these verses do not necessarily reflect the features of early Christian hymns that we have seen in many other instances in the New Testament. In this approach we may agree with Achtemeier, who explained: "The best conclusion remains to see traditional elements underlying these verses, traditions that were probably familiar to the readers and hence needed only allusive reference (thus contributing to our difficulty in

---

[62]Deichgräber, *Gotteshymnus und Christushymnus*, 170-73.

[63]See Deichgräber's critique of Bultmann in ibid., 172. Boismard's proposal that an original hymn can be formed from 1 Pet 1:20; 3:18, 22; and 4:6 has not been accepted either. In addition to the critiques of Deichgräber, see C. J. A. Lash, "Fashionable Sports: Hymn-Hunting in 1 Peter," in *Studia Evangelica*, vol. 7, *Papers Presented to the Fifth International Congress on Biblical Studies*, ed. E. A. Livingstone, TUGAL 126 (Berlin: Akademie-Verlag, 1982), 293-97.

[64]Translation adapted from the NRSV.

determining their precise meaning), but whose original form must necessarily elude us."[65]

Some concepts and expressions in 1 Peter 3:18-22 we have seen elsewhere.
The contrast of "put to death in the flesh" and "made alive by the spirit" (1 Pet
3:18b) calls to mind the similar phrasing in 1 Timothy 3:16, where "flesh" and
"spirit" are at the end of their lines as dative nouns following passive verbs.
There Christ was "manifested in flesh" and "vindicated in spirit." Unlike the
interpretive challenges those phrases created, the referents in 1 Peter 3:18 are
quite clearly the crucifixion and resurrection.

The suffering of Christ is made explicit in 1 Peter 3:18. This aligns with what
we saw in Philippians 2. However, here the author in his prefatory comments
has made the claim that the suffering was "for sins" (1 Peter 3:18a), a concept
that is not mentioned in Philippians. However, as we saw in Hebrews 1:1-4,
there the work of Christ is explicitly connected with sin: "When he had made
purification for sins, he sat down at the right hand of the Majesty on high,
having become as much superior to angels as the name he has inherited is
more excellent than theirs" (Heb 1:3). Notably, creating a further connection
with Hebrews, 1 Peter 3:22 concludes with the same idea of exaltation over
angels that Hebrews does: "who is at the right hand of God, having gone into
heaven, with angels, authorities, and powers made subject to him" (1 Pet 3:22).

The hymnic lines in 1 Peter 3:22 describe the ascension and exaltation of
Christ, as well as the subjection of all things to him. Each of these elements is
seen in other places in the New Testament, as well as in other hymns. However,
the specific combination of these elements is unique to 1 Peter. For Achtemeier,
this observation "shows the extent to which the author was independent in
his use and combination of such traditions. . . . The similarities that exist are
more likely due to common use of early tradition than to such direct
borrowing."[66] As we have seen, these themes are not only part of early tradition but also part of early Christian hymnic expression.

The notion that Christ is at the right hand of God is seen in Hebrews 1:3
and Ephesians 1:20. This idea derives from early Christian interpretation of
Psalm 110:1, although the psalm is not specifically quoted here.[67] The phrase
"having gone into heaven" (1 Pet 3:22a) is not seen in any of the hymns we have

---

[65]Achtemeier, *1 Peter*, 242-43.
[66]Ibid., 273.
[67]Ibid. For more on the influence of Ps 110 in early Christianity see Juel, *Messianic Exegesis*, 135-50.

looked at, but the subjugation of powers certainly is. In addition to Hebrews 1:2-4, this subjugation is evident in Philippians 2:10-11 where all creatures, in heaven, on earth, and under the earth, bow and confess the lordship of Christ.

Although not part of the hymnic lines we are focusing on, an interesting aspect of this passage is its reference to Christ's "making a proclamation" to the spirits in prison from the days of Noah (1 Pet 3:19-20). Gundry thinks this same idea is found in 1 Timothy 3:16 in the phrase "seen by angels."[68] If so, then this passage mirrors the first half of 1 Timothy 3:16 and may perhaps be an independent expansion on the traditions represented in it. Overall, it is difficult to see that the kind of exegetical explanations developed here (i.e., connecting baptism with Noah's ark in a midrashic style) are hymnic. Accordingly, we have focused only on the lines with clear hymnic style. Nevertheless, the connection is intriguing.

Deichgräber also identifies a verse from earlier in 1 Peter as a similarly styled hymnic fragment. First Peter 1:20 reads: "He was destined before the foundation of the world, but was revealed at the end of the ages for your sake."[69] Deichgräber notes the antithetical parallelism and the contrast between the two lines, as well as the participial style, all of which is similar to 1 Peter 3:18. Again, this line also reflects aspects of other early christological hymns. We have seen the notion of preexistence in Colossians 1:15 and John 1:1-3, as well as possibly in Philippians 2:6. The revelatory dimension of Christ's advent is also something we have encountered, clearly seen in the Colossian hymn and the Johannine prologue. This revelatory dimension of the advent of Christ is also emphasized in Hebrews 1:1-4. These connections are noteworthy, but the prior life of these lines in 1 Peter 1:20 cannot be discerned with any certainty.

What do we learn about early Christian worship from this passage? First, this passage reminds us that it is not just in the Pauline epistles or in the Pauline tradition that we find these hymnic passages. They are widely represented in the New Testament. Second, though each one is unique, they are all clearly united in their focus on Christ. Third, like other passages we have seen, these hymnic lines are informed by Jewish thought. Specifically, they show a close connection to the Jewish Scriptures as scriptural themes and motifs provide a way of understanding the significance of the Christ event as part of God's larger plan of redemption. Finally, in the way this hymn is utilized in its

---

[68]Gundry, "Form, Meaning and Background," 213.
[69]Deichgräber, *Gotteshymnus und Christushymnus*, 169-70.

context, we can see a close connection between hymnic praise of Christ and practical implications for believers. In this case, the suffering and ultimate exaltation of Christ offer hope to followers of Jesus who themselves are suffering. They can be assured of ultimate vindication through the victory of Christ over all powers, whether earthly Roman political powers or hostile spiritual ones.

HYMNS IN THE LUKAN INFANCY NARRATIVE

While the hymnic acclamations we looked at above are, for the most part, fragmentary, Luke's Gospel contains complete hymns. In the first two chapters of the Gospel of Luke, four different characters respond to news of God's salvation with joyful song that sounds very much like the psalmody of the Jewish Scriptures and the words of the prophets. Like characters in biblical narratives and other early Jewish texts, they respond to good news with a psalm of praise. These four psalms are commonly referred to by their Latin names. Mary's song is the Magnificat (Lk 1:46-55), Zechariah's is the Benedictus (Lk 1:68-79), the angels' song of praise is the Gloria in excelsis (Lk 2:14), and Simeon's is the Nunc Dimittis (Lk 2:29-32). As we look at the hymns from the mouths of these characters we will notice right from the outset that the hymns themselves are a bit different from the early christological hymns in the other passages. Luke's hymns do not have their focus on Christ as much as they do on the redemptive work that God is doing in the world. In this way the hymns of the infancy narrative bring into focus that what is about to happen in the narrative through Jesus and John the Baptist is part of God's larger plan for salvation. And yet, taken as a whole, these hymns do have a lot in common with early Christian hymnody.[70]

A good deal of attention has been devoted to the form, content, background, and function of these passages over the years.[71] These passages show a close

---

[70]Notably, the hymns of Luke's Gospel were the only New Testament hymns to be preserved and collected separately as part of a larger collection of biblical odes, perhaps as early as the late second century CE. See Jennifer Knust and Tommy Wasserman, "The Biblical Odes and the Text of the Christian Bible: A Reconsideration of the Impact of Liturgical Singing on the Transmission of the Gospel of Luke," *JBL* 133 (2014): 341-65.

[71]Most recently, see Richard J. Dillon, *The Hymns of Saint Luke: Lyricism and Narrative Strategy in Luke 1–2*, CBQMS (Washington, DC: Catholic Biblical Association, 2013). Earlier influential studies include Raymond E. Brown, *The Birth of the Messiah: A Commentary on the Infancy Narratives in Matthew and Luke*, ABRL (New York: Doubleday, 1993); Mark Coleridge, *The Birth of the Lukan Narrative: Narrative as Christology in Luke 1–2*, JSNTSup 88 (Sheffield, England: JSOT Press, 1993); Stephen Farris, *The Hymns of Luke's Infancy Narratives: Their Origin, Meaning and*

connection to the tradition of declarative psalms of praise. Not only in their form but also in their content and language, they demonstrate a robust engagement with the Jewish Scriptures. As for their function, Stephen Farris has argued that they serve as "the overture which sets out certain motifs which will recur in the body of the composition."[72] As we will see, two important motifs of the hymns are the themes of promise and fulfillment and the restoration of Israel. In addition to these motifs, the hymns show an expanding focus, moving from an initial concentration on God's fulfillment of God's promise to Israel to a final focus on the idea that this divine visitation is a light for Gentiles as well.

Magnificat. The Magnificat is Mary's response to the news that she will bear a son who is to be the Savior. This psalm divides readily into two sections. The first strophe (Lk 1:46-50) includes the hymnic opening and Mary's praise for what God has done for her personally. The second strophe (Lk 1:51-55) describes God's actions of reversal in the past and present with a particular emphasis on God's fulfillment of his promise to Israel. In their content and style, these two strophes show strong connections with a number of scriptural passages, including the Song of Hannah (1 Sam 2:1-10), Psalm 97 (LXX), and a number of passages from Isaiah.[73] The text reads, in English translation:

And Mary said:
My soul magnifies the Lord
And my spirit has found joy in God my Savior,
Because he considered the humble state of his servant.
For behold, from now on all generations will consider me blessed.
Because the Mighty One performed great things for me,
And holy is his name.
And his mercy is from generation to generation to those fearing him. (Lk 1:46-50)

He performed mighty deeds with his arm,
He scattered the arrogant in the thought of their heart
He pulled down rulers from thrones

Significance, JSNTSup 9 (Sheffield: JSOT Press, 1985); Ulrike Mittmann-Richert, *Magnifikat und Benediktus: die ältesten Zeugnisse der judenchristlichen Tradition von der Geburt des Messias*, WUNT 2/90 (Tübingen: Mohr Siebeck, 1996).
[72]Farris, *Hymns*, 151.
[73]See especially Is 7:14; 9:1-6; 11:1-10, and the song of praise in Is 12:1-6. Mittmann-Richert, *Magnifikat und Benediktus*, 144-53. For an extensive list of possible allusions in the Magnificat, see Brown, *Birth of the Messiah*, 358-60.

but raised up the humble.
He filled the hungry with good things
but the rich he sent away empty
He has come to the aid of Israel his child
In remembrance of his mercy
Just as he said to our fathers,
To Abraham and to his seed forever. (Lk 1:51-55)

As we noted at the beginning of this section, there is little here that calls to mind the language and imagery of the New Testament christological hymns we have been examining. There is no mention of Jesus or of the incarnation, crucifixion, resurrection, or exaltation. However, there are some important points of contact between this psalm and the christological hymn tradition. First, there is a clear mention of the redemptive work of God. Here it is described in the language of coming to the aid of Israel his child. In the christological hymns this notion is expressed quite differently, but there is often an explicit mention of the redemptive work that God has done through Christ (e.g., Jn 1:17).

Second, the underlying idea behind this psalm is that what God is doing in Christ is a continuation of God's past deeds of redemption and is just what God had promised to do for Abraham and his descendants. Thus the life of Christ is a life of fulfillment of God's promises. The use of scripturesque language that calls to mind a number of different possible intertexts helps to support this understanding. John Nolland explains, "The Magnificat (vv. 46–55) is at times marked by specific OT allusions, but more commonly OT motifs and language are used in fresh coinage which evokes more generally the whole thought world of OT faith and declares its eschatological fulfillment, at least in principle, in God's present activity with Mary."[74]

Third, there is explicit mention of rulers being pulled down from their thrones while the humble are raised up. While Christ is not mentioned here, at least the idea of enthronement and the issue of who is the ultimate ruler are raised. Just as God has done this kind of thing in the past, so in Christ the reader of Luke's Gospel will see the same. In this way we can anticipate the political implications of the advent of Christ, aspects of which are present in the hymns in Philippians, Colossians, and John.

---

[74]John Nolland, *Luke 1–9:20*, WBC 35A (Dallas: Word, 1989), 74.

Fourth, that Mary responds to this news with a psalm of joyous praise is also significant. In this she paves the way for the joyous reception of the good news that is a theme of Luke's Gospel.[75] She also indicates through her praise that the time of eschatological visitation has arrived. The prophets promised an outpouring of joy when God began to fulfill his promises of restoration (Joel 2:26-27; Zeph 3:14-15; Zech 9:9-10; Is 66:7-11).[76] Mary's praise thus begins the joyous symphony that follows. In this respect Mary may be considered a model for early Christian worship.

Benedictus. Each of these points, which are faintly suggested by the Magnificat, are made explicit and highlighted further by the song of Zechariah. A temple priest, Zechariah lost his voice when he did not believe the angelic announcement that Elizabeth would have a son (Lk 1:5-22). After the child was born Zechariah affirmed that the child should be named John (Lk 1:63). Upon doing so, according to Luke, "Immediately his mouth was opened and his tongue freed, and he began to speak, praising God" (Lk 1:64). Luke also tells the reader that Zechariah was filled with the Holy Spirit and that he "prophesied saying" (Lk 1:67):

> Blessed be the Lord the God of Israel,
> Because he visited and brought about redemption for his people,
> And raised a horn of salvation for us
> In the house of his servant David.
> Just as he said through the mouth of his holy prophets from ages long past.
> Salvation from our enemies and from the hand of all who hate us,
> To make mercy according to our fathers
> And to remember his holy covenant,
> An oath which he swore to Abraham our father.
> To grant us, without fear, rescued from the hand of enemies,
> To serve him in holiness and righteousness
> Before him all our days. (Lk 1:68-75)

In the second strophe (Lk 1:76-79) the temporal register and focus switch to a prophecy directed to Zechariah's son John. The second strophe reads:

---

[75]Kindalee Pfremmer De Long, *Surprised by God: Praise Responses in the Narrative of Luke-Acts*, BZNW 166 (Berlin: de Gruyter, 2009), 134.

[76]See also Ps 97 LXX and songs of praise in the Isaianic birth cycle, which also share the foundational perspective that God will act decisively on behalf of his people (Is 12:1-3; Ps 97:1-3 LXX) and that this will result in joyful song and praise (Is 12:4-6; Ps 97:4-9).

And you, child, will be called a prophet of the Most High.
For you will go before the Lord to prepare his way,
To give knowledge of salvation to his people
    through the forgiveness of sins,
According to the compassionate mercy of our God
In which dawn will visit us from on high,
To shine on those in darkness and residing in the shadow of death,
To direct our feet in the way of peace. (Lk 1:76-79)

Zechariah's song highlights a number of themes: divine visitation, redemption, salvation from enemies through a Davidic ruler, fulfillment of
prophetic promises, forgiveness of sins, and light dawning from on high.
Through language reflective of biblical passages like Psalm 97 (LXX), Psalm
105, Psalm 106, Isaiah 40:3, Malachi 3:1, Zechariah 3:8, and Zechariah 6:6,
this psalm positions the births of John and Jesus as the fulfillment of God's
promises of salvation.[77] These themes resonate closely with the same kinds
of ideas expressed in a first-century-BCE collection of Jewish psalms we
have examined: the Psalms of Solomon. As we saw in chapter two, Psalms
of Solomon 17 and 18 demonstrate this same language of expectation of a
Davidic messiah in psalm-like form that can be considered as resistance
poetry. In the same vein, the songs of both Mary and Zechariah have explicit
references to political reversals that would result in deliverance and a new
political reality for the descendants of Abraham. A new theme that Zechariah introduces is the idea of light. The phrases in Luke 1:78-79 relating to
the breaking in of dawn and the giving of "light to those who sit in darkness"
call to mind the Johannine prologue and its use of the imagery of light (mentioned six times) to describe the Logos in history as well as in the incarnation (cf. Jn 1:4-9).

In addition to these themes, Zechariah's song also explicitly raises the issue
of worship. The divine rescue from their enemies will allow the people of God
to worship him without fear and to "serve [Greek: *latreuein*] him in holiness
and righteousness" (Lk 1:75). Through this phrase, Luke Timothy Johnson
points out, "Luke has thereby made the experience of Zechariah a miniature
enactment of his own canticle: God's mercy liberates the people to worship
fearlessly; Zechariah's release from muteness is expressed in praise."[78]

---

[77]See also Mittmann-Richert, *Magnifikat und Benediktus*, 144-53.
[78]Luke Timothy Johnson, *The Gospel of Luke*, SP 3 (Collegeville, MN: Liturgical Press, 1991), 47.

Zechariah himself models a worshipful response to the deliverance of God. This idea that the song itself is an enactment of the reality it describes represents a significant function of the hymn as a whole.

Gloria in excelsis. After beginning with the song of a young woman and moving on to the song of a priest, the third song in Luke's overture of praise is the song of the angels. This short, two-line acclamation follows the angelic announcement to the shepherds in Luke 2:8-12. After the birth announcement, a multitude of the heavenly host appears with the first angel. They are described as "praising God and saying" (Lk 2:13):

> Glory to God in the highest
> And upon earth peace among men with whom he is pleased. (Lk 2:14)[79]

There is nothing explicitly christological to be seen here. The idea that the glory belongs to God is seen in the final line of the Philippian hymn (Phil 2:11), and as we will see it is also a feature of the hymns in Revelation 4–5. The theme of peace is highlighted here as a specific outcome of the divine visitation, perhaps alluding to Zechariah's prophecy in Luke 1:79.[80] *Peace* is an important term in Luke's hymns: it is the final word in the Benedictus and is also used in the Nunc Dimittis. This theme of peace is also reflected in at least two early christological hymns, including Colossians 1:18b-20 and Ephesians 2:18.

Nunc Dimittis. The final hymn in Luke's overture, the Nunc Dimittis, has much in common with the other three songs.[81] In the same familiar style that echoes key passages from the Jewish Scriptures, a fourth character, Simeon, blesses God as a result of the divine visitation. According to Luke, Simeon "blessed God and said" (Lk 2:28):

> Now dismiss your servant, Master,
> According to your word, in peace.
> For my eyes have seen your salvation,
> Which you prepared before all the peoples,
> A light for revelation to the Gentiles
> And glory for your people Israel. (Lk 2:29-32)

---

[79]The translation and arrangement of this brief angelic hymn is widely debated. I read it as a bicolon following Brown, *Birth of the Messiah*, 404-5.

[80]Johnson, *Gospel of Luke*, 51.

[81]Thematically it shows two close connections with earlier songs: a focus on Israel as the people of God (see Lk 1:54, 68; 2:32), and a focus on salvation and/or God as a savior (see Lk 1:47, 68; 2:30). Michael Wolter, *Das Lukasevangelium*, HNT 5 (Tübingen: Mohr Siebeck, 2008), 138.

Peace, salvation, fulfillment, and glory are all ideas that have been introduced previously. Even the concept of a "light for revelation" (Lk 2:32) has
been introduced in the Benedictus. However, here for the first time, the idea
that this light is not just for Israel but extends to the Gentiles is explicitly
spelled out. Looking back at the other songs, the song of the angels may be
interpreted to include the Gentiles. In addition, the light dawning on "those
in darkness and residing in the shadow of death" (Lk 1:78-79) in Zechariah's
song could conceivably include Gentiles. However, what was only hinted at
earlier is now made explicit by Simeon. Like the theme of fulfillment, the inclusion of the Gentiles in the salvation plan of God is another theme that is
echoed in the final verses of Luke's Gospel (Lk 24:47). It is also echoed
throughout the entire two-volume work and is prominent in the concluding
verses of Acts (see Acts 28:28).[82] We have seen this in the early christological
hymns as well. For example, 1 Timothy 3:16 and Ephesians 2:18-22 both explicitly include the Gentiles, while Colossians 1:15-20 includes the reconciliation of all things. Philippians 2:6-11 includes a vision of universal acknowledgment of the lordship of Jesus by all beings.

The collective impact of Luke's hymns. Taken together, these hymns play
some important roles in the overall strategy of these opening chapters of
Luke's Gospel. More than just supplying the interpretation to the narrative,
however, the hymns are also an important part of the narrative itself. Kindalee
Pfremmer De Long has noted several interrelated functions of the hymns of
the infancy narratives. First, as they interpret the narrative for the reader, they
invite the reader to embrace the view held by the characters: that the events
in the narrative represent the divine visitation. Second, they describe this
visitation and restoration using scriptural language. This kind of language
connects the narrative that follows with the world of the earlier biblical narratives, suggesting a continuity rather than a disjuncture. Third, as suggested
above, the presence of these psalms in the narrative fulfills scriptural expectations that praise would break forth at the dawn of the time of restoration. In
other words, as De Long succinctly points out, "Praise in the infancy narrative
asserts that the divine visitation has begun."[83] Thus the songs of Luke's infancy

---

[82]Ibid., 138-41. For Luke's purposes, Wolter notes that this verse "makes clear that the post-Easter
Gentile mission is already from the beginning a firm component of the realization of the salvation work of God among humanity" (141). Wolter notes that what Simeon knew will later be
revealed to the Roman Jews in Acts 28:28 (141).

[83]De Long, *Surprised by God*, 179.

narrative both show and tell the reader some very important information about the account that follows.

As we noted briefly, these hymns also strike some overtones of a resistant response to the prevailing Roman imperial ideology. At the very least they strike notes of divine reversal (the Magnificat), deliverance from enemies (the Benedictus), peace (the Gloria in excelsis), and blessings for Gentiles and Jews alike (the Nunc Dimittis). The significance of these connections with the broader political context of the Roman Empire is debated. However, in addition to the hymns themselves, the surrounding narrative in which they are included also strongly conveys a political and social message in addition to a religious one.[84] Citing numerous examples of Roman propaganda, Mark Wegener concludes that the kinds of imagery and terminology used in Luke 1–2 echoed the political rhetoric of the Roman era. He explains that, as literate readers, "[Luke's] first audience would have known they were reading a political manifesto couched in the rhetoric of traditional images. In all likelihood, they would have heard it as a subversive political tract."[85] Further, when considered in the larger context of early christological hymns that portray Christ in exalted language ordinarily ascribed to the emperor, the political implications of the hymns of the infancy narrative for first-century readers of Luke's Gospel should not be dismissed. Where modern readers would encounter these hymns as primarily (or exclusively) religious in nature, our awareness of first-century imperial rhetoric invites us to hear a broader message with political implications as well.

In terms of the connections of Luke's hymns with the more explicitly christological hymns of the New Testament, the findings are somewhat mixed. Missing from these hymns are some of the primary features of the christological hymns: a focus on Christ, his preexistence, the incarnation, the death of Christ, the cross, the resurrection, the ascension, the exaltation, and universal worship. Granted, most of these missing elements are included as features in Luke's narrative, so it is not necessarily a lack of interest in these dimensions that explains their omission from these psalms. Rather than recount the salient contents of the life, death, and resurrection of Christ, these four psalms portray the responses of a range of devout characters to the news that the time of redemption has begun. In common with the christological

---

[84]Mark I. Wegener, "The Arrival of Jesus as a Politically Subversive Event According to Luke 1–2," *CurTM* 44, no. 1 (2017): 15-23.
[85]Ibid., 23.

hymns, however, is an emphasis on the birth of Christ as signaling the initiation of the new age in which God fulfills the expectations of the prophets. Specific touch points with the early Christian hymns are the idea that Christ brings about peace, that his advent enlightens humanity, and that Gentiles and Jews alike are included as beneficiaries of God's actions in Christ. One final point of connection is the idea that God's redemptive activities in and through Christ result in glory to God. Turning to Revelation, we will see that this final point is of particular emphasis.

HYMNS IN REVELATION 4–5

The hymns, doxologies, and acclamations in Revelation are a diverse collection of praise and prophetic announcements found in sixteen passages.[86] According to Josephine Massyngbaerde Ford, "The hymns carry the 'story line' of the Apocalypse, and through them the work gradually moves into a crescendo and reaches a climax which becomes the proclamation of the establishment of the kingdom of God and the enthronement of the Lamb."[87] Since our study focuses on christological hymns, we will confine our analysis to Revelation 4–5, a pivotal passage that describes a scene in which Christ is the recipient of worship alongside God. The hymns of Revelation 4–5 thus have the clearest christological orientation of any in Revelation. While praise of the Lamb may be assumed in other passages, in Revelation 4–5 the scope of worship widens to include praise of both the one seated on the throne and the Lamb. Indeed, the idea that the Lamb is worthy of the same worship accorded to God is a primary point of the passage.[88]

A great deal has been written about the hymns in Revelation from a number of perspectives. One important line of investigation has been the extent to which these hymns reflect the practices of early Christian worship.[89]

---

[86]Klaus-Peter Jörns identified sixteen passages within the narrative vision descriptions of Revelation that are generally accepted as hymnic. Klaus-Peter Jörns, *Das hymnische Evangelium: Untersuchungen z. Aufbau, Funktion u. Herkunft d. hymnischen Stücke in d. Johannesoffenbarung,* SNT 5 (Gütersloh: Mohn, 1971), 19. By combining several of these and adding two more passages, Josephine Massyngbaerde Ford identified ten sections of Revelation that could be considered hymnic. These included: Rev 4:8b-11; 5:9-10, 12, 13b; 7:10, 12, 15-17; 11:15, 17-18; 12:10-12; 14:3-5; 15:3-4; 16:5-7; 18:2-3, 4-8, 10, 14, 16, 19-23; 19:1-8. See Josephine Massyngbaerde Ford, "The Christological Function of the Hymns in the Apocalypse of John," *AUSS* 56 (1998): 207-29.

[87]Ford, "Christological Function," 208.

[88]Bauckham, *Jesus and the God of Israel,* 141-42.

[89]Deichgräber, *Gotteshymnus und Christushymnus,* 44-59; Lucetta Mowry, "Revelation 4–5 and Early Christian Liturgical Usage," *JBL* 71 (1952): 75-84; John J. O'Rourke, "The Hymns of the

Although attempts to discover the elements of an early Christian liturgy underlying Revelation have not been persuasive, it is still highly likely that Revelation reflects the kinds of worship practices that were occurring in the early church. Further, whether these hymns are preexisting materials or freshly composed by the author is another question. Here we will follow David Aune's view that these passages are likely not taken over from the early church's liturgical practice, though they are certainly reflective of early Christian worship practices. Accordingly, the author is not quoting early Christian sources, but rather crafting these expressions of praise according to the custom of early Christians for the purposes of his larger composition.[90] In addition to these questions, others have explored the ways in which the hymns function in the narrative.[91] The role of these hymns is increasingly being explored with regard to their rhetorical function and the impact that the rhetoric has on the reader.[92] In my own earlier investigation of Revelation 4–5 I considered the ways in which these hymns might be understood as didactic hymns.[93] I argued that they played a significant role in constructing a compelling portrait of ultimate reality, which is a major aim of the Apocalypse as a whole. This social imaginary was in close dialogue with Jewish visions of God's ultimate purposes for the world. It was also in implicit conversation and even dispute with the Roman imperial vision of reality. Along these lines Brian Blount refers to the hymns of Revelation as "a celebration of confrontational resistance."[94]

Apocalypse," *CBQ* 30 (1968): 399-409. The question of the extent to which the hymns of the Apocalypse reflect an early Christian liturgy are addressed most recently in Ardea Russo, "Behind the Heavenly Door: Earthly Liturgy and Heavenly Worship in the Apocalypse of John" (PhD diss., University of Notre Dame, 2009), 39-102.

[90]David E. Aune, *Revelation 1–5*, WBC 52a (Dallas: Word, 1997), 315-17; Russo, "Behind the Heavenly Door," 101-2.

[91]For a review of scholarship on how these chapters fit into the larger context of Revelation, see Russell S. Morton, *One upon the Throne and the Lamb: A Tradition Historical/Theological Analysis of Revelation 4–5* (New York: Peter Lang, 2007), 39-82. For their function as hymns in light of the function of tragic choral lyric, see Justin Jeffcoat Schedtler, *A Heavenly Chorus: The Dramatic Function of Revelation's Hymns*, WUNT 2/381 (Tübingen: Mohr Siebeck, 2014).

[92]Robyn J. Whitaker, *Ekphrasis, Vision, and Persuasion in the Book of Revelation*, WUNT 2/410 (Tübingen: Mohr Siebeck); David A. deSilva, *Seeing Things John's Way: The Rhetoric of the Book of Revelation* (Louisville, KY: Westminster John Knox, 2009).

[93]Matthew E. Gordley, *Teaching Through Song in Antiquity: Didactic Hymnody Among Greeks, Romans, Jews and Christians*, WUNT 2/331 (Tübingen: Mohr Siebeck, 2011), 335-47.

[94]Brian K. Blount, *Revelation: A Commentary*, NTL (Louisville, KY: Westminster John Knox, 2009), 98.

The extent to which Revelation engages Roman imperial realities has been extensively discussed.[95] That the false worship of the emperor is in view, however, is made clear by references later in Revelation.[96] Larry Hurtado explains that a major emphasis of the author was "to urge perseverance in faith among the intended readers" demonstrated by renouncing idolatry and being willing to die rather than "participate in the ungodly and cruel system of political and economic power this figure [the beast] represents."[97] Recently, however, Steven Grabiner has proposed that efforts to read Revelation in its Roman imperial context have fostered an undervaluing of the extent to which Revelation actually focuses on a larger cosmic conflict.[98] However, Grabiner's emphasis on the cosmic conflict causes him to overlook the importance of the actual conflict occurring on the ground for believers in Jesus in Asia Minor. David deSilva's approach is much more helpful in appreciating the ways in which the author addresses the Roman imperial context of the Christians in Asia Minor. After reviewing the evidence for the ways in which the Roman imperial ideology and its manifestations in Asia Minor shaped people's lives, deSilva explains, "Roman imperialism, with its seductive economy and blasphemous imperial cult, is the main challenge John identifies in Revelation 4–22."[99] Pointing readers to the ultimate victory of God in the cosmic conflict is thus part of a strategy for helping readers negotiate their earthly context.

An important recognition deSilva makes in this regard is the way in which the author makes his case in Revelation. His primary mode of argumentation is not through a treatise or epistle but rather through narrative demonstration and graphic depiction. DeSilva explains the way this works for readers: "As they engage the vision, they are positioned to examine their current situation and possible courses of action in light of the standard deliberative topics explored in the previous chapters [i.e., the letters to the seven churches]. The explicit argumentation and appeals to emotion are all embedded within this

---

[95]See the discussion of the way that Revelation "though passionately resistant to Roman imperial ideology, paradoxically and persistently reinscribes its terms" in Stephen D. Moore, "The Revelation to John," in *A Postcolonial Commentary on the New Testament Writings*, ed. Fernando F. Segovia and R. S. Sugirtharajah, The Bible and Postcolonialism 13 (London: T&T Clark, 2007), 436-55, here 451-52.

[96]Cf. the description of the worship of the beast in Rev 13, especially Rev 13:4, 8.

[97]Hurtado, *Lord Jesus Christ*, 590.

[98]Steven Grabiner, *Revelation's Hymns: Commentary on the Cosmic Conflict*, LNTS 511 (New York: Bloomsbury T&T Clark, 2015).

[99]DeSilva, *Seeing Things John's Way*, 48.

narrative demonstration."[100] One might say that the author makes effective use of an emotionally charged narrative strategy to persuade readers to accept the claims he is making.

In this regard, the mode of persuasion in Revelation is similar to what we have seen in the christological hymns: "Rational persuasion is more allusive and associative than overtly argumentative, more experiential than explicated."[101] The singing of hymns by the various characters, and the content of these hymns are a significant part of this narrative demonstration. The author depicts the kinds of activities in which the audience can also participate in their own way as part of the Christian worshiping community. In this and other ways the hymns of Revelation 4–5, and of the entire Apocalypse, could have played an important role in the process of communal formation for an early Christian community in Roman Asia. While keeping such didactic functions in mind, here we explore these poetic passages for the ways in which they reflect what we have encountered in the other christological hymns of the New Testament.

The five discrete hymnic passages of Revelation 4–5 are (1) the trisagion (Rev 4:8b); (2) a second-person acclamation of God's worthiness (Rev 4:11); (3) a second-person acclamation of the Lamb's worthiness (Rev 5:9); (4) a third-person acclamation of the Lamb's worthiness (Rev 5:12); and (5) a doxology (Rev 5:13b). We will see that, despite their difference in presentation, the hymns in Revelation 4–5 exhibit many of the features of earlier christological hymns. Specifically, they include a focus on creation (Rev 4:11b); explicit mention of the death of Christ (Rev 5:9, 12); the redemptive work of God through Christ (Rev 5:9-10); emphasis on "all things" and other expansive phrases (Rev 4:11; 5:9-10, 12); a very close association of Christ with God (Rev 5:13b); mention of the supremacy of Christ; and explicit inclusion of the Gentiles in the people of God (Rev 5:9). In addition to these matters of content, the hymns in Revelation 4–5 participate in the broader project of going beyond rational or logical claims about Christ to include persuasion through affective, nonrational means. Furthermore, like the early christological hymns, these passages demonstrate deep connections with Jewish scriptural traditions in describing the work of God through Christ.

After citing the five praise passages, we will look more closely at the contents of these hymns. For clarity I include in italics an indication of who is reciting the particular hymn.

---

[100]Ibid., 296.
[101]Ibid., 295.

The four living creatures:
Holy, Holy, Holy Lord God Almighty,
the one who was and who is and who is to come. (Rev 4:8b)

The twenty-four elders:
You are worthy, our Lord and our God,
to receive the glory and the honor and the power,
for you created all things,
and according to your will they exist and were created. (Rev 4:11)

The twenty-four elders and the four living creatures:
You are worthy to take the book and to open its seals,
for you were slain and purchased for God by your blood
those from every tribe and tongue and people and ethnic group,
and made them a kingdom and priests to our God,
and they will rule upon the earth. (Rev 5:9-10)

Myriads and myriads of angels:
Worthy is the Lamb that was slain
to receive the power and wealth and wisdom
and strength and honor and glory and blessing. (Rev 5:12)

Every creature everywhere:
To the one seated upon the throne and to the Lamb
be the blessing and the honor and the glory and the power forever and ever.
        (Rev 5:13b)

The two instances of praise in Revelation 4 (Rev 4:8b and Rev 4:11) are very clearly tied to Jewish expressions of praise of God found in the Old Testament. The connections of each of these phrases with earlier Jewish literature have been widely discussed.[102] The first line of the two-line hymn in Revelation 4:8b reflects Isaiah 6:3, and the second line reflects Jewish exegetical traditions relating to Exodus 3:14 and Deuteronomy 32:39.[103] Without going into detail, it is important to note for our purposes that the heavenly worship begins in a way that is vitally connected with the language and thought of Second Temple Jewish theology. The change in style from third-person description in Revelation 4:8b to second person (direct address) in Revelation 4:11 is noteworthy. As we have seen, the early christological hymns are primarily third-person

---

[102]Jörns, *Das hymnische Evangelium*, 24-31. See also Aune, *Revelation 1–5*, 302-7.
[103]Jörns, *Das hymnische Evangelium*, 26-27.

compositions. Second-person acclamations are rare in the New Testament but do occur frequently in the Didache.[104] In addition, as I have already noted, the emphasis on creation is a feature of early Christian hymns (Jn 1:1-3; Col 1:15-16; Heb 1:1-4). The hymns in Revelation 4, however, have their focus solely on God, with no mention of an agent or mediator, as we saw in other christological hymns. This lack of ascription to Christ of agency in creation raises the question as to what the particular emphasis of these hymns will be. We will see below that the focus is on Christ as the Lamb that was slain.

While the hymnic praise in Revelation 4 directs the focus of the reader to God as the center of all things, the focus of the hymns in Revelation 5 is quite different. The four living creatures and the twenty-four elders together "sing a new song" (Rev 5:9). This new song (*ōdēn kainēn*) is explicitly directed to the Lamb in second-person address, just as the previous song was addressed to God. Just as God was declared worthy, so the Lamb is declared worthy. While God was worthy to receive honorific acclamations due to his role in creation, the Lamb is worthy to inaugurate the final judgment (i.e., take the book and open its seals) due to his sacrificial and redemptive death. The mention of "by your blood" (Rev 5:9) is noteworthy, as we saw a similar expression in Colossians 1:20. This hymn thus focuses on the death of Christ and specifically its redemptive function.[105] Hurtado explains, "The designation of Jesus as the Lamb reflects the author's emphasis on Jesus' sacrificial death as the key event that both secured the redemption of the elect and also serves as the model for their own commitment."[106] Christ's sacrificial death enables people from throughout the world to become a part of the kingdom of God. Here we can call to mind the universal dimension we saw in the Nunc Dimittis in Luke 2:29-32, discussed above. In this emphasis on the universal scope of God's redemptive work in Christ we also see some language potentially at odds with a Roman imperial perspective. The Roman emperor was thought to be the one to take individuals from throughout the

---

[104]Cf. Did. 8.2; 9.3-4; 10.2, 4-5. For a fuller discussion of connections with early Jewish and Christian writings, see Jörns, *Das hymnische Evangelium*, 34-37.

[105]Interestingly, Christ's work is described in both past and future tenses in language that has been described as "liturgical prose." He was slain, purchased people, and made them a kingdom and priests. This much is accomplished already. Still to come is the future aspect of this redemption: they will rule on the earth. This brief hymn thus taps into a multitude of temporal registers as did the hymns of Rev 4. In this way it reminds us of the mixed message about a realized eschatology versus a hope for the future as seen in several of the hymns we explored.

[106]Hurtado, *Lord Jesus Christ*, 592

known world and to civilize them and enable them to be full participants in the new world order.[107]

The fourth song in Revelation 4–5 features an expanded choir, which now includes the voices of many angels numbering "myriads of myriads and thousands of thousands" (Rev 5:11). Like the third song, this one is also focused on the Lamb, but this time in the third person rather than in the second person. The acclamations to the Lamb echo the acclamations to God in Revelation 4:11, especially power, honor, and glory. In addition, this song adds other acclamations, including wealth, wisdom, strength, and blessing. Such an expansion of praise attributes has the effect of indicating that the Lamb is truly and fully worthy, just as the one on the throne was.[108]

The fifth and final song, Revelation 5:13b, represents the climax of the chapter and is the most intriguing of all. In it the Lamb and "the one seated upon the throne" together receive worship, this time not just from the four living creatures or the twenty-four elders, but from "every creature in heaven and on earth and under the earth and in the sea" (Rev 5:13). In this sense we find a clear echo of the confession of the lordship of Christ in Philippians 2:6-11 by every tongue "in heaven, on earth, and under the earth." Honor and glory are ascribed to both and are picked up from Revelation 4:11 (where they are ascribed to God) and Revelation 5:12 (where they are ascribed to the Lamb). Blessing is again included, also picked up from Revelation 5:12. This short doxology adds one new element to what has already been said: power (*kratos*).[109] The final praises of Revelation 5 take the focus that has already been established and extend it into the eternal future by adding "forever and ever." The ultimate response to this acclamation of praise is a verbal "amen" from the four living beings (Rev 5:14) and a physical act of falling and worshiping by the elders. According to Hurtado, "It would be difficult to imagine a more direct and forceful way to express Jesus' divine status."[110] The appropriateness of the worship of Christ alongside God on the throne is thus reinforced verbally and physically by the description of this scene of heavenly worship.

In Revelation 4–5, then, we are introduced to heavenly worship of God that expands from four living creatures around the throne to include every

---

[107]Philo, *Legat.* 147.

[108]Bauckham, *Jesus and the God of Israel*, 178-79.

[109]Jörns, *Das hymnische Evangelium*, 55. The praise of God in Rev 4:11 and of the Lamb in Rev 5:12 uses the term *dynamis* rather than *kratos*. Cf. 1 Tim 6:16; 1 Pet 4:11; 5:11; Rev 1:6.

[110]Hurtado, *Lord Jesus Christ*, 592-93.

creature everywhere. We are also introduced to worship that expands its focus to include not only God but also the Lamb, and concludes in praise of God and the Lamb together in what amounts to a Christology of divine identity.[111] Further, as we saw in the hymns themselves, temporally the focus of worship extends from the distant past of creation, to the recent past of the death of Christ and redemption, to the present and future of the redeemed, to the eternal worship of God and the Lamb. Interestingly, as Steven Friesen notes, "John did not attempt to work out the relationship between the Lamb and the One on the throne through discussions of ontology or through abstract reasoning. His vision report works through the logic of worship and of apocalyptic symbol."[112] In this light, the strategic inclusion of hymnic praise is one means that John uses to paint a vision of past, present, and future in which the Christians of Asia Minor can locate themselves, form their communal identity, and live accordingly as worshipers of God and the Lamb.

To what extent does this vision connect with early christological hymns and their place in early Christian worship? The hymns in Revelation clearly share some key ideas and reinforce much of what we have seen reflected in early Christian hymnody. First of all, they promote the primacy of God the creator as reflective of the worship of God in the Jewish Scriptures. Second, they remember Christ specifically for his death on the cross ("the Lamb that was slain"). Significantly, this death was remembered as a redemptive act that benefits all humanity regardless of ethnicity. Third, though not narrated in the hymns, the exaltation of Christ is graphically portrayed through the overall narrative in which the hymns play a role. Fourth, like many hymns, these together suggest a hopeful future; in this case a future in which those redeemed by the Lamb rule the earth. This idea may be part of a larger counter-discourse in Revelation that resists the ultimacy of Rome or any human empire, but as we have seen it is also at play to some degree in other hymnic praises of Christ as supreme. Finally, the giving of honor, blessing, glory, and power by all creatures everywhere is a reflection of the kind of worship that the author promotes. As Hurtado explains, "The elaborate description of worship in Revelation 5 surely was intended to reinforce in the strongest terms

---

[111]Bauckham, *Jesus and the God of Israel*, 178-79.

[112]Steven J. Friesen, *Imperial Cults and the Apocalypse of John: Reading Revelation in the Ruins* (New York: Oxford University Press, 2001), 198.

the early Christian practice of including Jesus with God as recipients of worship on earth."[113] In its own unique way, then, the hymns around the throne in Revelation 4–5 provide a powerful encore and fitting conclusion to the symphony of christological hymns in the New Testament.

CONCLUSIONS

The psalms, hymns, hymn fragments, and hymnic lines we have examined in this chapter are remarkably diverse. They come from many different authors and stem from multiple early Christian traditions (i.e., Pauline, Petrine, Lukan, and Johannine). They also are found in multiple literary contexts, playing important roles in epistles, as well as in a Gospel and an apocalypse. At the same time, in spite of this diversity their contents and themes are surprisingly consistent. The hymns and lines that are explicitly christological have their focus on one or more of the following: the incarnation, the death of Christ, the resurrection, the exaltation, and the ultimate subjection of all things to the authority of Christ. A number of these passages also include an emphasis on the results of these activities in terms of redemption and its significance for all of humanity. In all but the Lukan hymns, the hymns are used in contexts that draw practical implications from the hymns for the audience. Ephesians 2:14-16 is utilized to urge the fostering of unity between Jews and Gentiles who are following Jesus. First Timothy 3:16 is used to help promote adherence to sound teaching and to combat false teaching that may have undervalued the earthly, physical aspects of Christ's work. Hebrews 1:1-4 is used to prepare the reader for what follows as it sets out a pattern of descent and ascent that will also mark the lives of those who follow the exalted Son. In 1 Peter 3:18-22 the example of Christ in his suffering and his ultimate victory are used to encourage those who are suffering that they too will be vindicated. The hymns in Revelation 4–5 model appropriate worship of God and the Lamb in a larger visionary context in which true versus false worship is at issue. And while Luke's hymns do not have a hortatory application, nevertheless through their modeling of a joyous response to the birth of Jesus and through their portrayal of Christ's advent in terms of the fulfillment of the prophetic promises of renewal and reversal, they encourage the reader to adopt the same view of the events about which they are reading.

---

[113]Hurtado, *Lord Jesus Christ*, 593.

Finally, though we are not able in every case to make a direct connection to these passages as hymns that were utilized in the worship gatherings of the early Christians, it is nevertheless highly likely that the language used in these passages is reflective of the practices of the worshiping communities. While being careful not to overstate this, we must also not overlook the clear patterns of connection that are present. Even if the authors are not quoting preexisting hymns, their compositions seem to reflect already accepted traditions about Christ that are expressed in the kind of hymnic conventions with which their audiences were familiar. Further, some of these passages became influential in the early church's worship in a very short time.[114] As we listen to them with an ear for what they tell us about early Christian worship, we may be hearing echoes of the earliest hymnic praise of Jesus.

---

[114]As noted by Knust and Wasserman, "Biblical Odes," 344.

CONCLUSION

$\mathcal{T}$ his exploration of the hymnic praise of Christ in the New Testament has taken us from the letters of Paul to the Gospel of Luke, from Hebrews to the Pastoral Epistles, and from the Gospel of John to the Apocalypse. We have seen the rich diversity in these expressions of praise while at the same time noting similarities and common threads running between many of these passages. We have also seen the ways in which many of these passages show connections to Jewish traditions as well as to conventions and ideas associated with contemporary Greco-Roman culture. We have certainly seen that these individual passages did not exist in a vacuum but were part of a larger tapestry of ancient ways of reflecting on ultimate reality through hymnic compositions. We are now in a position to reflect on all that we have seen and to draw some final conclusions.

RETRACING THE STEPS OF OUR JOURNEY

At the outset of this study it was necessary to address a significant challenge. While the recognition and study of early christological hymns has been a feature of New Testament scholarship for over a century, we saw that recent decades have seen an increased skepticism about the methodologies utilized and the results obtained. As we explored the writings of scholars critical of the "hymn-hunting" enterprise, it became clear that a major difficulty was the conflating of two distinct issues: recognition of hymnic features and the identification of preexisting materials. Specifically, the common claim that some or all of these New Testament christological texts may represent preexisting

materials that have been adapted to their present epistolary or literary contexts has been challenged as methodologically problematic. The criteria used
to make those determinations, many of which are based on actual observable
features in the text, do not necessarily lead to the conclusion that these texts
were preexisting materials. The features can be interpreted in other ways, including leading to a conclusion that these passages are a reflection of the
creativity and rhetorical skill of the writer, who may simply be reflecting the
kinds of claims made about Christ in worship contexts. In response to this
line of critique, we had to agree with critics that the attempt to identify preexisting material, and from it to then reconstruct an original hymn, is often
speculative to a significant degree. Further, from that starting point, drawing
conclusions about early Christian worship from a reconstructed early hymn
would then be all the more speculative. In light of these methodological
concerns, the approach in this volume has been to focus less on the question
of whether these passages are preexisting materials, and more on the question of
the extent to which the passages under consideration demonstrate observable
features that connect them with the conventions of Greco-Roman hymnody
and Jewish psalmody. My claim is that the features which unite these passages,
across all of their diversity, justify considering them collectively as early christological hymns. Further, following such an approach these passages can still
inform us about early Christian worship: either they were hymns themselves
or, if not actual hymns, they are at least reflective of the language and practice
of early Christian hymnody.

With that broader approach in view we then examined in chapter two some
important evidence about hymns in antiquity in both Greco-Roman and
Jewish contexts. From literary descriptions of ancient worship practices,
whether Jewish, Greek, or Roman; from inscriptional evidence; from ancient
writers who discuss hymns in terms of their rhetoric, style, and content; as
well as from individual hymns, hymns embedded in other genres, and from
collections of hymns preserved from the ancient world, it is clear that hymnody
was a widespread phenomenon in antiquity. In widely diverse settings and
contexts, we saw that poets utilized hymns to praise the divine, whether gods
or divinized rulers, and to invite their audiences into an encounter with ultimate reality through their lyrics. Through the choice of their subject matter
and its relationship to inherited traditions as well as to the present experiences
of their communities, ancient poets and hymnographers helped shape their

audiences' understanding of reality, promoting a way of seeing their place within the larger world as well as suggesting what was (or should be) of ultimate value to the community. The content of hymns joined with their elevated style to create a kind of discourse that had the ability to engage its hearers' minds as well as their emotions. Whether the hymns were in praise of Asclepius, the emperor, or divine Wisdom, they helped shape a worldview for their hearers. With this understanding of key features of the ancient context of early Christian worship, we then turned to analysis of the hymnic materials of the New Testament.

In the Philippian hymn we encountered several key aspects of the developing tradition of christological hymns. The hymn emphasizes Christ and, in particular, his humiliation and exaltation, which are couched in phrases and terms that evoke Jewish scriptural motifs. The explicit mention of the cross, a Roman tool for the subjection of Rome's enemies, is the focal point and a turning point of the hymn. Christ is exalted, invested with the divine name, and given worship and homage by all creatures, all of this culminating in the acclamation "Jesus Christ is Lord" (Phil 2:11). The action of the hymn occurs entirely within the framework of glory being given to God (Phil 2:11). Finally, with its focus on remembering Christ in this particular way, we noted that the hymn supported a set of beliefs, values, and practices that gave the Philippian believers the resources necessary to enact a spirituality of resistance within their context of Roman Philippi.

In the Colossian hymn we saw an apparent further development from the contents of the Philippian hymn even as central ideas were maintained. The hymn again emphasizes Christ, mentioning the cross at a key point (Col 1:20). The hymn also draws on Jewish motifs in abundance. In Colossians, however, the description of the supremacy of Christ strikes some different notes with new titles and descriptors such as "firstborn" (used twice; Col 1:15 and 18), "image of the invisible God" (Col 1:15), and "head of the body" (Col 1:18). In addition the connections to the wisdom tradition and the role of Christ as God's agent in both creation and redemption are new. The Philippian hymn makes mention of neither. Furthermore, the portrayal of Christ in the Colossian hymn offers a unique and subversive employment of themes normally associated with Roman imperial ideology. Like the Philippian hymn, the Colossian hymn through its memory of Christ offers a portrait of ultimate reality that would enable its readers to live their lives within the kingdom of the beloved Son.

The third and latest of the three major passages, the Johannine prologue, continues the emphasis on Christ as agent of God, who played a role in the creation of all things. It likewise draws heavily on wisdom traditions as well as temple imagery and covenantal themes associated with Moses. Without explicit mention of the cross or the resurrection, this passage demonstrates through a hymnic review of history that what God has accomplished through Jesus is the ultimate revelation of the glory of God—an event through which all the manifestations of the wisdom of God throughout history must now be understood. In its literary context it thus provides a fitting introduction to the Gospel of John as it models for the reader the kind of worshipful acknowledgment of Christ that the author intended for all readers and that is reinforced throughout the narrative by the worshipful responses of key characters. Such a worshipful response contrasts sharply with the response of those who rejected the Logos in history and those who rejected Jesus in the community's more recent past.

One thread visible throughout these passages is the engagement with Jewish prophetic promises related to the inauguration of the new age, the eschatological age of renewal. Though expressed differently and alluded to in unique ways in each hymn, there are clear connections with these traditions. The connections with Isaiah 40–66 are particularly noteworthy. In this regard all three hymns portray Christ as distinct from God, and yet fully included in the divine work of the redemption of humanity that God promised through the prophets of old.

Another thread is the employment of concepts and imagery that were also at home in the praises offered to the Roman emperor in association with the Roman imperial ideology. The portrayal of Christ as the one before whom every knee will bow (Philippians), as the one who has the supremacy in all things (Colossians), and as the one who has divine origins, who enlightens humanity with his presence, and who is a gracious benefactor (John) can arguably be seen as encroaching on the kinds of accolades and honors offered to the emperor. In addition, the explicit mention of the cross (in Philippians and Colossians) and the notion of the rejection of Jesus by the world (John) prevent worshipers of Christ from ignoring the historical fact of the ways in which the powers of the world refused to recognize Christ. The implications are both that Christ is greater than Caesar and that those who follow Christ should not be surprised to find themselves at odds with the prevailing forces in their day.

When we turned to the hymn fragments and shorter passages from throughout the New Testament, and to hymns embedded in narrative contexts, we found a range of variation and similarity that mirror the hymns in Philippians, Colossians, and John. Continued emphasis on the incarnation, death, resurrection, ascension, and exaltation of Christ is evident, though never identical in any two passages. Close connections with Jewish conceptions of God and God's plans for the redemption of humanity are noteworthy, but again they draw from a wide range of Jewish scriptural traditions. In the epistles and Hebrews, the emphases appear to be more on inclusion of the hymnic praise of Christ in support of the message of the writer. The hymns of Luke and Revelation give enough context to enable us to detect explicit engagement with Roman imperial themes. In those passages the hymns model a devout, worshipful response to the work of God through Christ. In Revelation, in both the narrative context and the words of praise themselves, Jesus is shown to be worthy of the worship traditionally reserved only for the one true God.

PUTTING THE PIECES TOGETHER

I concluded the introduction to this volume by outlining a set of claims about early Christian worship. Having examined those New Testament texts widely considered to be christological hymns or, at the very least, hymnic or poetic in nature, we can now return to those claims with a greater sense of their significance.

To begin with, it is clear that early Christian worship was centered on Christ. This conclusion seems not at all surprising or even all that interesting given that I have chosen here to explore *christological* hymns. Still, the fact that the early Christian milieu was generative of passages that offer hymnic declarations about Christ in elevated style and poetic form is foundational for this study. In a range of ways these passages invite readers to embrace a particular view of reality centered on the events surrounding the life, death, and resurrection of Jesus. I suggest that it is not these hymnic passages alone that give rise to this dynamic. What we know of early Christian worship as a whole indicates that much of it was similarly centered on Christ. Though we have little direct evidence of early Christian worship, there are good reasons to see these passages as a reflection of an already widespread emphasis on the centrality of Christ among these communities. Apart from the existence of such a prevalent christological perspective within the Christian communities, it is difficult to imagine a scenario that would result in such diverse yet related Christ-centered passages with hymnic features embedded throughout the New Testament writings.

While Christocentric in focus, the view of Jesus promoted in these passages is deeply rooted in a Jewish conception of the divine, so much so that Jesus is shown to be worthy of receiving the honor that was due in early Judaism to the one true God. In light of this it was not surprising to see that these early christological hymns were creatively and critically engaged with Jewish scriptural traditions. One way they reflect this is through their engagement with passages of Scripture relating to prophetic promises of renewal and restoration, particularly as seen in Isaiah 40–66. Scriptures relating to the glory of God, the temple, and personified Wisdom also are important in many of the hymns we examined. The New Testament christological hymns also seem to have maintained a meaningful connection to the Jewish psalm tradition, a tradition that was alive and well during the Second Temple period. These early christological hymns thereby show themselves to be connected to a living tradition of psalm composition and religious poetry, a genre that itself had a long pedigree of engaging culture, drawing on even earlier traditions, and resisting easy answers to the problem of suffering.

At the same time, in a number of instances it was clear that the early Christian praise of Jesus also appropriated aspects of Greek and Roman culture, albeit to varied degrees. Rhetorical features including the topoi of encomia and other kinds of praise writings are present in numerous instances. Greek philosophical ideas, most likely mediated through Hellenistic Judaism, are also present in some instances. The end result is that the New Testament christological hymns present us with a unique fusion of Jewish and Greco-Roman literary conventions and styles.

Early Christian worship was also apparently quite conscious of its imperial context. Many of the christological hymns demonstrate some degree of resonance with ideas that were present in Roman imperial ideology as it was promoted throughout the Roman world. By drawing on some of those themes in subversive ways, early Christian worship appears to have provided its participants with resources to resist the norms espoused through Roman imperial ideology and pagan religious beliefs. In that imperial context early Christian worship promoted an alternative view of reality in which God was redeeming humanity through a divinely appointed agent, namely, Jesus.

Finally, with their high concentration of poetic features or elevated stylistic features, their focus on divine realities associated with God's plan for humanity through Christ, together with their use of imagery and themes that resonated with their cultural contexts, it seems that the early christological hymns were far more than just a codification of doctrine or a logical statement of Christian beliefs. Rather, as hymns these passages also had an affective dimension and an allusive quality that had the potential to engage the emotions as well as the mind. Accordingly, early Christian worship offered imagery and language that had an evocative power capable of engaging the emotions of its participants and enabling them to see themselves as part of an imaginal world in which all powers are subject to the exalted Jesus. In some instances early Christian hymns explicitly brought into view a verbal picture of the exalted Jesus. In all cases, through language associated with praise of the divine, they invited their listeners as worshipers into an experience of the realities about which they spoke.

Given our recognition of these features, it is fair to say that the individuals who composed these hymns drew on rich resources available to them in their culture and, based on their experience of the risen and exalted Jesus, composed hymnic praise of a sort that had not existed previously. Whether drawing on the tradition of thanksgiving hymns or adapting the encomiastic praise of exalted humans, in the end the christological hymns of the New Testament amount to a unique Christian expression drawn from the context of their reflections on what God had accomplished through Christ. The widespread representation of this material throughout all of the various types of New Testament writings and genres, and from multiple time periods within the first century, suggests its importance from the earliest times. In this way we can agree with Richard Bauckham, who writes, "As the one exalted to participation in God's unique divine lordship, Jesus was the object of religious attention in Christian worship from the beginning."[1] The findings in this volume support such a claim.

Within this study I have attempted to articulate the primary themes and emphases of these hymns both individually and as a whole. In many ways, my

---

[1] Richard Bauckham, *Jesus and the God of Israel: God Crucified and Other Studies on the New Testament's Christology of Divine Identity* (Grand Rapids: Eerdmans, 2009), 130.

findings align with Richard Longenecker's in his articulation of nine major themes of the early confessions.[2] For Longenecker these include the following: God is the initiator, sustainer, and ultimate agent of redemption; Jesus is Israel's Messiah; the eschatological age of redemption has been inaugurated; Jesus is God's obedient Son; Jesus is humanity's redemptive Lord; Jesus is truly human; Christ died a redemptive death on the cross; Christ was resurrected/ exalted to new life; and new relationships were established through the work of Christ. While each of Longenecker's assertions is found in one or more of the passages examined in these pages, several additions need to be made to his list of major themes. First, the christological hymns as a whole portray Christ as the exalted Lord who is the ultimate victor over all powers. This victor motif was important to vindicate Christ in light of his shameful death on the cross. It was also important in drawing out the implications of Christ's present status for the daily practical realities of his followers. Christ's exalted status offered hope to believers in the midst of the Roman world in which Christ was not yet obviously reigning as Lord.

Second, as a result of this exalted status above all powers, Christ is understood to be worthy of worship alongside God. This participation in receiving worship was implicit in some hymns but explicit in others. These two themes cohere with Ralph Martin's summary statement: "If there is one motif that pervades the New Testament hymns, it is this ringing assurance that Christ is victor over all man's enemies, and is rightly worshipped as the Image of the God who is over all."[3] Bauckham expresses something similar when he writes, "The earliest hymns celebrated the saving death and heavenly exaltation of Jesus as the one who now shares the divine throne and, as God's plenipotentiary, receives the homage of all creation."[4] The exalted status of Jesus is closely connected with the idea that he is worthy of divine worship.

A third theme we must add is the following: The Christ of the christological hymns can only be fully appreciated by understanding the Jewish milieu and the Roman context in which the hymns emerged. A neglect of either context leads to an unintentional devaluing of the lived experience of those individuals who crafted these hymns at a specific time and in a specific place. A

---

[2]Richard N. Longenecker, *New Wine into Fresh Wineskins: Contextualizing the Early Christian Confessions* (Peabody, MA: Hendrickson, 1999), 34-43.

[3]Ralph P. Martin, *Worship in the Early Church* (Grand Rapids: Eerdmans, 1974), 52.

[4]Bauckham, *Jesus and the God of Israel*, 138.

full appreciation of both contexts enables us to understand how followers of Jesus understood him to be not only God's agent of redemption but also one to whom and through whom they could direct their worship of God. In addition, this awareness of Jewish and Greco-Roman contexts may help us appreciate the polyvalence of many of the expressions of praise in these hymns. Furthermore, the resonance of these hymns with both Jewish and Greco-Roman ideas may not have been simply an accident of a multicultural context but actually part of a very deliberate strategy. N. T. Wright suggests as much for Paul: "What Paul wanted to see as the result of his labors was cross-culturally united *worship* . . . namely, a *cult* in which the One God would be worshipped by people of every kind and kin."[5] The thematic and stylistic breadth of the New Testament christological hymns suggests that such a project was underway early on in the Christian movement.

AFTER THE NEW TESTAMENT CHRISTOLOGICAL HYMNS

As we noted in the introduction, with the exception of the hymns in Luke's infancy narrative we have no indication that any writers in the second or third centuries referred to these New Testament passages as hymns, psalms, or songs. On the other hand, we do have evidence that these passages (particularly Phil 2:5-11 and Col 1:15-20) were among the most quoted in the early church.[6] Their emphasis on the person and significance of Christ made them particularly well suited for use with regard to the christological controversies of the second and third centuries. In that regard, it is clear that early on they were widely known and were recognized as having authority and applicability to current problems. But this later use as a source for doctrinal and creedal formulation has little bearing on the kinds of conclusions we have drawn about these passages based on the ways in which they reflect conventions and norms of first-century-CE hymnody.

We may ask at this point what became of this evidently widespread practice of composing hymns to Christ and of using hymnic language in other genres of writings, such as epistles, narratives, and apocalypses. As it turns out, the

---

[5]N. T. Wright, *Paul and the Faithfulness of God* (Minneapolis: Fortress, 2013), 1506 (emphasis original).

[6]Benjamin Edsall and Jennifer R. Strawbridge, "The Songs We Used to Sing? Hymn 'Traditions' and Reception in Pauline Letters," *JSNT* 37 (2015): 290-311, esp. 300-305.

evidence from the second century CE shows that this impulse continued on in full force, and that hymnody continued to play an important role in the development of Christian thought and practice.[7] From the early part of the second century we have the frequently quoted remark by Pliny the Younger in his letter to Trajan about the actions of the early Christians. In his investigation Pliny found that "on a certain day prior to sunrise they were accustomed to gather, to sing antiphonally about Christ as their God" (*Ep.* 10.96.7).[8] And if this was happening at the beginning of the second century, it was certainly widespread at the end of that century as well. Eusebius preserved a few lines from *Against Artemon*, a work written around 200 CE, in which the author asks an intriguing rhetorical question. Seeking to refute the teaching of Artemon in his own day he called on earlier authoritative teachings about the nature of Christ and asked, "For who is ignorant of the books of Irenaeus, Melito, and the rest who proclaim Christ as God and man, and how many psalms and odes, written from the beginning by brothers in the faith, hymn Christ, the word of God, proclaiming him as a god?"[9] Whether or not this author's comments about "psalms and odes written from the beginning" includes within its scope any of the New Testament passages we have studied here, it certainly encompasses the time of the New Testament writings up through the second century. At least in some circles, the vitality of the rich tradition of christological hymns was apparently widely known by the end of the second century.

While it is clear that hymnody remained vital in the second century, we actually have relatively few hymnic texts preserved from that time period.[10] The texts we do have, however, tell quite a story about the development of early Christian hymnody. The earliest hymns found outside of the New Testament are from the first decade or two of the second century and, like those in the New Testament, are embedded in epistles. Three passages in the letters of Ignatius have been identified as hymns: *To the Ephesians* 19.2-3 (the "star hymn"),

---

[7]For a historical survey of early Christian hymnody, see John Anthony McGuckin, *The Path of Christianity: The First Thousand Years* (Downers Grove, IL: IVP Academic, 2017), 815-27.

[8]Martin Hengel, "The Song About Christ in Earliest Worship," in *Studies in Early Christology* (Edinburgh: T&T Clark, 1995), 227-91, esp. 262-64.

[9]Eusebius of Caesarea, *Hist. eccl.* 5.28.5. Trans. mine based on the Greek text in Eusebius, *Histoire Ecclésiastique: Livres V–VII*, trans. Gustave Bardy, SC 41 (Paris: Éditions du Cerf, 1994).

[10]See my study of some of this material in Matthew E. Gordley, *Teaching Through Song in Antiquity: Didactic Hymnody Among Greeks, Romans, Jews and Christians*, WUNT 2/331 (Tübingen: Mohr Siebeck, 2011), 350-82.

To the Ephesians 7.2, and *To Polycarp* 3.2. These remarkable passages show many of the features we have already seen in the New Testament christological hymns. On the one hand, within their epistolary contexts they provide strong support for the claims of the letters in which they are found. They also engage with earlier tradition, including Jewish traditions. But they also engage with and build on the early Christian traditions that developed in the first century CE and that we have seen in the New Testament christological hymns. These hymns of Ignatius have their focus on "Jesus Christ, our Lord" (Ign. *Eph.* 7.2) and utilize a number of common motifs, including the emphasis on the incarnation, the divine and human nature, the redemptive work of Jesus, and cosmological dimensions of his advent. Beyond these motifs, they also show some new developments that appear to reflect the developing needs of the early Christian communities. Additional language from other places in the New Testament is used to describe Jesus as a star that shone forth from heaven (Ign. *Eph.* 19.2) and as the "one physician" (Ign. *Eph.* 7.2). There is also notable use of metaphysical language, including philosophical paradoxes. The net result is that the hymnic passages embedded within the letters of Ignatius exhibit the use of imagery not found in the New Testament christological hymns. This leads to a hymnic portrayal of Jesus and his accomplishments that, while tied to the New Testament hymnic traditions, is much more philosophical in its presentation.[11]

These novel features of the hymns of Ignatius continue to develop within the second century. By the end of the second century, we find a christological hymn written in Greek metrical verse as an epilogue in Clement of Alexandria's *Paedagogus*.[12] In this elaborate hymn Clement uses language, concepts, and metaphors that would have been familiar to well-educated individuals within the Greek tradition. He also draws on the traditions about Christ found in the New Testament, but the echoes of Greek poetry are more prevalent than the biblical allusions.[13] Clement was not the only one to utilize Greek meter and Greek literature in hymnic compositions for followers of Jesus. We also find an emphasis on hymnody among groups that would later be identified

---

[11]Ibid., 351-58.

[12]For analysis and bibliography see Annewies van den Hoek, "Hymn of the Holy Clement to Christ the Saviour," in *Prayer from Alexander to Constantine: A Critical Anthology*, ed. Mark Christopher Kiley (London: Routledge, 1997), 296-303; Gordley, *Teaching Through Song in Antiquity*, 371-81.

[13]Van den Hoek, "Hymn of the Holy Clement," 298.

with the developing complex of ideas associated with Gnosticism. Second-century hymns such as the psalm of Valentinus and the Naassene hymn show clear associations with Gnostic thought and seem to represent a move away from the picture of Jesus that one gets from the first-century sources.[14]

Taken as a whole we can see that the hymns of the second century reflect a milieu that is much different from that in which the New Testament christological hymns were written. John McGuckin rightly notes that the second-century hymns show a greater emphasis on "personal mystical union" than we saw in the New Testament christological hymns, which were more concerned to narrate and illuminate the incarnation, death, resurrection, and exaltation of Jesus.[15] In addition, Martin Hengel has suggested that an association of hymns with continued revelation and the inspiration of the Spirit was at odds with a move toward conformity to apostolic teaching. Hengel associates the psalmody of the New Testament with songs inspired by the Spirit, and the relative paucity of similar texts in the second century and beyond as indications of structures and forces that "dammed up this enthusiastic freedom of the Spirit."[16] While Hengel's claims are worth considering, some of the findings of this study suggest a different explanation.

We have good reason to believe that the New Testament christological hymns, whether they were actual sung hymns or were composed by the authors of the letters in which we find them, reflect aspects of the worship of the early Christians as well as their engagement with the traditions they inherited. They engage with the Jewish Scriptures and early Jewish traditions; they also engage with the realities of their present cultural and historical contexts. Through these features they helped to shape the thinking and perceptions of the communities that chanted them (in the case of real hymns) or read them (in the case of hymns or hymnic passages embedded in other writings). These same dynamics—which I have argued are present in the use of hymns in many contexts in the ancient world—are surely present in the hymns of the second century as well. However, poets and writers in the second century were dealing with a different set of traditions

---

[14]For general bibliography on Gnostic hymns, see Michael Lattke, *Hymnus: Materialen zu einer Geschichte der antiken Hymnologie*, NTOA 19 (Göttingen: Vandenhoeck & Ruprecht, 1991), 254-60. On the Gnostic hymns preserved in Hippolytus see Gordley, *Teaching Through Song in Antiquity*, 358-63.

[15]McGuckin, *Path of Christianity*, 826.

[16]Hengel, "Song About Christ," 291.

than were the first-century writers. In addition to the messianically interpreted psalms of the Jewish Scriptures, and key biblical texts favored by the
early Christians, their inherited traditions also now included letters, Gospels,
and an Apocalypse. They also had the examples of christological reflection
in the New Testament hymns (though they did not refer to them as such,
other than the psalms in Luke's Gospel). In addition they had the traditions
and values associated with their own educational backgrounds, which were
different from those of the first-century believers. Christians of the second
century were no longer predominantly from Hellenistic Jewish backgrounds
(e.g., the Godfearers of Acts) or necessarily of low social status. Instead a
larger number were well educated in Greek and Roman literary culture and
were associated with a correspondingly higher social status. These are some
of the factors that enabled (and required) second-century Christian poets
and writers to take their hymnody in some new directions beyond what had
been possible in the first century.

   Hengel expands on this latter dynamic: "More and more educated people
entered the Church and sought songs there that were consistent with their
aesthetic taste. The Gnostic teachers, who themselves had an equivalent education and who wished to be considered philosophers, catered to this group."[17]
I would add that it is not only the aesthetic tastes of the educated but also the
broader range of Greek and Roman traditions that were available to them and
were part of their own formation through their education. These cultural resources shaped their view of the inherited Christian traditions and also helped
shape their hymnic praise of Christ in their own day. It is from within this
reality of emerging hymns with greater philosophical sophistication and
Gnostic tendencies that Hengel points to the "unfortunate counterreaction" of
the church leaders who then sought officially to emphasize the biblical psalms
alone rather than new songs.[18]

   From the third century onward, our knowledge of Christian hymnody is
fuller and more robust. We have the first early Christian hymn collection in
the Odes of Solomon, a text that reveals a great deal about the development
of hymnody in the Syriac tradition. The role of hymnody in the "heterodox-
orthodox" struggles of the third and fourth centuries has been noted, especially the hymnody associated with Marcion as well as several Gnostic teachers,

---

[17]Ibid., 242.
[18]Ibid., 244.

including Valentinus and Bardesanes.[19] One third-century hymn, "Phos Hilaron [Jesus Christ the cheerful light]," is still in use today.[20] The developments in these later hymns are noted by McGuckin, who explains that those "tendencies toward personal mystical union evoked in the second-century materials" were later set aside in favor of more dogmatic and instructive hymnody in the post-Nicene era.[21] But he also notes that this dimension of early Christian worship was not entirely lost: "This more intimate psychic aspect of hymnic writing passed on into the ascetical literature of the Eastern church."[22] And with these brief observations we have now moved far beyond the scope of the present study.

In these comments about the changes and developments in early Christian hymns from the first to the second to the third century, we have touched on significant changes of emphasis, content, and style. As hymns were composed and utilized by each new generation, it appears that the genre was adapted to address the needs of the day while also remaining connected to the traditions and texts of the past. In my thinking the three main factors that led to second-century hymnody's taking on a different tone than that of the New Testament are the changing needs of a new era, more and more Christians coming from educated backgrounds who were drawing on their own traditions, and the impact of a broader set of inherited traditions that now included the New Testament with its hymnic depictions of Christ. The New Testament christological hymns had now become part of the tradition—a tradition that could be drawn on but also adapted to suit the needs of these new generations just as the hymnographers of the New Testament era had drawn on the psalms and hymns that were part of their cultural inheritance.

CONTEMPORARY IMPLICATIONS

Two millennia later, the Christian imagination is still being shaped by the New Testament christological hymns. Most if not all of these texts have been set to music and are, in this way, used in services of worship in some traditions. For the most part, however, the significance of these hymns is that they are now read and interpreted by believers as sacred Scripture: God's Word. As such,

---

[19]McGuckin, *Path of Christianity*, 824-27.
[20]Ibid., 843.
[21]Ibid., 826.
[22]Ibid., 826-27.

they carry special authority in the Christian life and invite ongoing consideration by the faithful, who seek to make sense of their lives here and now in light of the realities about Jesus described in the New Testament. In what ways can the findings of this study about the hymns of the earliest Christian worshipers be a resource to enrich, inform, and foster reflection about worship in the modern church?

In order to answer this question in a way that is in keeping with the focus of this volume, let us return briefly to the way in which we have sought to understand the phenomenon of worship as whole. We have worked from an understanding that worship is more than just spoken words or ritual actions or inner thoughts and beliefs. Worship certainly can include those things, but it also cannot be reduced to any one of them. Instead, worship is, in its broadest scope, an intentional practice of affirming, proclaiming, and confessing an allegiance to God that, among other things, enables the worshiper to see himself or herself as part of a reality that is larger than the visible reality on offer within the world in which the worshiper lives. Worship, in this sense, would include words, actions, and rituals, together with an overall pattern of values and priorities that constitute the orientation of one's life. Within this broad way of thinking about worship, one can worship God through song, prayer, sacrament, and meditation in a congregational or other religious setting (1 Cor 14:26; Col 3:16). But one can also worship God through the performance of one's day-to-day responsibilities. Even the most mundane of activities can be considered worship of God when acted out with an awareness that it is being done "in the name of the Lord Jesus, giving thanks to God the Father through him" (Col 3:17; cf. Rom 12:1).

With this broad frame of reference for worship in mind, the New Testament christological hymns can be seen as threads within the larger tapestry of early Christian worship. To the extent that they were read, recited, or chanted in communal gatherings, they would seem to reflect more directly on the formal aspect of worship in my definition above. But since they describe the reality of God's redemptive work in the world centered on the person of Jesus, they also provide a framework for a way of viewing the world that can enable a worshiper to live every moment of her or his daily life as an act of worship. By following both of these threads, the New Testament hymns have the potential to be a resource for contemporary believers both in terms of formal, communal dimensions of worship and in terms of living one's life with a mindset of worship.

As we have discovered, the New Testament christological hymns reveal several important things about the nature and focus of early Christian worship:

▸ A reliance on and engagement with inherited tradition is clearly present.

▸ An engagement with current cultural values and practices is unmistakable.

▸ An undercurrent of resistance to dominant imperial regimes is particularly noteworthy.

▸ Throughout the hymns there is a pervasive recognition of Jesus as inaugurating a new era.

▸ The christological hymns of the New Testament remind us of the centrality of the cross, resurrection, and exaltation of Jesus.

With these features in view, it is important to note that the New Testament christological hymns do not prescribe or require that contemporary worship should reflect their style or their disposition. Nor do they prescribe that contemporary worship imitate their specific contents. In fact, these passages are not prescriptive at all. Yet with their recognition as Scripture they invite us to engage with their content and to consider the kind of responses to the good news about Jesus that they model.

First, as a starting point for contemporary reflection, a deeper understanding of these texts in their cultural contexts can facilitate our asking new questions about our own practices. From the observations above about what the hymns tell us about early Christian worship, we can pose an initial set of basic questions about the extent to which contemporary hymnody or liturgical song or worship music reflects the features of the earliest Christian hymns. These questions might be seen as taking inventory of the state of our worship without necessarily passing any judgment on the findings. For example, how does today's worship through song demonstrate a connection to inherited tradition? In what ways does it engage with current cultures? How does it resist competing ideologies that embody values contrary to the way of Jesus? Does it acknowledge and celebrate the reality of the new era inaugurated by Jesus? To what extent are the cross, resurrection, and exaltation features of contemporary worship songs? The spirit of these questions is not evaluative or judgmental. Rather, these are descriptive questions that ask us to think about the ways in which our worship currently reflects these dynamics.

Second, with answers to those descriptive questions in view as a starting point we may then proceed to ask a more challenging set of questions about what contemporary worship *could* or *should* be like. These questions invite us to consider the extent to which it would be valuable to *enhance* those features that were apparently a part of early Christian worship of Jesus. This second set of questions summons us to consider what might need to change in order for our current worship practices to more fully embody the spirit of early Christian worship. Is there a need to enhance the connections with inherited traditions? Is more or deeper cultural engagement needed? Is there a need to be more intentional in calling out and resisting dominant ideologies of the current era? Is more explicit celebration of the new age in which believers are living needed? Is there a need to deepen the ways in which the cross, resurrection, and exaltation are celebrated? Questions like these, which relate to the central themes of the New Testament christological hymns, can be a lens through which we take a fresh view of our worship practices. By asking these questions of our own worship practices and arriving at answers suited to particular contexts we may be able to plan for worship services that, while necessarily very different from the gatherings of the early Christians, will be linked to them in fundamental ways.

Third, if the two sets of questions above can lead us to a new understanding of formal aspects of worship, a similar set of questions can invite us to reflect on our own Christian worldview and the ways in which our daily lives reflect a worshipful orientation. We can consider what stories are shaping our own view of the world and of our place in it. We can consider whether we are valuing the traditions we have inherited while at the same time being mindful of the cultures in which we live. We can ask ourselves whether we are appropriately critical of values or norms of our culture that we may take for granted but that Jesus expressly opposed through his teaching or example. We can consider the extent to which we live our lives as citizens of the new era inaugurated by Jesus and as people whose lives are marked by the humility of the cross and the hope of resurrection.

At the most basic level, whether we ask these kinds of questions of our congregations or of our individual selves, the New Testament christological hymns have the potential to challenge contemporary Christians to consider whether our view of Jesus is expansive enough. The remarkable portrait of reality painted by the New Testament christological hymns is that of an imaginal world—a real world but one that cannot yet be perceived in the visible space around us—in which Jesus is Lord of all, the unique agent of God's work of redemption inclusive of Jews and Gentiles, inclusive of all people. If the church was born in the matrix of worship, and worship was centered on the crucified, risen, and exalted Jesus to the glory of God, then Christian vitality depends on growing and maturing in relationship with these origins. The New Testament christological hymns bring us with laser focus to the birth and infancy of the early church as it wrestled with its culture, its traditions, and its message of good news for all people. Our deep reflection and appropriation of the meaning of the New Testament christological hymns today could be a catalyst to a renewal and rebirth that is needed in the present moment as much as it ever has been.

BIBLIOGRAPHY

Achtemeier, Paul J. *A Commentary on First Peter*. Hermeneia. Minneapolis: Fortress, 1996.

Adams, Samuel V. *The Reality of God and Historical Method: Apocalyptic Theology in Conversation with N. T. Wright*. New Explorations in Theology. Downers Grove, IL: IVP Academic, 2015.

Aletti, Jean Noël. *Saint Paul Épitre aux Colossiens*. Paris: Éditions J. Gabalda, 1993.

Alter, Robert. *The Art of Biblical Poetry*. Edinburgh: T&T Clark, 1990.

Arnold, Clinton E. *Ephesians*. Zondervan Exegetical Commentary on the New Testament 10. Grand Rapids: Zondervan, 2010.

Atkinson, Kenneth. *I Cried to the Lord: A Study of the Psalms of Solomon's Historical Background and Social Setting*. JSJSup 84. Leiden: Brill, 2004.

Attridge, Harold W. *A Commentary on the Epistle to the Hebrews*. Hermeneia. Philadelphia: Fortress, 1989.

Aune, David E. "Hymn." In *The Westminster Dictionary of New Testament and Early Christian Literature and Rhetoric*, 222-24. Louisville, KY: Westminster John Knox, 2003.

———. *Revelation 1–5*. WBC 52a. Dallas: Word, 1997.

———. "Worship, Early Christian." In *Anchor Bible Dictionary*, edited by David Noel Freedman, 6:973-89. New York: Doubleday, 1992.

Bastiaensen, Antoon A. R. "*Psalmi, Hymni* and *Cantica* in Early Jewish-Christian Tradition." *StPatr* 21 (1989): 15-26.

Bauckham, Richard. *Jesus and the God of Israel: God Crucified and Other Studies on the New Testament's Christology of Divine Identity*. Grand Rapids: Eerdmans, 2009.

———. "The Worship of Jesus in Early Christianity." In *Jesus and the God of Israel: God Crucified and Other Studies on the New Testament's Christology of Divine Identity*, 127-51. Grand Rapids: Eerdmans, 2009.

Beasley-Murray, George R. *John*. WBC 36. Waco, TX: Word, 1987.

Bevere, Allan R. "Colossians and the Rhetoric of Empire: A New Battle Zone." In *Jesus Is Lord, Caesar Is Not: Evaluating Empire in New Testament Studies*, edited by Scot McKnight and Joseph B. Modica, 183-96. Downers Grove, IL: IVP Academic, 2013.

Bird, Michael F. *Colossians and Philemon: A New Covenant Commentary.* New Covenant Commentary. Havertown, UK: Lutterworth, 2011.

Blount, Brian K. *Revelation: A Commentary.* NTL. Louisville, KY: Westminster John Knox, 2009.

Bockmuehl, Markus N. A. *The Epistle to the Philippians.* BNTC 11. Peabody, MA: Hendrickson, 1998.

Bodel, John P., and Saul M. Olyan. *Household and Family Religion in Antiquity.* Ancient World—Comparative Histories. Malden, MA: Blackwell, 2008.

Boer, Martinus C. de. "The Original Prologue to the Gospel of John." *NTS* 61 (2015): 448-67.

Borgen, Peder. "The Gospel of John and Hellenism." In *The Gospel of John: More Light from Philo, Paul and Archaeology: The Scriptures, Tradition, Exposition, Settings, Meaning,* edited by Peder Borgen, 79-99. NovTSup 154. Leiden: Brill, 2014.

Bowra, C. M. "Melinno's Hymn to Rome." *JRS* 47 (1957): 21-28.

Boyarin, Daniel. "The Gospel of the *Memra*: Jewish Binitarianism and the Prologue to John." *HTR* 94 (2001): 243-84.

Bradshaw, Paul F. *Reconstructing Early Christian Worship.* London: SPCK, 2009.

———. *The Search for the Origins of Christian Worship: Sources and Methods for the Study of Early Liturgy.* 2nd ed. New York: Oxford University Press, 2002.

Bremer, Jan Maarten. "Greek Hymns." In *Faith, Hope and Worship: Aspects of Religious Mentality in the Ancient World,* edited by H. S. Versnel, 193-215. Studies in Greek and Roman Religion 2. Leiden: Brill, 1981.

Brooke, George. "Aspects of the Theological Significance of Prayer and Worship in the Qumran Scrolls." In *Prayer and Poetry in the Dead Sea Scrolls and Related Literature: Essays in Honor of Eileen Schuller on the Occasion of Her 65th Birthday,* edited by Jeremy Penner, Ken M. Penner, and Cecilia Wassen, 34-54. STDJ 98. Leiden: Brill, 2012.

Brown, Raymond E. *The Birth of the Messiah: A Commentary on the Infancy Narratives in Matthew and Luke.* ABRL. New York: Doubleday, 1993.

———. *The Community of the Beloved Disciple.* New York: Paulist, 1979.

———. *The Gospel According to John I–XII.* 2nd ed. AB 29. Garden City, NY: Doubleday, 1986.

Brucker, Ralph. *"Christushymnen" oder "epideiktische Passagen"? Studien zum Stilwechsel im Neuen Testament und seiner Umwelt.* FRLANT 176. Göttingen: Vandenhoeck & Ruprecht, 1997.

———. "'Songs,' 'Hymns,' and 'Encomia' in the New Testament?" In *Literature or Liturgy? Early Christian Hymns and Prayers in Their Literary and Liturgical*

Context in Antiquity, edited by Clemens Leonhard and Hermut Löhr, 1-14. WUNT 2/363. Tübingen: Mohr Siebeck, 2014.

Burger, Christoph. *Schöpfung und Versöhnung: Studien zum liturgischen Gut im Kolosser- und Epheserbrief.* WMANT 46. Neukirchen-Vluyn: Neukirchener Verlag, 1975.

Burney, C. F. "Christ as the ΑΡΧΗ of Creation." *JTS* 27 (1926): 160-77.

Carter, Warren. *John and Empire: Initial Explorations.* New York: T&T Clark, 2008.

Chaniotis, Angelos. "Der Kaiserkult im Osten des Römischen Reiches im Kontext der zeitgenössischen Ritualpraxis." In *Die Praxis der Herrscherverehrung in Rom und seinen Provinzen*, edited by Hubert Cancik and Konrad Hitzl, 3-28. Tübingen: Mohr Siebeck, 2003.

Charlesworth, James H. "Jewish Hymns, Odes, and Prayers (ca 167 BCE–135 CE)." In *Early Judaism and Its Modern Interpreters*, 411-36. Philadelphia: Fortress, 1986.

Chazon, Esther G. "Tradition and Innovation in Sectarian Religious Poetry." In *Prayer and Poetry in the Dead Sea Scrolls and Related Literature: Essays in Honor of Eileen Schuller on the Occasion of Her 65th Birthday*, edited by Jeremy Penner, Ken M. Penner, and Cecilia Wassen, 55-67. STDJ 98. Leiden: Brill, 2012.

Childs, Brevard S. *Memory and Tradition in Israel.* Naperville, IL: Allenson, 1962.

Cohick, Lynn H. "Philippians and Empire: Paul's Engagement with Imperialism and the Imperial Cult." In *Jesus Is Lord, Caesar Is Not: Evaluating Empire in New Testament Studies*, edited by Scot McKnight and Joseph B. Modica, 166-82. Downers Grove, IL: IVP Academic, 2013.

Coleridge, Mark. *The Birth of the Lukan Narrative: Narrative as Christology in Luke 1–2.* JSNTSup 88. Sheffield: JSOT Press, 1993.

Collins, Adela Yarbro. "Psalms, Philippians 2:6-11, and the Origins of Christology." *BibInt* 11 (2002): 361-72.

———. "The Second Temple and the Arts of Resistance." In *From Judaism to Christianity: Tradition and Transition: A Festschrift for Thomas H. Tobin, S.J., on the Occasion of His Sixty-Fifth Birthday*, edited by Patricia Walters, 115-29. NovTSup 136. Leiden: Brill, 2010.

———. "The Worship of Jesus and the Imperial Cult." In *The Jewish Roots of Christological Monotheism: Papers from the St. Andrews Conference on the Historical Origins of the Worship of Jesus*, edited by Carey C. Newman, James R. Davila, and Gladys S. Lewis, 234-57. Leiden: Brill, 1999.

Colpe, Carsten. *Die religionsgeschichtliche Schule: Darstellung und Kritik ihres Bildes vom gnostischen Erlösermythus.* FRLANT 60. Göttingen: Vandenhoeck & Ruprecht, 1961.

Cook, W. Robert. "Eschatology in John's Gospel." *CTR* 3 (1988): 79-99.

Cosgrove, Charles H. *An Ancient Christian Hymn with Musical Notation: Papyrus Oxyrhynchus 1786: Text and Commentary.* STAC 65. Tübingen: Mohr Siebeck, 2011.

Cousar, Charles B. "The Function of the Christ-Hymn (2.6-11) in Philippians." In *The Impartial God: Essays in Biblical Studies in Honor of Jouette M. Bassler,* edited by Calvin J. Roetzel, Robert L. Foster, and Jouette M. Bassler, 212-18. Sheffield: Sheffield Phoenix Press, 2007.

Cox, Ronald R. *By the Same Word: Creation and Salvation in Hellenistic Judaism and Early Christianity,* 212-18. BZNW 145. Berlin: de Gruyter, 2007.

Culpepper, Richard Alan. "The Pivot of John's Prologue." *NTS* 27 (1980): 1-31.

————. "The Prologue as Theological Prolegomenon to the Gospel of John." In *The Prologue of the Gospel of John: Its Literary, Theological, and Philosophical Contexts: Papers Read at the Colloquium Ioanneum 2013,* edited by Jan G. Van der Watt, Richard Alan Culpepper, and Udo Schnelle, 3-26. WUNT 359. Tübingen: Mohr Siebeck, 2016.

Danker, Frederick W. *Benefactor: Epigraphic Study of a Graeco-Roman and New Testament Semantic Field.* St. Louis: Clayton, 1982.

De Long, Kindalee Pfremmer. *Surprised by God: Praise Responses in the Narrative of Luke-Acts.* BZNW 166. Berlin: de Gruyter, 2009.

Deichgräber, Reinhard. *Gotteshymnus und Christushymnus in der frühen Christenheit.* SUNT 5. Göttingen: Vandenhoeck & Ruprecht, 1967.

Delling, Gerhard. *Worship in the New Testament.* London: Darton, Longman & Todd, 1962.

deSilva, David A. *Seeing Things John's Way: The Rhetoric of the Book of Revelation.* Louisville, KY: Westminster John Knox, 2009.

Dillon, Richard J. *The Hymns of Saint Luke: Lyricism and Narrative Strategy in Luke 1-2.* CBQMS 50. Washington, DC: Catholic Biblical Association, 2013.

Dodd, C. H. *The Interpretation of the Fourth Gospel.* Cambridge: Cambridge University Press, 1968.

Dunn, James D. G. *Christology in the Making: A New Testament Inquiry into the Origins of the Doctrine of the Incarnation.* 2nd ed. Grand Rapids: Eerdmans, 1996.

————. *Did the First Christians Worship Jesus? The New Testament Evidence.* Louisville, KY: Westminster John Knox, 2010.

———. *The Epistles to the Colossians and to Philemon: A Commentary on the Greek Text.* NIGTC. Grand Rapids: Eerdmans, 1996.

Eastman, Susan Grove. "Philippians 2:6-11: Incarnation as Mimetic Participation." *Journal for the Study of Paul and His Letters* 1 (2010): 1-22.

Edelstein, Emma J., and Ludwig Edelstein. *Asclepius: Collection and Interpretation of the Testimonies.* Baltimore: Johns Hopkins University Press, 1998.

Edsall, Benjamin, and Jennifer R. Strawbridge. "The Songs We Used to Sing? Hymn 'Traditions' and Reception in Pauline Letters." *JSNT* 37 (2015): 290-311.

Ehrman, Bart D. *Forgery and Counterforgery: The Use of Literary Deceit in Early Christian Polemics.* New York: Oxford University Press, 2013.

Elliott, Neil. "Paul and the Politics of Empire: Problems and Prospects." In *Paul and Politics: Ekklesia, Israel, Imperium, Interpretation; Essays in Honor of Krister Stendahl*, edited by Richard A. Horsley, 17-39. Harrisburg, PA: Trinity Press International, 2000.

Embry, Brad. "Some Thoughts on and Implications from Genre Categorization in the *Psalms of Solomon.*" In *The Psalms of Solomon: Language, History, Theology*, edited by Eberhard Bons and Patrick Pouchelle, 59-78. EJL 40. Atlanta: SBL Press, 2015.

Eusebius. *Histoire Ecclésiastique: Livres V-VII.* Translated by Gustave Bardy. 4th ed. SC 41. Paris: Éditions du Cerf, 1994.

Falk, Daniel. "Psalms and Prayers." In *Justification and Variegated Nomism.* Vol. 1, *The Complexities of Second Temple Judaism*, edited by D. A. Carson, Peter T. O'Brien, and Mark A. Seifrid, 7-56. Grand Rapids: Baker Academic, 2001.

Farris, Stephen. *The Hymns of Luke's Infancy Narratives: Their Origin, Meaning and Significance.* JSNTSup 9. Sheffield: JSOT Press, 1985.

Fee, Gordon D. *Pauline Christology: An Exegetical-Theological Study.* Peabody, MA: Hendrickson, 2007.

———. "Philippians 2:5-11: Hymn or Exalted Pauline Prose." *BBR* 2 (1992): 29-46.

Fewster, Gregory P. "The Philippians 'Christ Hymn': Trends in Critical Scholarship." *CurBR* 13 (2015): 191-206.

Flusser, David. "Psalms, Hymns, and Prayers." In *Jewish Writings of the Second Temple Period: Apocrypha, Pseudepigrapha, Qumran Sectarian Writings, Philo, Josephus*, edited by Michael E. Stone, 551-77. Philadelphia: Fortress, 1984.

Foley, Helene P. *The Homeric Hymn to Demeter: Translation, Commentary, and Interpretive Essays.* Princeton, NJ: Princeton University Press, 1994.

Forché, Carolyn. *Against Forgetting: Twentieth-Century Poetry of Witness.* New York: W. W. Norton, 1993.

Ford, Josephine Massyngbaerde. "The Christological Function of the Hymns in the Apocalypse of John." *AUSS* 56 (1998): 207-29.

Fossum, Jarl E. "In the Beginning Was the Name: Onomanology as the Key to Johannine Christology." In *The Image of the Invisible God: Essays on the Influence of Jewish Mysticism on Early Christology*, edited by Jarl E. Fossum, 109-34. NTOA 30. Göttingen: Vandenhoeck & Ruprecht, 1995.

Foster, Paul. *Colossians*. BNTC. New York: Bloomsbury T&T Clark, 2016.

Fowl, Stephen E. *Philippians*. Two Horizons New Testament Commentary. Grand Rapids: Eerdmans 2005.

———. *The Story of Christ in the Ethics of Paul: An Analysis of the Function of the Hymnic Material in the Pauline Corpus*. JSNTSup 36. Sheffield: Sheffield Academic, 1990.

Friesen, Steven J. *Imperial Cults and the Apocalypse of John: Reading Revelation in the Ruins*. New York: Oxford University Press, 2001.

Furley, William D., and Jan Maarten Bremer. *Greek Hymns: Selected Cult Songs from the Archaic to the Hellenistic Period*. 2 vols. STAC 9-10. Tübingen: Mohr Siebeck, 2001.

Gese, Hartmut. *Essays on Biblical Theology*. Minneapolis: Augsburg, 1981.

Giblin, Charles Homer. "Two Complementary Literary Structures in John 1:1-18." *JBL* 104 (1985): 87-103.

Gilbert, Maurice. "The Review of History in Ben Sira 44–50 and Wisdom 10–19." In *Rewriting Biblical History: Essays on Chronicles and Ben Sira in Honour of Pancratius C. Beentjes de Gruyter*, edited by Jeremy Corley and Harm van Grol, 319-34. DCLS 7. Berlin: de Gruyter, 2011.

Giles, Terry, and William Doan. *Twice Used Songs: Performance Criticism of the Songs of Ancient Israel*. Peabody, MA: Hendrickson, 2009.

Gloer, W. Hulitt. "Homologies and Hymns in the New Testament: Form, Content and Criteria for Identification." *PRSt* 11 (1984): 115-32.

Gordley, Matthew E. *The Colossian Hymn in Context: An Exegesis in Light of Jewish and Greco-Roman Hymnic and Epistolary Conventions*. WUNT 2/228. Tübingen: Mohr Siebeck, 2007.

———. "Creating Meaning in the Present by Reviewing the Past: Communal Memory in the *Psalms of Solomon*." *JAJ* 5 (2014): 368-92.

———. "The Johannine Prologue and Jewish Didactic Hymn Traditions: A New Case for Reading the Prologue as a Hymn." *JBL* 128 (2009): 781-802.

———. "Psalms of Solomon as Resistance Poetry." *JAJ* (forthcoming 2018).

———. "*Psalms of Solomon* as Solomonic Discourse: The Nature and Function of Attribution to Solomon in a Pseudonymous Psalm Collection." *JSP* 25 (2015): 52-88.

———. *Teaching Through Song in Antiquity: Didactic Hymnody Among Greeks, Romans, Jews and Christians.* WUNT 2/331. Tübingen: Mohr Siebeck, 2011.

Grabiner, Steven. *Revelation's Hymns: Commentary on the Cosmic Conflict.* LNTS 511. New York: Bloomsbury T&T Clark, 2015.

Gradel, Ittai. *Emperor Worship and Roman Religion.* OCM. Oxford: Clarendon, 2002.

Gundry, Robert H. "The Form, Meaning and Background of the Hymn Quoted in 1 Timothy 3:16." In *Apostolic History and the Gospel: Biblical and Historical Essays Presented to F. F. Bruce on His 60th Birthday*, edited by W. Ward Gasque and Ralph P. Martin, 203-22. Exeter, UK: Paternoster, 1970.

Haenchen, Ernst. *A Commentary on the Gospel of John.* Translated by Robert W. Funk. Hermeneia. Philadelphia: Fortress, 1984.

Harland, Philip A. *Greco-Roman Associations: Texts, Translations, and Commentary.* Vol. 2, *North Coast of the Black Sea, Asia Minor.* BZNW 204. Berlin: de Gruyter, 2011.

Harlow, Barbara. *Resistance Literature.* New York: Methuen, 1987.

Heen, Erik M. "Phil 2:6-11 and Resistance to Local Timocratic Rule: Isa theō and the Cult of the Emperor in the East." In *Paul and the Roman Imperial Order*, edited by Richard A Horsley, 125-53. Harrisburg, PA: Trinity Press International, 2004.

Hellerman, Joseph H. "The Humiliation of Christ in the Social World of Roman Philippi, Part 1." *BibSac* 160 (2003): 321-36.

———. "The Humiliation of Christ in the Social World of Roman Philippi, Part 2." *BibSac* 160 (2003): 421-33.

———. *Reconstructing Honor in Roman Philippi: Carmen Christi as Cursus Pudorum.* SNTSMS 132. Cambridge: Cambridge University Press, 2005.

Hengel, Martin. "The Prologue of the Gospel of John as the Gateway to Christological Truth." In *The Gospel of John and Christian Theology*, edited by Richard Bauckham and Carl Mosser, 265-93. Grand Rapids: Eerdmans, 2008.

———. "The Song About Christ in Earliest Worship." In *Studies in Early Christology*, 227-91. Edinburgh: T&T Clark, 1995.

Hermogenes. *Hermogenes' On Types of Style.* Translated by Cecil W. Wooten. Chapel Hill: University of North Carolina Press, 1987.

Hoek, Annewies van den. "Hymn of the Holy Clement to Christ the Saviour." In *Prayer from Alexander to Constantine: A Critical Anthology*, edited by Mark Christopher Kiley, 296-303. London: Routledge, 1997.

Hofius, Otfried. *Der Christushymnus Philipper 2, 6-11: Untersuchungen zu Gestalt und Aussage eines urchristlichen Psalms.* 2nd ed. WUNT 17. Tübingen: Mohr, 1991.

Homer. *Iliad*. Translated by A. T. Murray and William F. Wyatt. 2nd ed. 2 vols. LCL 170-71. Cambridge, MA: Harvard University Press, 1999.

Horace. *Odes and Epodes*. Translated by Niall Rudd. LCL 33. Cambridge, MA: Harvard University Press, 2004.

Horsley, Richard A. *Revolt of the Scribes: Resistance and Apocalyptic Origins*. Minneapolis: Fortress, 2010.

Hübner, Hans. *Die Weisheit Salomons*. ATDA 4. Göttingen: Vandenhoeck & Ruprecht, 1999.

Hurtado, Larry W. *At the Origins of Christian Worship: The Context and Character of Earliest Christian Devotion*. Grand Rapids: Eerdmans, 2000.

———. *Lord Jesus Christ: Devotion to Jesus in Earliest Christianity*. Grand Rapids: Eerdmans, 2003.

Huttner, Ulrich. *Early Christianity in the Lycus Valley*. Translated by David Green. AJEC 85. Leiden: Brill, 2013.

Jeffery, Peter. "Philo's Impact on Christian Psalmody." In *Psalms in Community: Jewish and Christian Textual, Liturgical, and Artistic Traditions*, edited by Harold W. Attridge and Margot E. Fassler, 147-87. Atlanta: Society of Biblical Literature, 2003.

Johnson, Luke Timothy. *The Gospel of Luke*. SP 3. Collegeville, MN: Liturgical Press, 1991.

Johnson, Timothy S. *A Symposion of Praise: Horace Returns to Lyric in Odes IV*. Wisconsin Studies in Classics. Madison: University of Wisconsin Press, 2004.

Jörns, Klaus-Peter. *Das hymnische Evangelium: Untersuchungen z. Aufbau, Funktion u. Herkunft d. hymnischen Stücke in d. Johannesoffenbarung*. SNT 5. Gütersloh: Mohn, 1971.

Juel, Donald. *Messianic Exegesis: Christological Interpretation of the Old Testament in Early Christianity*. Philadelphia: Fortress, 1988.

Karris, Robert J. *A Symphony of New Testament Hymns*. Collegeville, MN: Liturgical Press, 1996.

Käsemann, Ernst. "A Critical Analysis of Philippians 2:5-11." *JTC* 5 (1968): 45-88.

———. "A Primitive Christian Baptismal Liturgy." In *Essays on New Testament Themes*, 149-68. Studies in Biblical Theology. Naperville, IL: Allenson, 1964.

———. "The Structure and Purpose of the Prologue to John's Gospel." In *New Testament Questions of Today*, 138-67. Philadelphia: Fortress, 1969.

Keener, Craig S. *The Gospel of John: A Commentary*. 2 vols. Peabody, MA: Hendrickson, 2003.

Kennedy, George Alexander. *Aristotle: On Rhetoric*. New York: Oxford University Press, 1991.

Kiley, Mark Christopher. *Colossians as Pseudepigraphy.* BibSem. Sheffield: JSOT Press, 1986.

Kloppenborg, John S. "Isis and Sophia in the Book of Wisdom." *HTR* 75 (1982): 57-84.

Knust, Jennifer, and Tommy Wasserman. "The Biblical Odes and the Text of the Christian Bible: A Reconsideration of the Impact of Liturgical Singing on the Transmission of the Gospel of Luke." *JBL* 133 (2014): 341-65.

Koester, Craig R. *Hebrews: A New Translation with Introduction and Commentary.* AB 36. New York: Doubleday, 2001.

Kotrosits, Maia. *Rethinking Early Christian Identity: Affect, Violence, Belonging.* Minneapolis: Fortress, 2015.

Kraemer, Ross Shepard. *Her Share of the Blessings: Women's Religions Among Pagans, Jews, and Christians in the Greco-Roman World.* New York: Oxford University Press, 1992.

Krause, Deborah. *1 Timothy.* Readings, a New Biblical Commentary. London: T&T Clark, 2004.

Krentz, Edgar. "Epideiktik and Hymnody: The New Testament and Its World." *BR* 40 (1995): 50-97.

Kroll, Josef. *Die christliche Hymnodik bis zu Klemens von Alexandria.* Reprint of *Darmstadt 1968.* 2nd ed. Darmstadt: Wissenschaftliche Buchgesellschaft, 1968.

Kugel, James L. *The Idea of Biblical Poetry: Parallelism and its History.* New Haven, CT: Yale University Press, 1981.

Lash, C. J. A. "Fashionable Sports: Hymn-Hunting in 1 Peter." In *Studia Evangelica.* Vol. 7, *Papers Presented to the Fifth International Congress on Biblical Studies,* edited by E. A. Livingstone, 293-97. TUGAL 126. Berlin: Akademie-Verlag, 1982.

Lattke, Michael. *Hymnus: Materialen zu einer Geschichte der antiken Hymnologie.* NTOA 19. Göttingen: Vandenhoeck & Ruprecht, 1991.

Lausberg, Heinrich. *Handbook of Literary Rhetoric: A Foundation for Literary Study.* Translated by Matthew T. Bliss, Annemiek Jansen, and David E. Orton. Leiden: Brill, 1998.

Lee, Dorothy. "In the Spirit of Truth: Worship and Prayer in the Gospel of John and the Early Fathers." *VC* 58 (2004): 277-97.

Leonhard, Jutta. *Jewish Worship in Philo of Alexandria.* TSAJ 84. Tübingen: Mohr Siebeck, 2001.

Leppä, Outi. *The Making of Colossians: A Study on the Formation and Purpose of a Deutero-Pauline Letter.* Publications of the Finnish Exegetical Society 86. Göttingen: Vandenhoeck & Ruprecht, 2003.

Litwa, M. David. *Iesus Deus: The Early Christian Depiction of Jesus as a Mediterranean God.* Minneapolis: Fortress, 2014.

Lohmeyer, Ernst. *Die Briefe an die Philipper, an die Kolosser und an Philemon.* KEK 9. Göttingen: Vandenhoeck & Ruprecht, 1954.

———. *Kyrios Jesus: Eine Untersuchung zu Phil. 2, 5-11.* SHAW, Philosophisch-Historische Klasse, 1927/28:4. Heidelberg: Winter, 1928.

Löhr, Hermut. "What Can We Know About the Beginnings of Christian Hymnody?" In *Literature or Liturgy? Early Christian Hymns and Prayers in Their Literary and Liturgical Context in Antiquity,* edited by Clemens Leonhard and Hermut Löhr, 157-74. WUNT 2/363. Tübingen: Mohr Siebeck, 2014.

Lohse, Eduard. *A Commentary on the Epistles to the Colossians and to Philemon.* Hermeneia. Philadelphia: Fortress, 1971.

Longenecker, Bruce W. *The Crosses of Pompeii: Jesus-Devotion in a Vesuvian Town.* Minneapolis: Fortress, 2016.

Longenecker, Richard N. *New Wine into Fresh Wineskins: Contextualizing the Early Christian Confessions.* Peabody, MA: Hendrickson, 1999.

Mack, Burton L. *Wisdom and the Hebrew Epic: Ben Sira's Hymn in Praise of the Fathers.* CSHJ. Chicago: University of Chicago Press, 1985.

Maier, Harry O. "Reading Colossians in the Ruins: Roman Imperial Iconography, Moral Transformation, and the Construction of Christian Identity in the Lycus Valley." In *Colossae in Space and Time: Linking to an Ancient City,* edited by Alan H. Cadwallader and Michael Trainor, 212-31. NTOA, SUNT 94. Göttingen: Vandenhoeck & Ruprecht, 2011.

———. "A Sly Civility: Colossians and Empire." *JSNT* 27 (2005): 323-49.

Malina, Bruce J., and Jerome H. Neyrey. *Portraits of Paul: An Archaeology of Ancient Personality.* Louisville, KY: Westminster John Knox, 1996.

Martin, Michael Wade, and Bryan A. Nash. "Philippians 2:6-11 as Subversive *Hymnos*: A Study in the Light of Ancient Rhetorical Theory." *JTS* 66 (2015): 90-138.

Martin, Ralph P. *Ephesians, Colossians, and Philemon.* IBC. Atlanta: John Knox Press, 1991.

———. *A Hymn of Christ: Philippians 2:5-11 in Recent Interpretation and in the Setting of Early Christian Worship.* Downers Grove, IL: InterVarsity Press, 1997.

———. *Worship in the Early Church.* Grand Rapids: Eerdmans, 1974.

McDonough, Sean M. *Christ as Creator: Origins of a New Testament Doctrine.* Oxford: Oxford University Press, 2009.

McGowan, Andrew B. *Ancient Christian Worship: Early Church Practices in Social, Historical, and Theological Perspective.* Grand Rapids: Baker Academic, 2014.

McGuckin, John Anthony. *The Path of Christianity: The First Thousand Years.* Downers Grove, IL: IVP Academic, 2017.

McHugh, John F. *A Critical and Exegetical Commentary on John 1–4.* Edited by Graham Stanton. ICC. London: T&T Clark, 2009.

Meier, John P. "Structure and Theology in Heb 1,1-14." *Bib* 66 (1985): 168-89.

———. "Symmetry and Theology in the Old Testament Citations of Heb 1:5–14." *Bib* 66 (1985): 504-33.

Mellor, Ronald. *ΘΕΑ ΡΩΜΗ: The Worship of the Goddess Roma in the Greek World.* Hypomnemata: Untersuchungen zur Antike und zu ihrer Nachleben Heft 42. Göttingen: Vandenhoeck & Ruprecht, 1975.

Michaels, J. Ramsey. *The Gospel of John.* NICNT. Grand Rapids: Eerdmans, 2010.

Minear, Paul S. "Singing and Suffering in Philippi." In *The Conversation Continues: Studies in Paul & John in Honor of J. Louis Martyn,* edited by J. Louis Martyn, Robert Tomson Fortna, and Beverly Roberts Gaventa, 202-19. Nashville: Abingdon, 1990.

Mittmann-Richert, Ulrike. *Magnifikat und Benediktus: die ältesten Zeugnisse der judenchristlichen Tradition von der Geburt des Messias.* WUNT 2/90. Tübingen: Mohr Siebeck, 1996.

Moore, Stephen D. *Empire and Apocalypse: Postcolonialism and the New Testament.* Bible in the Modern World 12. Sheffield: Sheffield Phoenix, 2006.

———. "The Revelation to John." In *A Postcolonial Commentary on the New Testament Writings,* edited by Fernando F. Segovia and R. S. Sugirtharajah, 436-55. The Bible and Postcolonialism 13. London: T&T Clark, 2007.

Morton, Russell S. *One upon the Throne and the Lamb: A Tradition Historical/ Theological Analysis of Revelation 4–5.* New York: Peter Lang, 2007.

Mowinckel, Sigmund. "Psalms and Wisdom." In *Wisdom in Israel and in the Ancient Near East,* edited by M. Noth and D. Winton Thomas, 205-24. VTSup 3. Leiden: Brill, 1955.

———. *The Psalms in Israel's Worship.* Translated by D. R. Ap-Thomas. 2 vols. 1962. Reprint, Grand Rapids: Eerdmans, 2004.

Mowry, Lucetta. "Revelation 4–5 and Early Christian Liturgical Usage." *JBL* 71 (1952): 75-84.

Murphy-O'Connor, Jerome. *Paul: A Critical Life.* Oxford: Clarendon, 1996.

Nasrallah, Laura Salah. *Christian Responses to Roman Art and Architecture: The Second-Century Church amid the Spaces of Empire*. Cambridge: Cambridge University Press, 2010.

Newsom, Carol A. *The Self as Symbolic Space: Constructing Identity and Community at Qumran*. STDJ 52. Leiden: Brill, 2004.

Neyrey, Jerome. "Worship in the Fourth Gospel: A Cultural Interpretation of John 14–17." *BTB* 36 (2006): 107-17.

Nolland, John. *Luke 1–9:20*. WBC 35A. Dallas: Word, 1989.

Norden, Eduard. *Agnostos Theos: Untersuchungen zur Formengeschichte religiöser Rede*. Stuttgart: Teubner, 1956.

O'Brien, Peter T. *Colossians, Philemon*. WBC 44. Waco, TX: Word, 1982.

O'Grady, John F. "The Prologue and Chapter 17 of the Gospel of John." In *What We Have Heard from the Beginning: The Past, Present, and Future of Johannine Studies*, edited by Tom Thatcher, 215-28. Waco, TX: Baylor University Press, 2007.

Oropeza, B. J. *Jews, Gentiles, and the Opponents of Paul: Apostasy in the New Testament Communities*. Apostasy in the New Testament Communities 2. Eugene, OR: Cascade, 2012.

O'Rourke, John J. "The Hymns of the Apocalypse." *CBQ* 30 (1968): 399-409.

Page, Hugh R., Jr. *Israel's Poetry of Resistance: Africana Perspectives on Early Hebrew Verse*. Minneapolis: Fortress, 2013.

Penner, Jeremy, Ken M. Penner, and Cecilia Wassen, eds. *Prayer and Poetry in the Dead Sea Scrolls and Related Literature: Essays in Honor of Eileen Schuller on the Occasion of Her 65th Birthday*. STDJ 98. Leiden: Brill, 2012.

Peppard, Michael. "'Poetry,' 'Hymns' and 'Traditional Material' in New Testament Epistles or How to Do Things with Indentations." *JSNT* 30 (2008): 319-42.

Pernot, Laurent. "The Rhetoric of Religion." *Rhetorica* 24 (2006): 235-54.

Pizzuto, Vincent A. *A Cosmic Leap of Faith: An Authorial, Structural, and Theological Investigation of the Cosmic Christology in Col. 1:15-20*. CBET 41. Leuven: Peeters, 2006.

Plant, I. M. *Women Writers of Ancient Greece and Rome: An Anthology*. Norman: University of Oklahoma Press, 2004.

Portier-Young, Anathea. *Apocalypse Against Empire: Theologies of Resistance in Early Judaism*. Grand Rapids: Eerdmans, 2011.

———. "Jewish Apocalyptic Literature as Resistance Literature." In *The Oxford Handbook of Apocalyptic Literature*, edited by John J. Collins, 135-62. Oxford: Oxford University Press, 2014.

Price, S. R. F. *Rituals and Power: The Roman Imperial Cult in Asia Minor.* Cambridge: Cambridge University Press, 1986.

Putnam, Michael C. J. *Artifices of Eternity: Horace's Fourth Book of Odes.* Ithaca, NY: Cornell University Press, 1986.

Quinn, Jerome D., and William C. Wacker. *The First and Second Letters to Timothy: A New Translation with Notes and Commentary.* ECC. Grand Rapids: Eerdmans, 2000.

Race, William H. "Aspects of Rhetoric and Form in Greek Hymns." *GRBS* 23 (1982): 5-14.

———. *Style and Rhetoric in Pindar's Odes.* Atlanta: Scholars Press, 1990.

Rader, William Harry. *The Church and Racial Hostility: A History of Interpretation of Ephesians 2, 11-22.* BGBE 20. Tübingen: Mohr, 1978.

Reese, James M. *Hellenistic Influence on the Book of Wisdom and Its Consequences.* AnBib 41. Rome: Biblical Institute Press, 1970.

Reumann, John. *Philippians: A New Translation with Introduction and Commentary.* AYB 33B. New Haven, CT: Yale University Press, 2008.

Reyes, Luis Carlos. "The Structure and Rhetoric of Colossians 1:15-20." *FN* 12 (1999): 139-54.

Richey, Lance Byron. *Roman Imperial Ideology and the Gospel of John.* CBQMS 43. Washington, DC: Catholic Biblical Association of America, 2007.

Robinson, J. A. T. "The Relation of the Prologue to the Gospel of St. John." *NTS* 9 (1962): 120-29.

Rosell Nebreda, Sergio. *Christ Identity: A Social-Scientific Reading of Philippians 2.5-11.* FRLANT 240. Göttingen: Vandenhoeck & Ruprecht, 2011.

Russell, D. A. "Aristides and the Prose Hymn." In *Antonine Literature,* edited by D. A. Russell, 199-216. Oxford: Clarendon, 1990.

Russo, Ardea. "Behind the Heavenly Door: Earthly Liturgy and Heavenly Worship in the Apocalypse of John." PhD diss. University of Notre Dame, 2009.

Sanders, Jack T. *The New Testament Christological Hymns: Their Historical Religious Background.* SNTSMS 15. Cambridge: Cambridge University Press, 1971.

Sawyer, Deborah F. *God, Gender, and the Bible.* London: Routledge, 2002.

Schedtler, Justin Jeffcoat. *A Heavenly Chorus: The Dramatic Function of Revelation's Hymns.* WUNT 2/381. Tübingen: Mohr Siebeck, 2014.

Scott, James C. *Domination and the Arts of Resistance: Hidden Transcripts.* New Haven, CT: Yale University Press, 1990.

Scott, Martin. *Sophia and the Johannine Jesus.* LNTS 71. Sheffield: JSOT Press, 1992.

Selby, Gary S. *Not with Wisdom of Words: Nonrational Persuasion in the New Testament.* Grand Rapids: Eerdmans, 2016.

Shaner, Kathryn A. "Seeing Rape and Robbery: ἁρπαγμός and the Philippians Christ Hymn (Phil. 2:5-11)." *BibInt* 25 (2017): 342-63.

Skehan, Patrick W. "Borrowings from the Psalms in the Book of Wisdom." *CBQ* 10 (1948): 384-97.

Skehan, Patrick W., and Alexander A. Di Lella. *The Wisdom of Ben Sira: A New Translation with Notes and Commentary.* AB 39. New York: Doubleday, 1987.

Skinner, Christopher W. "John's Gospel and the Roman Imperial Context: An Evaluation of Recent Proposals." In *Jesus Is Lord, Caesar Is Not: Evaluating Empire in New Testament Studies,* edited by Scot McKnight and Joseph B. Modica, 116-29. Downers Grove, IL: IVP Academic, 2013.

Smith, D. Moody. *John.* ANTC. Nashville: Abingdon, 1999.

Smith, J. A. "The Ancient Synagogue, the Early Church, and Singing." *Music and Letters* 65 (1984): 1-16.

———. "First-Century Christian Singing and Its Relationship to Contemporary Jewish Religious Song." *Music and Letters* 75 (1994): 1-15.

Stauffer, Ethelbert. *New Testament Theology.* Translated by John Marsh. London: SCM, 1955.

Sterling, Gregory E. "Prepositional Metaphysics in Jewish Wisdom Speculation and Early Christological Hymns." In *Wisdom and Logos: Studies in Jewish Thought in Honor of David Winston,* edited by D. T. Runia and Gregory E. Sterling, 219-38. SPhiloA 9. Atlanta: Scholars Press, 1997.

Stettler, Christian. *Der Kolosserhymnus: Untersuchungen zu Form, traditionsgeschichtlichem Hintergrund und Aussage von Kol 1, 15-20.* WUNT 2/131. Tübingen: Mohr Siebeck, 2000.

Stone, Michael E. *Jewish Writings of the Second Temple Period: Apocrypha, Pseudepigrapha, Qumran, Sectarian Writings, Philo, Josephus.* CRINT. Section 2, LJPSTT 2. Assen, Netherlands: Van Gorcum; Philadelphia: Fortress, 1984.

Sumney, Jerry L. *Colossians: A Commentary.* NTL. Louisville, KY: Westminster John Knox, 2008.

———. *"Servants of Satan," "False Brothers" and Other Opponents of Paul.* JSNTSup 188. Sheffield: Sheffield Academic, 1999.

———. "Writing 'In the Image' of Scripture: The Form and Function of References to Scripture in Colossians." In *Paul and Scripture: Extending the Conversation,* edited by Christopher D. Stanley, 185-229. ECL 9. Atlanta: Society of Biblical Literature, 2012.

Taylor, Joan E. *Jewish Women Philosophers of First-Century Alexandria: Philo's "Therapeutae" Reconsidered*. Oxford: Oxford University Press, 2003.

Thatcher, Tom. *Greater Than Caesar: Christology and Empire in the Fourth Gospel*. Minneapolis: Fortress, 2009.

———. "'I Have Conquered the World': The Death of Jesus and the End of Empire in the Gospel of John." In *Empire in the New Testament*, edited by Stanley E. Porter and Cynthia Long Westfall, 140-63. McMaster New Testament Studies Series 10. Eugene, OR: Pickwick, 2011.

Theobald, Michael. *Die Fleischwerdung des Logos: Studien zum Verhältnis des Johannesprologs zum Corpus des Evangeliums und zu 1 Joh*. NTAbh 20. Münster: Aschendorff, 1988.

Thompson, Marianne Meye. *John: A Commentary*. NTL. Louisville, KY: Westminster John Knox, 2015.

Tobin, Thomas. "The Prologue of John and Hellenistic Jewish Speculation." *CBQ* 52 (1990): 252-69.

———. "The World of Thought in the Philippians Hymn (Philippians 2:6-11)." In *The New Testament and Early Christian Literature in Greco-Roman Context: Studies in Honor of David E. Aune*, edited by John Fotopoulos, 91-104. Leiden: Brill, 2006.

Trafton, Joseph L. "What Would David Do? Messianic Expectation and Surprise in Ps. Sol. 17." In *The Psalms of Solomon: Language, History, Theology*, edited by Eberhard Bons and Patrick Pouchelle, 155-74. EJL 40. Atlanta: SBL Press, 2015.

Van der Watt, Jan G., Richard Alan Culpepper, and Udo Schnelle. *The Prologue of the Gospel of John: Its Literary, Theological, and Philosophical Contexts: Papers Read at the Colloquium Ioanneum 2013*. WUNT 359. Tübingen: Mohr Siebeck, 2016.

Walker, Jeffrey. *Rhetoric and Poetics in Antiquity*. New York: Oxford University Press, 2000.

Walsh, Brian J., and Sylvia C. Keesmaat. *Colossians Remixed: Subverting the Empire*. Downers Grove, IL: IVP Academic, 2004.

Watts, James W. *Psalm and Story: Inset Hymns in Hebrew Narrative*. JSOTSup 139. Sheffield, England: JSOT Press, 1992.

Wegener, Mark I. "The Arrival of Jesus as a Politically Subversive Event According to Luke 1–2." *CurTM* 44 (2017): 15-23.

Werline, Rodney A. "The Experience of God's *Paideia* in the Psalms of Solomon." In *Experientia*. Vol. 2, *Linking Text and Experience*, edited by Colleen Shantz and Rodney A. Werline, 17-44. Atlanta: Society of Biblical Literature, 2012.

West, M. L. *Ancient Greek Music*. Oxford: Clarendon, 1992.

Whitaker, Robyn J. *Ekphrasis, Vision, and Persuasion in the Book of Revelation.* WUNT 2/410. Tübingen: Mohr Siebeck, 2015.

Williams, P. J. "Not the Prologue of John." *JSNT* 33 (2011): 375-86.

Wilson, R. McL. *Colossians and Philemon: A Critical and Exegetical Commentary.* ICC. London: T&T Clark, 2005.

Wilson, Stephen G. "Music in the Early Church." In *Common Life in the Early Church: Essays Honoring Graydon F. Snyder,* edited by Julian V. Hills and Richard B. Gardner, 390-401. Harrisburg, PA: Trinity Press International, 1998.

Wilson, Walter T. *The Hope of Glory: Education and Exhortation in the Epistle to the Colossians.* NovTSup 88. Leiden: Brill, 1997.

Winston, David. *The Wisdom of Solomon: A New Translation with Introduction and Commentary.* AB 43. Garden City, NY: Doubleday, 1979.

Witherington, Ben, III. *The Letters to Philemon, the Colossians, and the Ephesians: A Socio-rhetorical Commentary on the Captivity Epistles.* Grand Rapids: Eerdmans, 2007.

Wolter, Michael. *Das Lukasevangelium.* HNT 5. Tübingen: Mohr Siebeck, 2008.

Wright, N. T. *Jesus and the Victory of God.* Minneapolis: Fortress, 1996.

———. *The New Testament and the People of God.* Minneapolis: Fortress, 1992.

———. *Paul and the Faithfulness of God.* Minneapolis: Fortress, 2013.

———. "Poetry and Theology in Colossians 1:15-20." *NTS* 36 (1990): 444-68.

———. *The Resurrection of the Son of God.* Minneapolis: Fortress, 2003.

Wright, N. T., and J. P. Davies. "John, Jesus, and 'The Ruler of This World': Demonic Politics in the Fourth Gospel?" In *Conception, Reception, and the Spirit: Essays in Honor of Andrew T. Lincoln,* edited by J. G. McConville and Lloyd Pietersen, 71-89. Eugene, OR: Cascade, 2015.

Wright, Robert B. *The Psalms of Solomon: A Critical Edition of the Greek Text.* JCTCRS. New York: T&T Clark, 2007.

Yarbrough, Mark M. *Paul's Utilization of Preformed Traditions in 1 Timothy: An Evaluation of the Apostle's Literary, Rhetorical, and Theological Tactics.* LNTS 417. London: T&T Clark, 2009.

Yeung, Maureen W. *Faith in Jesus and Paul: A Comparison with Special Reference to "Faith That Can Remove Mountains" and "Your Faith Has Healed/Saved You."* WUNT 2/147. Tübingen: Mohr Siebeck, 2002.

AUTHOR INDEX

SUBJECT INDEX

SCRIPTURE INDEX

Finding the Textbook You Need

The IVP Academic Textbook Selector
is an online tool for instantly finding the IVP books
suitable for over 250 courses across 24 disciplines.

ivpacademic.com